Cinematic Reflections on the Legacy of the Holocaust

An international group of psychoanalysts and film scholars address the enduring emotional legacy of the Holocaust in *Cinematic Reflections on the Legacy of the Holocaust: Psychoanalytic Perspectives*. Particular focus is given to how second and third generation survivors have explored and confronted the psychic reverberations of Holocaust trauma in cinema.

This book focuses on how film is particularly suited to depict Holocaust experiences with vividness and immediacy. The similarity of moving images and sound to our dream experience allows access to unconscious processing. Film has the potential to reveal the vast panorama of Holocaust history as well as its intrapsychic reverberations. Yet despite the recent prominence of Holocaust films, documentaries, and TV series as well as scholarly books and memoirs, these works lack a psychoanalytic optic that elucidates themes such as the repetition compulsion, survival guilt, disturbances in identity, and disruption of mourning that are underlying leitmotifs.

Cinematic Reflections on the Legacy of the Holocaust will be of great interest to psychoanalysts and therapists as well as to scholars in trauma, film, and Jewish studies. It is also of interest to those concerned with the prevention of genocide and mass atrocities and their long-term effects.

Diana Diamond is Professor of Psychology at City University of New York, and is on the faculty of the NYU Postdoctoral Program in Psychotherapy and Psychoanalysis and the Weill Cornell Medical College. She has written numerous articles on personality disorders, attachment theory and research, mental representation and the application of psychoanalytic theory to the understanding of narrative and symbolism in cinema. She is the co-author or co-editor of four books, including *Attachment and Sexuality* (Routledge, 2008), and the forthcoming *A Clinical Guide to Treating Narcissistic Disorders: A Transference Focused Psychotherapy* (Guilford Press). She is also in private practice of individual and couple therapy and psychoanalysis in New York City.

Bruce Sklarew is a practicing psychoanalyst in Chevy Chase, MD who co-edited four books, including *The Last Emperor: Multiple Takes* (Wayne State) and *Bernardo Bertolucci: Interviews* (University of Mississippi), and authored over fifty papers on film and applied analysis in communities. He originated Recover, a bereavement program at the D.C. Morgue. He is the film editor for *The American Psychoanalyst and The International Journal for Applied Psychoanalytic Study*.

PSYCHOANALYTIC INQUIRY BOOK SERIES

SERIES EDITOR: JOSEPH D. LICHTENBERG

Like its counterpart, *Psychoanalytic Inquiry: A Topical Journal for Mental Health Professionals*, the Psychoanalytic Inquiry Book Series presents a diversity of subjects within a diversity of approaches to those subjects. Under the editorship of Joseph Lichtenberg, in collaboration with Melvin Bornstein and the editorial board of *Psychoanalytic Inquiry*, the volumes in this series strike a balance between research, theory, and clinical application. We are honored to have published the works of various innovators in psychoanalysis, including Frank Lachmann, James Fosshage, Robert Stolorow, Donna Orange, Louis Sander, Léon Wurmser, James Grotstein, Joseph Jones, Doris Brothers, Fredric Busch, and Joseph Lichtenberg, among others.

The series includes books and monographs on mainline psychoanalytic topics, such as sexuality, narcissism, trauma, homosexuality, jealousy, envy, and varied aspects of analytic process and technique. In our efforts to broaden the field of analytic interest, the series has incorporated and embraced innovative discoveries in infant research, self psychology, intersubjectivity, motivational systems, affects as process, responses to cancer, borderline states, contextualism, postmodernism, attachment research and theory, medication, and mentalization. As further investigations in psychoanalysis come to fruition, we seek to present them in readable, easily comprehensible writing.

After more than 25 years, the core vision of this series remains the investigation, analysis, and discussion of developments on the cutting edge of the psychoanalytic field, inspired by a boundless spirit of inquiry. A full list of all the titles available in the *Psychoanalytic Inquiry* Book Series is available at www.routledge.com/Psychoanalytic-Inquiry-Book-Series/book-series/LEAPIBS.

Cinematic Reflections on the Legacy of the Holocaust

Psychoanalytic Perspectives

Edited by Diana Diamond and Bruce Sklarew

Routledge
Taylor & Francis Group
LONDON AND NEW YORK

First published 2019
by Routledge
2 Park Square, Milton Park, Abingdon, Oxon OX14 4RN

and by Routledge
52 Vanderbilt Avenue, New York, NY 10017

Routledge is an imprint of the Taylor & Francis Group, an informa business

British Library Cataloguing-in-Publication Data
A catalogue record for this book is available from the British Library

Library of Congress Cataloging-in-Publication Data
Names: Diamond, Diana, 1948 editor. | Sklarew, Bruce H. editor.
Title: Cinematic reflections on the legacy of the Holocaust : psychoanalytic perspectives / edited by Diana Diamond and Bruce H. Sklarew.
Description: London ; New York, NY : Routledge, 2018. |
Series: Psychoanalytic inquiry book series ; 58 | Includes bibliographical references and index.
Identifiers: LCCN 2018009035 (print) | LCCN 2018016592 (ebook) | ISBN 9781315142159 (Master) | ISBN 9781351392532 (Web PDF) | ISBN 9781351392525 (ePub) | ISBN 9781351392518 (Mobipocket/Kindle) | ISBN 9781138306967 (hardback : alk. paper) | ISBN 9781138306981 (pbk. : alk. paper)
Subjects: LCSH: Holocaust, Jewish (1939–1945), in motion pictures. | Psychic trauma in motion pictures. | Motion pictures–Psychological aspects.
Classification: LCC PN1995.9.H53 (ebook) | LCC PN1995.9.H53 C553 2018 (print) | DDC 791.43/658405318–dc23
LC record available at https://lccn.loc.gov/2018009035

ISBN: 978-1-138-30696-7 (hbk)
ISBN: 978-1-138-30698-1 (pbk)
ISBN: 978-1-315-14215-9 (ebk)

Typeset in Times New Roman
by Wearset Ltd, Boldon, Tyne and Wear

This book is dedicated to Dori Laub and to the memory of Primo Levi

Contents

List of figures ix
Notes on contributors x
Acknowledgments xiv

Introduction 1
DIANA DIAMOND

1 **The art and angst of viewing Holocaust films** 34
BRUCE SKLAREW

2 ***Six Million and One*: a documentary** 40
ANNA ORNSTEIN

3 **Between forgetting and remembering: two films of Alain Resnais** 51
LISSA WEINSTEIN

4 ***The Pawnbroker*** 71
ROBERT WINER

5 **Multiplicity, dissociation, and mentalization in *Hannah Arendt* by Pam Katz and Margarethe von Trotta** 85
DIANA DIAMOND AND ELLIOT JURIST

6 From *Shoah* to *Son of Saul*: cinematic traces and intergenerational dialogues 122
CATHERINE PORTUGES

7 *Son of Saul*: the remains of civilization 161
CLARA MUCCI

8 Sadomasochistic regression in *The Night Porter* 184
BRUCE SKLAREW

9 To know or not to know? Common themes in *Ida* and *The Flat* 197
EMANUEL BERMAN

10 Inheriting Nazisim: reflections on the film *Two or Three Things I Know About Him* 211
RÉGINE WAINTRATER

11 Discussion 226
NANETTE AUERHAHN AND DORI LAUB

Index 247

Figures

2.1 Knoten_A8_1 41
5.1 Hannah Arendt watching the Eichmann trial from the press room 96
5.2 Hannah Arendt thinking 108
9.1 Hannah reads her grandmother's letter in Arnon's presence (from *The Flat*) 201
9.2 Edda reads her father's incriminating CV, in Arnon's company (from *The Flat*) 206

Notes on contributors

Nanette C. Auerhahn, Ph.D., is a clinical psychologist in private practice in Beachwood, O.H. She is a fourth-year candidate in the adult psychoanalyst training program at the Cleveland Psychoanalytic Center where she teaches in the Psychoanalytic Psychotherapy Program. Dr. Auerhahn has taught at Yale, Stanford, and Case Western Reserve Universities as well as the California School of Professional Psychology in San Francisco. She received her Ph.D. in 1980 from Yale University and was a postdoctoral fellow at Stanford University. Dr. Auerhahn was the recipient of fellowships from the National Science Foundation, the Mark Kanzer Foundation, the Stanford Humanities Center, and Stanford's Institute for Research on Women and Gender. She has been a researcher with the Fortunoff Videoarchive for Holocaust Testimonies at Yale University and a consultant at the Cleveland Rape Crisis Center, the Case Western Reserve University Counseling Center, Bellefaire Jewish Children's Bureau, Mt. Sinai Hospital, Laurelwood Hospital, and Menorah Park Center for Aging. Dr. Auerhahn has written numerous articles on trauma; her writing was awarded the Cleveland Psychoanalytic Center Essay Prize in 2011 and 2016.

Emanuel Berman, Ph.D. is a training and supervising analyst of the Israel Psychoanalytic Society. He is chief international editor of *Psychoanalytic Dialogues*, editor of *Essential Papers on Literature and Psychoanalysis* (1993), and author of *Impossible Training* (2004).

Diana Diamond, Ph.D., is a psychoanalyst and Professor in Clinical Psychology at City University of New York, as well as a Senior Fellow at the Personality Disorders Institute at Weill Medical College of Cornell University. She has published extensively in the areas of mental representation, attachment, and psychoanalysis, and the application of psychoanalytic concepts to understanding narrative and symbolism in cinema. She co-edited the book *Attachment and Sexuality* (Routledge, 2014) with the late Sidney J. Blatt and Joseph Lichtenberg. She is also author of the forthcoming *A Clinical Guide to Treating Narcissistic Disorders: A Transference Focused Psychotherapy* (with Frank Yeomans, Barry Stern, and Otto Kernberg, Guilford Press).

Elliot Jurist, Ph.D., is Professor of Psychology and Philosophy at the Graduate Center and The City College of New York, CUNY. From 2004 to 2013, he served as the Director of the Clinical Psychology Doctoral Program at CUNY. From 2008 to 2018, he was the Editor of *Psychoanalytic Psychology*, the journal of Division 39 of the APA. He is also the editor of a book series, Psychoanalysis and Psychological Science, from Guilford Publications, and author of *Minding Emotions,* from the same publisher (April 2018). He is the author of *Beyond Hegel and Nietzsche: Philosophy, Culture and Agency* (MIT Press, 2000) and co-author of *Affect Regulation, Mentalization and the Development of the Self* (Other Press, 2002), the latter of which has been translated into five languages and won two book prizes. He is also the co-editor of *Mind to Mind: Infant Research, Neuroscience, and Psychoanalysis* (Other Press, 2008).

Dori Laub, M.D., himself a child survivor of the Holocaust, is Clinical Professor of Psychiatry at the Yale University School of Medicine and a psychoanalyst in private practice. He has worked for decades with victims of genocidal, childhood sexual abuse, and combat trauma. Laub is cofounder of the Fortunoff video archive for Holocaust testimonies at Yale and has written extensively on the topic of testimony and basic witness, and on the relationship between testimony and psychoanalysis.

Clara Mucci, Ph.D., is Professor of Clinical Psychology at the University of Chieti, Italy, where she has been full Professor of English Literature (Shakespeare Studies) until recently. After a Ph.D. from Emory University on literature and psychoanalysis, she retrained in psychology to become a licensed psychotherapist psychoanalytically oriented and was for several months a Fellow at the Personality

Disorders Institute, New York, directed by Otto Kernberg. The author of several books on Shakesperean drama, of a monograph on trauma and psychoanalysis (*Beyond Individual and Collective Trauma: Intergenerational Transmission, Psychoanalytic Treatment, and the Dynamics of Forgiveness* (Karnac Books, London, 2013.), her latest book is *Borderline Bodies: Affect Regulation Therapy for Personality Disorders* (Norton, New York, 2018).

Anna Ornstein, M.D., is a retired Professor of Child Psychiatry, University of Cincinnati and Lecturer in Psychiatry, Harvard University. She is a supervising analyst at the Boston Psychoanalytic Institute and at the Massachusetts Institute for Psychoanalysis.

Catherine Portuges, Ph.D., is Founding Director, Interdepartmental Program in Film Studies; Professor Emerita, Comparative Literature; and Founding Curator, Massachusetts Multicultural Film Festival at the University of Massachusetts Amherst. Her books include *Cinemas in Transition in Central and Eastern Europe after 1989* (Temple, 2013); *Gendered Subjects* (Routledge, 2012); and *Screen Memories: The Hungarian Cinema of Márta Mészáros* (Indiana, 1993). She is Film Consultant, European Psychoanalytic Film Festival (UK), co-editor for Film for *American Imago*, and a member of the Academic Advisory Board for the Institute for Holocaust, Genocide and Memory Studies. She serves on the editorial boards of *Studies in Eastern European Cinema, Jewish Film and New Media*, and *Hungarian Studies*.

Bruce Sklarew, M.D., is a practicing psychoanalyst, Faculty Emeritus at the Baltimore-Washington Center for Psychoanalysis, and the Howard University College of Medicine. He has co-edited *The Last Emperor: Multiple Takes* (Wayne State, 1998), *Bernardo Bertolucci: Interviews* (University of Mississippi, 2000), *Analysts in the Trenches: Streets, Schools, War Zones* (Analytic Press, 2004), *A Journey of Child Development: Selected Papers of Joseph D. Noshpitz* (Analytic Press, 2011), and over 50 papers on film and applied analysis in communities. As Chair of the Forum for the Psychoanalytic Study of Film, he co-originated the award-winning *Projections: A Journal of Psychoanalysis and Film*. He is the Film Editor of the *International Journal of Applied Psychoanalysis* and *The American Psychoanalyst*. He organized retrospectives on the films of Bernardo Bertolucci with Bertolucci present, and approximately 60 other film programs, including a retrospective on Buñuel, co-sponsored by the embassies of Spain, Mexico, and France in Washington, D.C. In addition, he visits the sets of Bertolucci films. For over 20 years he has programed extensive film programs at meetings of the American Psychoanalytic Association. He originated Recover, a bereavement program at the D.C. Morgue and the School-Based Mourning Project in D.C. inner-city schools.

Régine Waintrater, Ph.D., is Associate Professor in Clinical Psychology and Psychopathology at the Department of Psychoanalytical Studies of the Paris Diderot University (Paris 7), France. She has written many articles and chapters of books on collective traumas and their transgenerationnal transmission. Her main book: *Sortir du génocide: Témoignage et survivance* (Paris: Payot, 2003 paperback 2011).

Lissa Weinstein, Ph.D., is a Professor in the Doctoral Program of Clinical Psychology at the City College of the City University of New York. She is on the faculty of the New York Psychoanalytic Institute and the Institute for Psychoanalytic Training and Research. She publishes in the areas of psychoanalytic theory, film, and literature and sleep research.

Robert Winer, M.D., has been responding to the cinema for decades, trying to see what the cinema can teach him about the human condition. He has started a number of training programs at the Washington Center for Psychoanalysis, including a national program, New Directions: Writing with a Psychoanalytic Edge. He is the author of *Close Encounters: A Relational View of the Therapeutic Process.*

Acknowledgments

We want to express our gratitude as we have been privileged over the years to collaborate with a talented group of psychoanalysts and film scholars who have enhanced our work, many of whom are represented in this book.

Thanks to the filmmakers who over the generations have continued to grapple with what it means to represent the Holocaust, and in so doing ensure it will never be forgotten. Through their haunting artistry, these finely textured films help us to mourn and commemorate both the survivors and the victims.

Thanks to Annette Insdorf, whose remarkably comprehensive book *Indelible Shadows: Film and the Holocaust* has been an encyclopedic resource for Holocaust film scholarship.

Special appreciation goes to Dori Laub, whose work on testimony, witnessing, and creative transformation of trauma has inspired us in the development of this manuscript.

We also want to express gratitude to Joseph Lichtenberg, whose steadfast commitment to applied psychoanalysis, among his vast interests and accomplishments, inspired us to expand what was originally slated to be an issue of *Psychoanalytic Inquiry* into a book.

Thanks also to our editors from Routledge Press Kate Hawes and Charles Bath for their patience and perseverance in helping to bring this book to fruition. We are grateful for the editorial assistance of James Splendore and Andrea Fortunato.

Diana Diamond expresses her gratitude to John Alschuler whose love always sustains and whose interest always inspires; and to Julia Rose Alschuler for her dedication to carrying on family traditions and stories. Thanks to Solomon Diamant who refused to exchange one ghetto for another, and who found in the US a door of hope.

Bruce Sklarew appreciates Margaret Meyers' continuous support and editing along with Bonnie Kaufman, psychoanalyst, and Myra Sklarew, a poet of the Holocaust and a chronicler of Holocaust memories and distortions in Lithuania.

Introduction

Diana Diamond

Introduction

"Why do we need another film about the Holocaust?" This is a question posed by Hungarian director László Nemes, whose film *Son of Saul* (Rajna, Sipos, & Nemes, 2015) won the Grand Prix Award and the Oscar for best foreign film. Nemes responded[1] that the generation that lived through WWII and the Holocaust is gradually disappearing, and that subsequent generations are getting more remote from these cataclysmic events. Although memoirs and histories about the Holocaust are plentiful, the Shoah is too vast an historical trauma to be represented in one modality or medium. In its blend of perception and fantasy, images and words, sound and music, both fictional narratives and documentary footage, film is an optimal medium for the representation of Holocaust atrocities. Holocaust films convey the subjectivity of the victims, the hellish minutiae of everyday life in the ghettos and concentration camps, and the nature and extent of the historical and individual traumas endured by victims and survivors. Despite the prominence of Holocaust films, memoirs, and scholarly books that address historical and cinematic issues in representing the Holocaust (Insdorf, 2003; Kerner, 2011), missing from the current literature on Holocaust film are psychoanalytic reflections on the major themes that have emerged from these films, which is the focus of the current volume. The contributors to this volume view Holocaust films through a psychoanalytic optic that elucidates themes such as the repetition compulsion, survival guilt, disturbances in identity, and disruption of mourning, which are underlying leitmotifs of the films discussed.

The Holocaust is so vast an historical trauma that it has been said to defy representation (Laub & Podell, 2012); yet since the camps were liberated, filmic depictions have been crucial in providing evidence for Holocaust atrocities (Delage, 2010, 2017).The Nazis created a machine for bureaucratically organized state-sanctioned violence, systematically annihilating whole groups in ways that are unprecedented in human history in that they strove not just for total physical destruction but also elimination of witnesses to their atrocities. Even among the survivors, bearing testimony was compromised. As Laub (1992) relates: "Massive trauma precludes its registration; the observing and recording mechanisms of the human mind are temporarily knocked out" (p. 57). The massive traumatization of the survivors initially had a silencing and numbing effect, necessary for some to reconstitute and rebuild their decimated lives and families (Berman, Chapter 9; Ornstein, Chapter 2); yet, with aging, maturation, and confrontation with mortality, many survivors have found their voice. Narratives long buried in individual journals and letters, archives recently opened, artfully concealed accounts, such as the diaries of the Sonderkommandos hidden under the crematoria at Auschwitz (Chare & Williams, 2015), continue to be found. Consequently, narratives, photographs, memoirs, data sources, even new film footage are still emerging, still being discovered and still being mentalized, that is, subject to an exploration of the various, searing, complex, contradictory mental states that were endured by survivors and their reverberations in their progeny. As a result, we the spectators, are better able to engage in the imaginative activity of bearing witness to these experiences. Witnessing involves not only seeing the evidence—that is, the original archival footage of the atrocities that attest to their veracity—but also reconstructing and empathizing with the complex, often devastating mental states that were endured by victims, survivors, and even perpetrators.

Underlying the disparate papers in this book are psychoanalytic perspectives on how the Holocaust legacy has been represented in film over several generations. Cinematic representations of the Holocaust reveal imagistically not only the consciously held or reconstructed historical experience but also the optics of the unconscious, that is, the unmodulated and unintegrated affects, fantasies, experiences and visual residues of them that are repressed or dissociated. Film is uniquely suited to capture individual and historical traumas that may overwhelm the individual's representational capacities. The visual mode conveys the full force of the "real"; that is, what is often unspeakable, unsymbolized, and unmentalized, which Laub and Podell (1995) refer to as the "black hole"

(p. 1002) of trauma. Indeed, in many Holocaust films, we find deranging montages, disorienting jump cuts, shifts from black and white to color that recreate subjective experiences of terror and dissociation, juxtaposed with documentary footage that grounds the Holocaust in the chain of events that comprise its historical reality. While Adorno (1955) initially stipulated that "to write lyric poetry after Auschwitz is barbaric," a statement that continues to be debated today, he (Adorno, 1962) subsequently modified this position, writing: "It is now virtually in art alone that suffering can still find its own voice, consolation without being immediately betrayed by it" (p. 318).

This prophecy is borne out by the filmic depictions of the Shoah. This introduction first offers a brief review of how the Holocaust has been represented in film over several generations, and then provides summaries of the chapters, with a focus on the psychoanalytic perspectives they bring to bear on the Holocaust experience.

Representation of the Holocaust in film

From the beginning, filmic portrayals of the Shoah were central in documenting the barbarism and dehumanization of the Holocaust experiences, including the concentration camps and their aftermath. In 2010, an exhibit entitled "Filming the Camps: From Hollywood to Nuremberg," curated by film historian Christian Delage (2010) at the Memorial de la Shoah in Paris, presented footage shot by Allied forces documenting the liberation of the concentration camps, as well as directors' notes, letters, daily military dispatches, and journal entries describing the unimaginable cruelties and hellish realties that they encountered.[2] This exhibit enabled the viewer to see original footage in its historical context and read the accompanying narratives written daily by the cameramen, officers, soldiers, and directors/photographers, so that one has the sense of witnessing the events in real time. These initial documentaries and photographs formed the first cut to the cinematic project of how to depict the Shoah in images and words; but as Kerner (2011) observes, the cinematographers who shot this archival footage "were not unreflective conduits of unmediated reality" (p. 192). In their quest to document history and to show the authenticity of what had taken place, they left a body of objective evidence used in the Nuremburg and other trials to bring the Nazis to justice. But they also created a "highly mediated visual record of the camps"

(Haggith, quoted in Kerner, 2011, pp. 192–193), a visual Procrustean bed that configured the work of subsequent directors who used the archival footage in their Holocaust films.

Indeed, there were differences in how the Americans, British, and Soviets shot footage about the liberation of the camps.[3] The U.S forces favored long tracking shots that panned over the emaciated bodies and excruciating expressions of inmates who gazed at the liberators with awe and apathy, duplicating for the viewer their experience as they entered the camps.[4] We see echoes of this technique in the use of hand-held cameras and naturalistic tracking shots in films such as *Son of Saul* (Rajna, Sipos, & Nemes, 2015), which immerses the spectator in the hellish and chaotic subjective world of Sonderkommandos (special squads of inmates and future victims).

By contrast, the British filmed in a more formal manner, with staged shots of Nazi guards lined up on the edge of gaping mass graves filled with murdered victims, while the British officers on high ground excoriated them, telling them to behold the bodies in the pits and their crimes against humanity for which they would be held accountable. We see echoes of this approach in the melancholic, almost elegiac tone of the narrator in films such as in *Night and Fog* (Dauman, Halfon, Lifchitz, & Resnais, 1955). The Soviets, on the other hand, sought to capture the full horror of the carnage in close-ups that revealed the raw brutality of it, with grainy images of decomposing bodies horribly mutilated in mass graves, or spilling out of ovens (Delage, 2010). The Soviet material also tends to push the victimization of Jews into the background, as the historian Liebman (2007) has remarked, as did Resnais in *Night in Fog* (Dauman, Halfon, Lifchitz, & Resnais, 1955), revealing the myriad moral ambiguities that characterized the experience of the Holocaust and its representation.

The films discussed in these papers include all of these techniques—the informal tracking shots that introduce us naturalistically to the camp and focus on close-ups of the survivors that characterized the technique characteristics of the U.S. forces, the distancing long shots favored by the British, and the grainy, horrific images of carnage shot by the Russians—all of which strove to capture distinct aspects of an incomprehensible reality. The original filmic representations of the Holocaust, in brutal raw footage shot by the Allies as they liberated the camps during WWII, initially formed the basis for a series of documentaries about the Holocaust such as *Death Mills* (Wilder, 1945) as well as films like *Night and Fog* (Dauman, Halfon, Lifchitz, & Resnais 1955). The next generation of filmmakers turned to fiction films that focus on the psychological legacy of the victims, survivors, and even perpetrators, with fictional accounts punctuated with original archival footage of the atrocities. These films explore how Holocaust trauma is registered and restructured within the individual psyche by depicting subjective experiences of unspeakable horrors that might defy signification in other narrative formats. Filmic narratives such as *The Pawnbroker* (Langer, Lewis, & Lumet, 1965), *The Night Porter* (Edwards, De Simone, & Cavani, 1974), *Hiroshima Mon Amour* (Dauman, Halfon, & Resnais, 1959) foster the resolution of trauma because they allow for the creative manipulation of categories of time, space, self, and other so that traumatic events may be explored metaphorically, ironically, or even perversely. Furthermore, the creative act of narration in film or other arts, bridges the chasm between self and other that is the legacy of trauma; for narratives are not told into a void but presuppose a witness who listens and empathizes within the framework of a shared cultural space (Laub & Podell, 1995; Rose, 1987; Laub & Hamburger, 2017).

Indeed, in the second and third generation of Holocaust films, the emphasis shifts to the significance of film as a vehicle for the survivors to give testimony, and for others to witness it. In his masterwork *Shoah* (Lanzmann, 1985), Lanzmann constructs a film that is comprised primarily of interviews with survivors, perpetrators, observers, and/or bystanders to the Holocaust in the present rather than of archival footage of the horrors themselves, eschewing any graphic depiction of the corpses (Lanzmann, 1994). In so doing he expands film into a vehicle for witnessing and testimony (Felman & Laub, 1992). In his view, the mindless repetition of Holocaust images with which most individuals are now familiar has a banalizing effect. The dearth of such stock images throws us back on mental representations of the Shoah that persist in the present, continuing to shape the psyches of subsequent generations (Lanzmann, 1994).

The anchoring of the Holocaust experience through interviews that demonstrate the vestiges of the past in the present attitudes and experiences of survivors, perpetrators, and bystanders evokes, in Lanzmann's (1985, 1994), view the ongoing horror of the Holocaust far more than the afterimages of the films and photos such as those in *Night and Fog* (Dauman, Halfon, Lifchitz, & Resnais 1955). As Cowie (2005) has observed, "seeing does not translate into simple and proper knowing" (quoted in Kerner, 2011, p. 188). One could also surmise that knowing the historical reality does not necessarily imply understanding it at a depth level, which is the goal of the papers in this book. However, as LaCapra (1998) asks, what will happen in a later generation that may not be familiar with the images Lanzmann excludes? "Moreover, is it possible that archival documents, images, and footage would not have a merely banalizing effect but might serve to provide reality tests for an imagination that can otherwise run rampant to the point of obsession and hallucination?" (LaCapra, 1998, p. 109).

For this reason, other filmmakers in the third generation, such as Nemes, in *Son of Saul* (Rajna, Sipos, & Nemes, 2015), have created a unique genre of film, blending documentary-like fiction films or documentaries that recreate Holocaust experiences in the present. *Son of Saul* (Rajna, Sipos, & Nemes, 2015), for example, takes the individual inside the subjective and corporeal experience of the Sonderkommandos, or special squads, assigned to operate the crematoria and thus caught up in the Nazi killing machine. By doing so, Nemes illustrates perhaps as effectively as any post-Holocaust survivor interview or horrific archival footage, how this state-sanctioned genocide precipitated, as Hannah Arendt (2006) put it, "the moral collapse that the Nazi's caused in respectable European societies, not only among the victimizers but also among the victims" (p. 122). Shot through a hand-held camera that virtually takes us inside the psyche of one Sonderkommando, in *Son of Saul* (2015) we witness, as though firsthand, the unspeakable chaos, irrationality, violence, and degradation, the organization and envisioning of which Levi (2015) has called the Nazi's "most diabolical crime" (p. 2443). Based on the actual writings of the Sonderkommandos (the scrolls of Auschwitz) found buried under the crematoria in Auschwitz in 1980, the film invites us to imagine how one can still strive for moral redemption in the midst of such hell, even as one contributes to the deaths of others and is certain to perish oneself.

Another type of cinematic Holocaust representation has emerged in the second and third generation of Holocaust filmmakers in which individuals, whose parents and/or grandparents have concealed as much as they have revealed about their Holocaust experience, both as perpetrators and survivors, attempt to piece together a more complete and comprehensive narrative (Kerner, 2011). Through examination of documents, letters, photographs, and diaries, as well as through extensive interviews with family members, extended kinship and friend networks, by returning to the scene of the camps or other sites of trauma and rescue, they attempt to imagine and relive their families' Holocaust experience. *Six Million and One* (Fisher, 2011), *The Flat* (Goldfinger & Kufus, 2011), and *Two or Three Things I Know About Him* (Svarcová & Ludin, 2005) are examples of such investigative documentaries that uncover layers of suffering, denial, betrayal in both Germans and Jews. In these films, we see the ways that making (and viewing) films about the Holocaust may catalyze a journey of self-discovery in second or third generation survivors when parents were not able to articulate or narrate their own traumatic experiences, but rather lived them out in distorted relational patterns, centering around denial or dissociation.

Just as filmic representations of the Holocaust experience continue to advance in technical complexity, emotional depth, and range, so also has the emotional reach of these films extended to encompass the meaning of the Shoah not only for the generation that experienced the Holocaust directly, but for subsequent generations who must try to make sense of how they reverberate in the representational worlds of the survivors and their offspring. For this reason, these films invite psychoanalytic exploration of the legacy of the Holocaust for survivors and subsequent generations, such as that found in these papers, which are described below.

Overview of chapters

In Chapter 1, "The art and angst of viewing Holocaust films," Bruce Sklarew compares how viewing Holocaust films and the dream experience are akin, because both realms can convey vital unimaginable and unspeakable experiences and horrors. In a state of confinement, the moviegoer is more attuned to the primary, preverbal infantile experience of visual and auditory stimuli—facial expressions, gestures, or body movements—than to language. Conveying almost unimaginable degrees of sadism and suffering, Holocaust films are commemorative works of art, which confront this suffering and bring us closer to absorbing the reality of the Holocaust. While reading, listening to speakers, visiting museums or memorials, or looking at still photographs can offer us knowledge and an array of meaningful images, none provide the finely integrated experience of watching a finely textured film that can stir unsettling feelings and help us mourn through its haunting artistry.

In Chapter 2, "*Six Million and One*: a documentary," Anna Ornstein writes about a film in which four adult siblings visited the Mauthausen camp complex in Austria where their father, Joseph Fisher, was a 17-year-old slave laborer. Hard labor combined with a starvation diet and sub-zero temperatures claimed the lives of many thousands as they assembled fighter planes in a tunnel system built deeply into the Austrian Alps. David, the filmmaker and mental health professional in the family, was inspired to make this film by his father's diary, which he wrote two years before his death as a gift to his children so that they might understand the unspeakable horrors he had witnessed, as well as the miraculous nature of his survival. Although Joseph Fisher was liberated, his children intuited that he was not free and remained a victim, who isolated himself emotionally to protect him and them from his horrific experiences, and the inner torment that they continued to cause him. The film records the changes in the siblings from reluctant observers to participants who imaginatively reconstructed their father's experiences. Ornstein discusses the different responses of the four Fisher siblings to the experience of returning to the camp, talking with veterans of the camps, and literally walking the ground and witnessing the terrain on which such cruelty and torture took place—responses that illuminate the variations on how the second generation experienced their parents' Holocaust history.

In Chapter 3, "Between forgetting and remembering: two films of Alain Resnais," Lissa Weinstein uses Resnais' *Night and Fog* (Dauman, Halfon, Lifchitz, & Resnais 1955) and *Hiroshima Mon Amour* (Dauman, Halfon, & Resnais, 1959) to reexamine assumptions about how film depicts historical trauma. At first glance, the subjects of the films (the Holocaust and the aftermath of the bombing of Hiroshima) as well as their chosen genres (documentary vs. fiction) appear disparate; yet a closer examination of both their form and content suggest they are successive iterations of a singular trauma. Both challenge one's capacity to truly see, metaphorically to "know," the experiences of another's trauma and the veracity of memory. In Weinstein's view, the construction of the traumatic narrative is never a singular narrative, but rather successive expansions of a network of images that are continually symbolized and increasingly integrated into novel narrative contexts.

In Chapter 4, "*The Pawnbroker*," one of the first films in the post-war era to explore the impact of the Holocaust on survivors after a period of culturally reinforced silence and denial, Robert Winer describes how a survivor, Sol Nazerman, has been so extraordinarily traumatized by the camp experience that he can no longer find a new lease on life. His pawnshop, in its iconography and social practice, has become the resurrection of the death camp, a camp in which he is now in command. As a reaction to his humiliating passivity in the camp, he has determined never to be powerless again. The only truth that really matters to him is the truth of the Holocaust, and that his life should bear witness to that suffering.

In Chapter 5, "Multiplicity, dissociation, and mentalization in *Hannah Arendt*," Diana Diamond and Elliot Jurist explore Pam Katz and Margarethe von Trotta's cinematic recreation of the fierce debate ignited over half a century ago when Arendt covered the trial of Adolf Eichmann, the former Nazi administrator of Jewish affairs. Arendt's argument in *Eichmann in Jerusalem* (Arendt, 2006), that Eichmann demonstrated an "inability to think," that is, to ever think from the perspective of the other, aroused suspicion and outrage, insofar as it was interpreted as minimizing Eichmann's guilt. They explore how the multiplicity of Arendt's identity, including contradictory selves—German and Jewish—that reflect the powerful and often conflictual historical currents of the twentieth century, provided Arendt with the capacity to explore the psyche and mental states of the victimizers and particularly the complexities of victim/victimizer dynamics. Arendt's determination, even compulsion, to cover the Eichmann trial could be seen as an attempt to bear witness to the Holocaust experiences of others that she so narrowly escaped, to transform her survival into an act of exploration of the mind of the perpetrators. It was also a quest to come to grips with her own survivor guilt that also may have been linked to her relationship with Heidegger, her former mentor and lover who was complicit with the Nazi regime.

In Chapter 6, "From *Shoah* to *Son of Saul*: cinematic traces and intergenerational dialogues," Catherine Portuges explores issues of memorialization and re-enactment of Holocaust histories in a Central European context where topographies have been redrawn, political alliances renegotiated, and once-sealed archives made accessible. She discusses the way Holocaust films from this region address the imperative to work through the silences and suppression that have characterized Holocaust memorialization. The paper provides an overview of multigenerational cinematic portrayals of the Holocaust, from Claude Lanzmann's nine-hour documentary masterpiece *Shoah* (1985) to Laszlo Nemes's *Son of*

Saul (Rajna, Sipos, & Nemes, 2015). Portuges explores how as the contested terrain of personal, familial, and collective experience is inscribed in the interplay among filmmakers and their subjects, new visual, textual, and emotional discoveries emerge in Central European cinema.

In Chapter 7, Clara Mucci, in discussing *Son of Saul* (Rajna, Sipos, & Nemes, 2015) by Hungarian director Lazlo Nemes, confronts a major riddle about what it means to be human when inhumanity and annihilation prevail. In the midst of the hellish atmosphere of Auschwitz near the end of the war, Saul Auslander, a Sonderkommando, is determined to find a rabbi to bury a preadolescent boy, who briefly survives the gas chamber and who may or may not be his son. Mucci takes up the issue of how, when individual and collective life has been stripped of meaning, the only surviving meaning becomes a ritual, which symbolically reinstates civilization against barbarity and bestiality. Comparing Saul's compulsion to bury the body of his son to Antigone's determination to bury her father against the law of the state, Mucci takes up how rituals of mourning, including the rites and prayers with which we bury the dead, function to symbolically affirm the sacredness of human life, connecting us to culture and civilization.

In Chapter 8, "Sadomasochistic regression in *The Night Porter*," Bruce Sklarew encounters the complexity of sadomasochistic engagement and vulnerability to retraumatization. Set in Vienna in 1957, Max, an ex-SS officer and photographer reunites, via a chance meeting in an elegant hotel, with the gentile daughter of a socialist, his 15-year-old "possession" in a concentration camp. She eventually surrenders to Max's interest. Contributions from Primo Levi's S*urvival in Auschwitz* (1947) and Susan Sontag's views on the Nazis are explored.

In Chapter 9, "To know or not to know? Common themes in *Ida* and *The Flat*," Emanuel Berman explicates the ways that two seemingly disparate films *Ida* (Pawlikowski, Abraham, & Dzieciol, 2013) *and The Flat* (Goldfinger & Kufus, 2011) are linked by the processes of denial and dissociation in the face of the brutal murder of family members in the Holocaust. In *the Flat* (Goldfinger & Kufus, 2011), the director's grandparents are unable to confront or acknowledge not only the loss of their murdered relatives, but also their own friendship with a Nazi official who helped to orchestrate the Final Solution—a friendship that continued after the war and which was built on denial, in both families, of the extent of this complicity. By contrast, in *Ida* (Abraham, Dzieciol, & Pawlikowski,

2013), a young Polish woman, who was sheltered in a convent with no awareness of her Jewish identity and tragic background, is reconnected with her aunt on the eve of taking her vows as a nun. Her aunt, who has avoided this painful history by her participation in the communist regime as a judge who wreaks vengeance on the enemies of the state, informs Ida that she is Jewish and that her parents and cousin (the aunt's son) were murdered by Polish peasants who initially sheltered them. Both films involve journeys—internal and external—in which as the painful realities are revealed, denial and dissociation break down. Berman focuses on the emotional upheavals from the return of the repressed and the reconnection with the dissociated among victims, perpetrators, and their next generation.

In Chapter 10, "Inheriting Nazism," Régine Waintrater explores how the aftermath of Nazism still reverberates not only in the lives of its victims, but also among perpetrators and their descendants. Discussing Malte Ludin's film, *Two or Three Things I Know About Him* (Svarcová & Ludin, 2005), the author analyzes how the son of a Nazi officer uses the creative process as a means to discover and integrate a traumatic legacy. His quest is played out on the levels of collective as well as familial history, levels intimately linked in cases of psychic and social catastrophe. Waintrater explores how creativity can allow the subject to disengage from family loyalties and restore a space of thought that had been overcome by trauma.

In Chapter 11, a discussion of the papers, Nanette Auerhahn and Dori Laub reflect on how the formal qualities of cinema, with its privileging of visual and imagistic modalities including "the pallet of techniques available to the filmmaker" (p. 226) such as flash cuts and long tracking shots, flashbacks, and interweaving of different time periods and realities both internal and external, are uniquely suited to depict the panoply of historical and individual traumas that comprise the Holocaust. They focus on how "the language of film … approximate(s) the language of a psychoanalysis" (p. 226). The discussants further develop the point made by Sklarew (Chapter 1) that the power of film to transform the spectator into a witness devolves in part from the regressive experience of film viewing, which induces a dream state in which affects and sensations depicted on the screen are experienced with an immediacy that catalyzes varying degrees of identification in the viewer. Just as traumatic dreams are not direct reflections of trauma, so do Holocaust films fail to fully embody the "Real of the Holocaust" (p. 227) in the view of Auerhahn and Laub. Both trauma and film are encoded in the imagistic rather than lexical mode, which makes possible the encapsulation of traumatic experiences in dissociative states that may both disrupt and preserve the mental apparatus so that they may be subsequently integrated. Laub and Auerhahn speak to the necessity for such an integration in their statement that "the only ethical response to trauma is bearing witness and transmitting information," which they see as one of the primary purposes of Holocaust films. Such was the case with Arendt, who, in covering the Eichmann trial, also bore witness not only to Holocaust atrocities, but also to her own dissociated experiences (Chapter 5). In their discussion of the compulsion of Saul, a Sonderkommando, to bury a boy who may or may not be his son, in *Son of Saul* (Rajina, Sipos, & Nemes, 2015), they see not only the quest for cultural continuity and transcendence of meaningless and barbarity through rituals of burial, but also the fetishizing of such rituals to screen out the full impact of an intolerable and heinous reality that cannot be thought or known. Auerhahn and Laub (Chapter 11) recognize that films represent "Only one step in an ongoing, never completed effort at symbolizing trauma" (p. 228). In their view, the narrative of the Holocaust is a process of never-ending construction since trauma short-circuits processes of symbolization, seeking expression in an ever-widening web of images that "are continually symbolized and increasingly integrated into novel narrative contexts" (p. 228).

Psychoanalytic themes in Holocaust film

The psychoanalytic optic of our contributors helps us to trace the psychoanalytic themes that underlie the papers including:

1 The meaning and variants of survival and survivor guilt, and the psychic mechanisms that survivors used to manage the devastating legacy of the Holocaust, include dissociation, repression, repetition compulsion, and attempts at restitution. These papers take up the soul-destroying as well as soul-preserving aspects of such mechanisms for survivors; that is, the ways that survival itself may constitute an art form (Laub & Podell, 1995) when it spurs reflection and creative transformation of traumatic experience in life or art.
2 The extent to which the Holocaust, which involved an unprecedented loss of life and the disruption of links between the individual and his

or her cultural identity, disrupted processes and rituals of mourning; and the way film-making and film viewing can catalyze collective mourning that inscribes the individual in culture and community.

3 The ways that the repetition compulsion, with its intertwined roots in aggression and eroticism, is inscribed in the victims and survivors.
4 The extent to which the massive historical trauma of the Shoah created ruptures in the sense of identity, at both the individual and group level.
5 The role of the witness in the Holocaust experience and the extent to which watching these films transforms the spectator into a witness to the testimony about the atrocities they represent.
6 The role of transitional phenomena, creativity, and narration in fostering understanding and integration, rather than dissociation and repetition in the face of the Holocaust legacy for individuals and social groups.
7 The ways that psychoanalytic concepts such as dream and the dream screen, transference and countertransference help illuminate aspects of the film and film viewing process. Each of these themes will be further discussed below.

The meaning and variants of survival and survivor guilt

These papers take up the theme of how survivors deal with the tormenting guilt about surviving family and community, and its psychological impact on subsequent relationships and generation. As Ida states in the film of the same name when viewing the remains of her parents and cousin who were murdered by the Polish peasant who initially hid them, "Why was I spared … why am I not here?" (Pawlikowski, Abraham, & Dzieciol, 2013). In similar fashion, Joseph Fisher writes in a journal he left for his children documenting the atrocities that he experienced at the slave labor camp Gusen, and that he could not share with them during his lifetime, "I felt guilty for having survived … I have felt this way all my life and I can't shake the feeling … I often regret having survived. I say why me?" (Fisher, 2011).

The concept of survivor guilt has received relatively scant attention in the psychoanalytic literature per se, with the exception of those who have worked closely with Holocaust survivors and their families (Danieli,

1985; Laub & Hamburger, 2017); but it is recognized as perhaps one of the most potent affects that reverberates through the generations of survivors (Chapter 4). The capacity to experience guilt is conceptualized as a developmental achievement that in Freudian terms involves the instantiation of an individualized, but socially sanctioned sense of morality, stemming from tension between id impulses, ego, and superego (Freud, 1923). In Kleinian terms, guilt is thought to be linked to the depressive position, where the individual develops the capacity to feel remorse in the face of hostility toward objects who are both loved and hated as whole complex individuals and involves strivings to make reparation for any damage done to them (Klein, 1935, 1997).

In situations of massive historical trauma, where individuals were subjected to the repeated violations of human needs, dehumanizing tortures, and multiple daily indignities, where they were forced to witness capricious cruelty, sadism, torture, and execution of others, a devastating sense of helplessness ensued. Despite this sense of induced helplessness in the face of such massive aggression, or perhaps because of it, survivor guilt has been observed to be a universal experience often involving a loss of belief in one's own goodness and/or the goodness of one's objects (Laub & Hamburger, 2017). We see examples of this in *The Pawnbroker* (Lumet, Langer, & Lewis, 1964) where Sol is helpless to stop the fatal fall of his son from his shoulders in the cattle car, or in which he is forced to witness the rape of his wife by a Nazi officer. The failure to protect and repair one's objects may mobilize intolerable levels of aggression and despair. The result may be a chronic need for punishment (Nunberg, 1926) leading to massive self-directed aggression, as when Sol impales his hand on the spike or Ida's aunt, Red Wanda, commits suicide after finally confronting the remains of her son, sister, and brother-in-law who were murdered by the Polish peasant who had previously hidden them.

In these scenes of self-mutilation, self-destruction, and destruction individuals attempt to turn passive into active, to reverse the total powerlessness and passivity that Danieli (1985) suggests might be "perhaps the most devastating experience for victim survivors, one that was existentially intolerable" (p. 7). In *the Pawnbroker*, Winer (Chapter 4) makes the point that survivor guilt is the driving force of Sol's existence, leading him in two directions—both toward horrific self-punishment, near-total decathexis from others that enable him to ruthlessly exploit his customers in the pawnshop—an identification with the aggressor that also harkens to the destruction of his good internal objects. Ultimately it is survival guilt in Winer's (Chapter 4) view that leads to a painful traumatic repetition of Sol's powerlessness in the face of the loss of his son and family.

Yet understanding survivor guilt requires that we understand the way the individual psyche bears the imprint of collective experience. Guilt implies the capacity for choice and agency. In situations where both are massively curtailed, where the individual was rendered helpless in the face of extreme brutality, hunger, cold, and deprivation, "the room for choices (especially moral choices) was reduced to nothing" (Levy, 2015, p. 2440). In such situations, psychoanalytic conceptualizations of guilt, and/or defenses against it, may be inadequate. A number of the papers point out how guilt, either conscious or unconscious, may be dealt with through defensive maneuvers, including massive denial, reaction formation, projection, or dissociation. But these mechanisms that operate on the individual level are reinforced by culturally sanctioned denials of the extent of losses and traumas endured, in part because of the guilt they evoke, as is the case in Israel today (Berman, Chapter 9).

It is particularly in the arena of showing the intersection of cultural with individual defense that these films reveal their brilliance. The documentaries *The Flat* (Goldfinger & Kufus, 2011), *Six Million and One* (Fisher, 2011), and *Two or Three Things I Know About Him* (Svarcová & Ludin, 2005) may be seen as works that reflect the legacy of survivor guilt now reverberating in the second and third generations. In his discussion of *The Flat* (Goldfinger & Kufus, 2011), Berman (Chapter 9) points out how Hannah, the filmmaker's mother has kept survivor guilt at bay by a stance of not knowing that her own mother perished in a concentration camp, or that her parents maintained an ongoing friendship with a Nazi functionary after the war. When the filmmaker confronts his mother about the silence that enshrouded these issues, she says, "It's interesting but I'm not going to start looking into it … I don't really care what happened years ago. Will it make me see them differently?" (Goldfinger & Kufus, 2011). This statement articulates the conflict between knowing and not knowing about the traumatic past, "the compulsion to complete the process of knowing and the inability and fear of doing so" (Laub and Hamburger, 2017, Kindle Edition, location 850) that characterizes so many survivor families. The dissociative mechanisms that Berman (Chapter 9) identifies as crucial to warding off aspects of the traumatic past, and thus of survivor guilt, are conveyed by close-ups, which capture how evasions are written in frozen expressions of indifference or refusal to make eye contact.

In sum, these papers illustrate, up close, the psychic mechanisms that survivors used to manage survival guilt, as well as how in some members (the filmmakers) it functioned as an impetus for restitution and reintegration of disavowed aspects of family history. By doing so, these papers take up the soul-destroying as well as soul-preserving aspects of such mechanisms for survivors; that is, the ways that survival itself may constitute an art form (Laub & Podell, 1995) when it spurs reflection and creative transformation of traumatic experience in life or art.

Moving beyond dissociation, denial, and disavowal, the papers in this volume reveal the readiness to explore "the gray zone," that space that Levi (2015, p. 2418) posited existed during the Holocaust between the victims and the victimizers. Levi (2015) defined the gray zone as a zone with "undefined contours," that both separates and connects victims and perpetrators. He insists that whatever individuals did to survive, the distinction between victims and perpetrators can never be eradicated. Rather, the relationships between them, including areas of complicity and collaboration, ought to be rendered in all their complexity. Survival guilt, as the papers in this volume indicate, is in part a legacy of this "gray zone."

While survival was largely due to luck and constitution and involved inevitable compromises (Levi, 2015), survival was also sometimes miraculous, inexplicable, and an art form in itself when it involved a transcendence of bodily limits and possibilities and an apprehension of reality that allows for symbolization of trauma (Laub & Podell, 1995). As the authors represented in this volume point out, in addressing the complexities of the gray zone these films involve the creative transformation of "the facts" of experience, embracing multiple perspectives on historical and individual trauma, and opening up spaces for fantasy and symbolization that allow for further integration.

Winer (Chapter 4) has observed that: "It is one of the great ironies of the Holocaust that the survivors, on the whole, seem to have felt more guilt than their persecutors" (p. 82). Again, guilt or the absence of guilt, cannot be thought of as an individual phenomenon but is rather an experience that cannot be separated from the collective. Indeed, there is massive denial of the extent of the barbarism and complicity of the Nazi era in the case of postwar Germany as Waintrater (Chapter 10) points out, where, in the quest for normalization, an excessive concern with reconstruction and productivity replaced reflection on the Nazi past. In her analysis of *Two or Three Things I know About Him* (Svarcová & Ludin, 2005), Waintrater (Chapter 10) explores the Holocaust legacy in the one German family where the father, a Nazi functionary, was hanged for his crimes, exposing the mechanisms of denial, repression, disavowal, and dissociation through which not only individuals who participated directly in the Nazi regime, but also several generations of the German people, eluded their responsibility and guilt for the Holocaust. This chapter poses the question of continuities and discontinuities between Ludin's attempt to exonerate himself ("I do not deserve to die. I cannot plead guilty. I acted under the constraints of the situation ... in the framework of orders and directive ... I was firm but I committed no crime ...") and his grandson's statement that while he deplores the Holocaust and finds the Holocaust "distasteful and sickening ... it's my grandfather's guilt ... it can't be handed down to my mother and me" (Svarcová & Ludin, 2005). By contrast, another family member dies of alcoholism, which is attributed by her siblings to her unresolved anger about her father's execution and her inability to mourn his death. Mediating between these two perspectives is the filmmaker who goes against family loyalty to ruthlessly pursue and film the truth about the extent of his father's complicity in the Final Solution. By so doing, he attempts to integrate the excruciating legacy of guilt and shame that is denied by some family members, but that has destroyed others.

Primo Levi (2015) warns against indulging in armchair psychoanalysis, leniency, or confusion when considering the guilt or lack of it in survivors and perpetrators, saying that not only the victims deserve our compassion and help, but also the perpetrators, who should be punished but also understood. These films, which reveal what survivor guilt or lack of it looks like in individuals and families, both German and Jewish, contributes to Levi's imperative to understand the terrifying pressure that "a modern totalitarian state can exert on the individual" (Levi, 2015, p. 2577).

The repetition compulsion

The ways that the repetition compulsion, with its twin roots in aggression and eroticism, casts a shadow over the lives of survivors and their progeny, distorting identity and relational capacities, is another major theme that unites the papers in this volume. Caruth (1996) reminds us that traumatic narratives are permeated with oscillations between devastating encounters with death and the often intolerable sense of having survived it, particularly when others have not. It is this dialectic that leads the individual to seek out experiences that repeat this duality, often leading to reimmersion in traumatic encounters.

These points are dramatically illustrated in Sklarew's (Chapter 8) paper on "Sadomasochistic regression in *The Night Porter*," which revolves around a reconnection in postwar Vienna between Max, a Nazi officer, now working in obscurity as a night porter, and Lucia who became his sex slave at the age of 15 in the camp. A chance meeting rekindles their sadomasochistic bond, the lure of which is revealed in a series of flashbacks that, as the film progresses, escalate in length and intensity, slowly revealing the perverse core of their relationship. Sklarew (Chapter 8) discusses the complex and compelling ways in which eroticism and aggression comingle in their relationship, and ultimately lead to their annihilation at the hands of a Nazi group. Sklarew analyzes Lucia's return to Max as an expression of the repetition of her traumatic experiences in the Lager, where she came to sexual maturity under the directive of Max's sadistically tinged adoration. For Lucia, the violent and perverse experiences induced states of unbearable fear, overstimulation, and excitation that congealed into an indelible unmentalized core of trauma, structuring her object relations along a sadomasochistic axis that propels her toward a deadly re-enactment in which she both courts and defies death.

While the psychoanalytic conception of repetition compulsion is an aspect of the death drive in which eroticism becomes yoked to aggression, and pain becomes a route to pleasure in the sadomasochistic trope, these formulations perhaps need further amplification when understood within the context of the vast historical trauma of the Holocaust. Levi (2015) has called *The Night Porter* (Edwards, De Simone, & Cavani, 1974) "a fine but mendacious film" (p. 2439), mendacious perhaps because of the director Cavani's explication of the film as revealing "a victim-tormenter dynamic more or less clearly expressed and generally experienced at an unconscious level" in every environment, and for her statement that "we are all victims or murderers and we accept these roles voluntarily" (quoted in Levi, 2015, p. 2439). Speaking to this point, Levi (1986) observes:

> It is naive, absurd, and historically false to believe that an infernal system such as National Socialism sanctifies its victims: on the contrary, it degrades them, it makes them resemble itself, and this all the more when they are available, blank, and lacking a political or moral armature. From many signs, it would seem the time has come to explore the space which separates (and not only in the Nazi Lagers) the victims from the persecutors, and to do so with a lighter hand, and with a less turbid spirit than has been done, for instance, in a number of films [we are told by the editor of Levi's complete works that he was referring here to *The Night Porter* (Cavani, Edwards, & De Simone, 1974)].
>
> (p. 29)

Laub and Hamburger (2017), working from a perspective that integrates multiple psychoanalytic perspectives (psychoeconomic and object relations) with trauma theory, offer another way of understanding the phenomenon of the repetition compulsion. They hypothesize that in situations of massive historical trauma in which individuals are stripped of identity and dignity, the individual is plunged into a black hole in which there is a loss of inner sustaining objects, leading to a sense of paralysis and helplessness. In such situations,

> the traumatizing other, the perpetrator, then becomes the sole object to which the self can turn for help in the traumatic situation, and traumatic experience becomes encapsulated in a self-object fusion that is difficult to resolve and persistently impairs identity.
>
> (Laub & Hamburger, 2017, Kindle edition, location 737–738)

Such a trauma-informed object relations formulation explicates Lucia's compulsion to return to the sadomasochistic bond with Max, as well as her ultimate choice to sacrifice herself to it. One can imagine that Max remained as a tantalizing, tormenting, negative object in her unconscious linked to a representation of self as deprived and tortured, if desired and seduced (Fairbairn, 1952).

It is difficult to understand the nature of Eros, or the interweaving of Eros and aggression in the face of massive historical trauma, without taking into account such formulations. The phenomenon of identification with the aggressor that has been used to explicate the persisting identification of survivors with their oppressors, is also amplified by a consideration of the internalization of such a pernicious, deadly object relational scenario. In situations of massive trauma, links to good internal objects may be obliterated and the individual is left at the mercy of an internalized object relational dyad (victim and oppressor) that is encapsulated in traumatic experiences, with one side usually experienced at the conscious level and the other enacted and projected in ways that affect their subsequent relational experiences, and distort external reality and even, in some cases, reality-testing itself.

Weinstein's paper, "Between forgetting and remembering: two films of Alain Resnais" (Chapter 3), also offers novel perspectives on the phenomenon of the repetition compulsion that amplify our psychoanalytic understanding of this concept, by expanding it into the realm of the repetition of socially and historically determined imagery. Weinstein suggests that *Hiroshima Mon Amour* (Dauman, Halfon, & Resnais, 1959), by eliding the boundary between past and present, prioritizes repetition by showing how it can stem from a re-enactment of aspects of traumatic experiences that remain unrepresented and unintegrated in the life- history and psyche of the individual in which they are driven to re-enact. Further, the repetition compulsion is given new meaning by Weinstein's point that the two films are linked through the recurring images of mountains of hair or use of skin as drawing paper in the camps in *Night and Fog* (Dauman, Halfon, Lifchitz, & Resnais, 1955) juxtaposed with clumps of hair falling out or human skin floating off individuals from radiation poisoning in *Hiroshima Mon Amour* (Dauman, Halfon, & Resnais, 1959). The repetition of these images constructs a latticework that connects these two films. Two separate narratives, one of the Holocaust itself and the other of a doomed love affair between a French woman and a German soldier, are intertwined through images that function as signifiers resonating in the unconscious of the viewers as well as the survivors, as evidenced by their universality in dreams and non-Holocaust-centered films.

Repetition compulsion in Weinstein's (Chapter 3) view is inevitable in the face of trauma in that it involves continual and progressively more complex and complete iterations of themes, objects, events, sensations, experiences related to the trauma in which the compulsion to repeat may be ameliorated by "objects of desire that support the capacity to change" (p. 68). Trauma, in *Hiroshima Mon Amour* (Dauman, Halfon, & Resnais, 1959) is not located in the original events but in "its very unassimilated nature—the way it was precisely not known in the first instance—returns to haunt the survivor later on…" (Caruth, 1996, pp. 3–4). Weinstein reminds us that it is in such repetitions of images, artifacts, phrases, flashbacks, memories, and dreams that trauma narratives are constructed, leading to the possibility for mourning and reintegration.

Mourning: impeded and reinstated

The ways that survivor guilt and the repetition compulsion impede the processes of mourning, even while they propel individuals endlessly toward it, are also addressed by the contributors to the volume. In fact, a number of the papers make reference to the ways in which these films made by the second and third generations of Holocaust survivors, function to reengage family members in a mourning process that was stalled or truncated by the unimaginable and massive losses endured by survivors. In the "univers concentrationnaire [a dehumanizing complex system that permeated all aspects of life inside and outside the camps]" (Levi, 2015, p. 2414), where parents and children were separated and even made to aggress against each other, the ability to mourn individual losses was often crushed under the massive wheel of violence and menace. Levi (2015) reminds us that "never have so many human lives been extinguished in such a short time and with such a shining combination of technological ingenuity fanaticism and cruelty" (p. 2419)." In watching David Fisher and his siblings trace the trajectories of their father's traumatic experiences in *Six Million and One* (Fisher, 2011), both internally and externally; in watching Malte Ludin, the director in *Two or Three Things I Know About Him* (Svarcová & Ludin, 2005) come to grips with the extent of his father's war crimes that led to his death; in witnessing Hannah Arendt bearing witness to Holocaust atrocities she narrowly escaped in covering the Eichmann trial; in watching Saul Auslander, a member of the Sonderkommando in *Son of Saul* (Rajna, Sipos, & Nimes, 2015) rescue a young man's body from the crematorium and strive to give him a Jewish burial; in seeing Ida and her aunt reunited at the gravesite of their family members; in watching Bomba the barber in *Shoah* (Lanzmann, 1985) break down while re-enacting the process of cutting the hair of his neighbors before sending them to the gas chamber, we also see the resuscitation of a mourning process.

Yet as much as reinstating a mourning process can be healing, the papers in this volume also reveal the extent to which it can be annihilating.

Mourning, particularly in the face of traumatic loss, inevitably involves a resuscitation of anxieties about aggression, regrets around harm or neglect of loved ones, and desire to repair such hurts and to make reparation for past failures to love fully and adequately (Klein, 1935; Kernberg, 2010). In situations when the trauma of loss is compounded by violence such as occurred during the Holocaust, the pain of loss may be laced with excruciating feelings of hostility and guilt. This does not, however, necessarily lead to pathological mourning.

There are certainly examples of pathological mourning in these films involving an inability to acknowledge and mourn losses, such as the example of Ida's aunt Wanda, who evaded mourning by repudiating her kin (Ida) and who commits suicide after burying the remains of her family. But for the most part, the papers attest to how films open up spaces for mourning at both the individual and the collective level. This is perhaps the greatest appeal of Nemes' film *Son of Saul* (Rajna, Sipos, & Nimes, 2015), which takes us into the bowels of Auschwitz where the Sonderkommando, enlisted as slave labor in the factories of annihilation, do the most heinous work of leading inmates to the crematoria and disposing of their remains. Saul's compulsion to find a rabbi to say the Kaddish and give his son a Jewish burial, Mucci reminds us, constitute "a novel version of Antigone's ethical gesture cast against an order not only of conflict between laws, (as was the case in Sophocles' play), but of total devastation and annihilation" (p. 161).

Mourning, which ordinarily links family members to each other through traditions of commemoration and remembrance, was made near impossible for victims of the Holocaust. The typical and expectable cycles of loss and mourning through the generations were disrupted by the massive causalities and the catastrophic losses endured by survivors. The sheer massiveness and rapidity of the industrialized killing necessarily disrupted processes of mourning, as did the transports that separated and fragmented families so that they were often unaware of each other's fate, or unable to accept it. "In my mind, my father and my sister didn't really die.... after all I didn't see them die," says Joseph Fisher (Fisher, 2011). Danieli (1985), an Israeli psychologist who has worked with Holocaust survivors for many years quotes a 74-year-old sole survivor of a family of 72 people who stated: "Even if it takes one year to mourn each loss, and even if I live to be 107 [and mourn all members of my family] what do I do with the rest of the six million?" (p. 11). Mucci

(Chapter 7), Auerhahn and Laub (Chapter 11), and others in this volume suggest that in *Son of Saul* (Rajina et al., 2015) we "become" Saul, the member of the Sonderkommando, who in his singular and even mad struggle to bury the one, helps us to mourn the six million.

The papers in this volume also help us to mourn and integrate aspects of the Holocaust experience that have been denied full exploration, such as those of the Sonderkommando, who along with others who were enlisted to aid in the work of the Nazis, were among the most compromised and degraded of the victims (see Levi, 2015, for a discussion). In the intensely realized portrait of Saul we are a long way from the leering, menacing figure of the Capo [functionaries who aided the Nazis] whose image is flashed before us in *Night and Fog* (Dauman, Halfon, Lifchitz, & Resnais, 1955) when the narrator intones, "Who was responsible?" He responds to his own question by saying, "Not me says the Capo, the guards, the commandants" as though they all bore equivalent complicity.[5]

Lanzmann's film *Shoah* (1985) also includes scenes in which mourning for the dead is resuscitated though a revisiting, in the present, the sites of trauma where excruciating losses and betrayals occurred. Perhaps the links between Lanzmann and Nemes, the two filmmakers who deal head-on with the Sonderkommando, reside in their capacity to resuscitate mourning not only for the dead but for all that was lost to our collective humanity in the Holocaust. In one scene in *Shoah* (1985), Lanzmann interviews Bomba, a Sonderkommando who survived by posing as a barber and was assigned to cut the hair of women and children before they were sent to the gas chamber. When asked by Lanzmann what his first impression was when he saw all these naked women and children entering the gas chamber, Bomba initially turns away and is unable to speak, in a visceral gesture that bespeaks denial of grief. But as the interview continues, with Bomba circling around a man in a barber's chair while he trims his hair, Bomba breaks down while recollecting an experience where the sister and wife of a friend from his hometown came into the gas chamber. The camera zooms in on his face contorted by grief and pain—in a moment that merges dramatic fiction with documentary (Kerner, 2011; Portuges, 2017). He tells Lanzmann that he can't go on, "I can't do it, it's too hard," but Lanzmann exhorts him, "Please we have to do it, you know it" (Lanzmann, 1985). It is almost as though Lanzmann, in his staged interview with Bomba, one of the most celebrated and criticized scenes in *Shoah* (Lanzmann, 1985), is opening up a space for mourning in the here and now, not only for Bomba but for himself and the viewer in a way that could not be experienced in either a fiction film or a more formal objective documentary. In sum, these papers and the films they discuss reinstate mourning as a creative and productive process that allows for the existential acceptance and working through of losses both of others and of aspects of self. Could it be that film viewing may function as a collective and culturally sanctioned ritual of mourning in and of itself that allows us to reintegrate lost or disavowed aspects of collective history and experience into our ongoing self-narrative?

Identity: fragmentation, recovery, and integration

How mourning processes are connected to the process of identity integration and recovery of identity is another unifying theme in these films. Mourning, when short-circuited or denied, distorts identity so that traumatic experiences, rather than be reintegrated, remain unaligned in the self. Danieli (1985, 1998) and Laub and Hamburger (2017) in their clinical work with Holocaust survivors, have observed that in situations where historical and individual trauma converge, psychoanalytic concepts of identity may be inadequate to understand the regressions, ruptures, or dislocation in sense of identity that may occur at the individual or group level. Under ordinary circumstances we think of identity as an evolving process over the life cycle, initially anchored in integrated concepts of self and others, derived from early family experiences, but influenced over the life cycle, by ever-widening sets of identifications with community, nationality, religious groups that are taken into the self-representation.

Massive trauma and victimization inevitably creates ruptures in identity, at both the individual and the group level, by introducing experiences of self so extreme that they must be dissociated. Laub (Laub & Hamburger, 2017), Danieli (1985, 1998), and others who have worked clinically with Holocaust survivors and their families have observed there is no uniform or singular way in which experiences of trauma are woven into the identity of survivors and their progeny; rather the extent of ruptures in identity depend on the nature of the Holocaust experience, the extent of the victimization, as well the degree of destruction of all the existing familial and cultural traditions and supports. Danieli (1981) questions "the possibility of full integration of the Holocaust by its survivors and their offspring alone, while humanity, Western culture, and society in general have not yet done so" (p. 13).[6]

The papers in this volume address the attempt on the part of survivors to recover or integrate aspects of individual and group identity lost or obscured in the Holocaust, while at the same attesting to the ways that identity may remain fragmented, unintegrated, or inauthentic. Individuals in the second and third generations may experience the sense of being overwhelmed or colonized by their parent's unassimilated, unverbalized, or unformulated Holocaust experiences, while others may experience a hole in their identity stemming from their parent's inability to share crucial aspects of their experiences with them. In such situations, dissociative mechanisms may lead to multiple unintegrated self-states in both survivors and their progeny. Several of the papers in this volume, such as those by Waintrater (Chapter 10), Berman (Chapter 9), Diamond and Jurist (Chapter 5), and Ornstein (Chapter 2), center on processes by which aspects of such dissociated identity, at both the personal and the group level, are recovered and reworked by survivors and their offspring. At the same time, these papers also celebrate how survival itself is often a testament to some identity integration and integrity based on the restoration of good internal objects as evidenced by the creation of new enduring relationships and families.

As Ornstein (Chapter 2) points out in her paper on *Six Million and One* (Fisher, 2011), there were variations among the Fisher siblings in their internal representation of their father and his holocaust history and the extent of their identification with it. They also vary in the extent to which they view his survival and the journal that documents it as a creative transformation of unformulated traumas that separated him emotionally from his children into a dialogue with them that would allow him to face horrors and losses. While the oldest sibling, David Fisher, the filmmaker and mental health professional, embraced his father's memoir, stating, "I journeyed in the footsteps of my father's memoir" (Fisher, 2011), other siblings refused to read it and even expressed anger at the father for surviving. However, as Ornstein points out, by actually experiencing the places and spaces where their father had suffered, he came alive for them, both internally and externally. "When we went into the gas chambers suddenly Poppa was there with all the torments he went through and all the intolerable suffering," said one sibling (Fisher, 2011). Such imaginative reconstructions of the parent's Holocaust experiences serve to consolidate the process of identification, which involves "the transformation of the self-representation under the influence of the internalized object representation" (Kernberg, 2010, p. 607). Perhaps this is why one sibling refers to the trip as "psychoanalysis on a couch in a tunnel" (Fisher, 2011).

The complexities of individual and group identity, along with the cycles of ruptures and recovery that they were subject to in a time of massive historical trauma, are also explored by Berman (2017) in his analysis of *Ida* (Pawlikowski, Abraham, & Dzieciol, 2013). Hidden by nuns during the war, Ida learns of her Jewish identity only on the eve of taking her vows, only when she reconnects with her aunt, a major figure in the Polish resistance, who tells her that her parents, like most Jews, have died in the Holocaust and have no grave. Do we see Ida's ultimate return to the convent as a foreclosure of developing a more complex and nuanced identity that would integrate her Polish/Catholic and Jewish origins, or as Berman (2017) stipulates, as reflecting the complexities of identity in postwar Poland where both Jewish identity and the extent of Polish anti-Semitism and collaboration with the Nazis were submerged in the postwar communist equalitarian materialist ethos? The enigma of Ida and her identity is presaged in the opening images of her painting the face on a statue of Christ just before she learns that she is Jewish. It is also reflected in the elegiac pace of the film and its prolonged silences in which the camera portrays the characters (particularly Ida's face), lingering over expressions, and movements, as if seeking to penetrate to her essential core. That her inner world of memory and desire is never revealed is consistent with the film's emphasis on the unfathomable nature of her identity, or perhaps to its frozenness or fixity (Laub & Hamburger, 2017)—the legacy of her traumatic past of which even after she learns of it, she remains unaware. Berman (2017) reminds us that the film, although it won the Palme d'Or in Cannes for best foreign film, had a mixed reception in Poland where some deplore the film's portrayal of Ida's aunt, a judge who organized her identity around prosecuting enemies of the communist regime and then collapsed into alcoholism and promiscuity, as anti-communist. Others criticized the film for being unpatriotic in its depiction of Poles as murderers, when in fact Nazis bore the responsibility for killing Jews. These reactions show how "subjective transferential responses play a major role in any interpretation in literature and film" (Berman, Chapter 7, p. 208) and how such transferences may devolve from the fluidity of identity and identifications in the postwar and post-communist eras.

The papers in this volume suggest that in the aftermath of historical collective identity traumas such as genocide and holocaust, individual and group identity formation are rendered increasingly complex and the task of identity integration more challenging. Speaking to the significance of group identity, in one study, collective identity trauma was found to be a more powerful predictor of individual symptoms than traumas related to personal identity (Hamburger, 2017). The challenge of identity in our time is to integrate a multiplicity of selves, that is, disparate experiences of self each with its own patterns and dimensions, into a unity that integrates discontinuities and contradictions (Bromberg, 1996; Kernberg, 2006). Diamond and Jurist (Chapter 5) in their paper on the film *Hannah Arendt* (Brokemper, Rexin, & von Trotta, 2012), explore the multiplicity of Hannah Arendt, perhaps one of the most influential and enigmatic figures of the twentieth century, whose concept of the banality of evil, honed in her experience of covering the Eichmann trial, has left its footprint across two centuries. It has forever changed the way we conceptualize the nature of evil and state-sanctioned violence. Hannah Arendt's identity—including her sometimes seemingly contradictory selves—German and Jewish, philosophy student of Heidegger, a Nazi sympathizer and political theorist of totalitarianism, Zionist and critic of Israel—reflects the powerful and often conflictual historical currents of the twentieth century. Diamond and Jurist (Chapter 5) suggest that covering the Eichmann trail provided the impetus for Arendt to confront dissociated aspects of her own history, including her narrow escape from Gurs, the French internment camp only days before the Nazis invaded, as well as her guilt over her association with Heidegger, her mentor and lover who repudiated her after he joined the Nazi party. It was Arendt's capacity to tolerate multiplicity and contradiction in self and others that sparked the extraordinary originality of her thinking and the boldness of her ideas, and enabled her to identify and explore the complexities of the victim/victimizer dynamic in our time.

Testimony, witnessing, transitional phenomena, and the psychoanalytic process

The papers in this volume and the films they discuss attest to the role of transitional phenomena, creativity, and narration in fostering understanding and integration, rather than dissociation and repetition in the face of the Holocaust legacy for individuals and social groups. Located in that liminal space between self and other, the internal world of fantasy and external reality, individual and culture, objective and subjective aspects of experience, the transitional dimension as Winnicott (1967, 1971, 1986) defined it, constitutes a sphere in which the cultural history of the group is conveyed through the singularity of the individual narrative. Caruth (1996) writes: "Traumatic experience … suggests a certain paradox: that the most direct seeing of a violent event may occur in an absolute inability to know it" (p. 91). Knowing or understanding is fostered by the process of testimony, defined by Laub and Hamberger (2017) as "a meeting place for mutual witnessing and repair of trauma-induced fragmented memories and psychic disruptions" (Laub & Hamburger, 2017; Kindle edition, location 429). Since it is likely that for subsequent generations film viewing will be a foremost vehicle for learning about the Holocaust, films become an important repository for testimony.

Watching these films discussed in these papers, potentially transforms the spectator into a witness to the testimony of Holocaust experiences and atrocities. For example, Diamond and Jurist (Chapter 5) discuss how the spectator is transformed into a witness through watching Arendt cover the Eichmann trial. As we witness the cascade of Holocaust horrors unfolding through the testimony of the victims and perpetrators during the trial, depicted in an artful mix of documentary and fiction footage, we identify with Arendt's compulsion to bear witness to these atrocities and to seek to understand them. Laub and Hamburger (2017) emphasize the importance of such collective witnessing of Holocaust history as it is represented through different modalities and reinstated in domains that can be shared.

What realities can be mentalized and shared may vary considerably according to the historical era in which narratives of historical and individual trauma are constructed. A case in point is the lack of attention to the plight of the Sonderkommando and their demonization in the films of the immediate postwar era versus the sanctification of their suffering in the recent *Son of Saul* (Rajna, Sipos, & Nemes, 2015). The latter film has inscribed their experience in the collective arena of public discourse, where it could be more readily discussed, shared, and understood. Interestingly enough, a prior film, entitled *The Grey Zone* (Koffler, Lerner, Lerner, & Nelson, 2001), about the struggles of the Sonderkommando to save a young woman who survived the gas chambers in the midst of a failed attempt to blow up the crematoria at Auschwitz, had a mixed reception in the U.S. because it looked at the moral ambiguities surrounding the Holocaust. Even the director, who wanted to call attention to the plight of the Sonderkommando, confessed that he had difficulty watching the rushes. "I'm sorry to say this, but I couldn't watch some of it because it was so strong," he said. "I really hope people will be brave enough to go and watch the movie" (Hohenadel, 2001).

It is for this reason that the Holocaust may be an inexhaustible text, always in the process of construction and reconstruction. As papers in this volume attest, every generation and historical era brings to light new narratives, new documents, and new ways of understanding and conceptualizing them, mirroring a psychoanalytic process in which narratives are constructed and reconstructed as new memories, dreams, associations, and transference manifestations emerge. A number of our contributors make reference to the elements of psychoanalytic narrative and psychoanalytic process in these films. For example, in both *Two or Three Things I Know About Him* (Svarcová & Ludin, 2005) and *The Flat* (Goldfinger & Kufus, 2011), the filmmakers are propelled into a process of self-discovery by reconstructing the narratives of their families' fates in the Holocaust; but we also see the characters at times resist their own disclosures and insights. Furthermore, transference is at play in the films discussed, particularly in moments of breakdown, strife, or intense affect between interviewers and interviewees in documentaries such as *Shoah* (Lanzmann, 1985), and is also involved in the ways that the films are interpreted or received (Berman, Chapter 9). Countertransference is also evident in the filmmaker's relationship to his or her subjects. For example, in *Shoah* (Lanzmann, 1985), in the urgency with which Lanzmann implores Bomba to express his anguish about his own complicity as he mimes the cutting of hair and recollects the incident discussed above, he reveals both an identification with his subject and an intrepid neutrality that enables him to elicit tortuous aspects of his subject's history. It is hoped that in depicting the myriad ways that historical and individual trauma is represented in film, the papers in this volume will catalyze new perspectives on the reconstruction of trauma narratives in clinical psychoanalysis. Most importantly, these papers continue the psychoanalytic enterprise of helping to envision and understand what we as human beings are capable of, what we can endure, what we must repeat, what we can imagine, what we can change or not. Caruth (1996) notes that works of art transcend the limits of Freud's theory of trauma and traumatic repetition, creating a "striking juxtaposition of the unknowing injurious repetition and the witness of the crying voice" (p. 85). In reading these papers and viewing the films they discuss, we bear witness to these crying voices, ensuring they will not be forgotten and silenced, thereby continuing the ceaseless task of imagining the unimaginable and representing that which resists representation.

Notes

1 Nemes was interviewed after the showing of *Son of Saul* at the Hamptons International Film Festival in October 2015.

2 Indeed, there are even multiple perspectives about whether Holocaust is an adequate term for the historical cataclysm to which it refers. Some scholars object to the connotation of ritual sacrifice implied by the term Holocaust which originates from the Greek term for burnt offering, and prefer the term, Shoah which means "great disaster" (Berman, Chapter 9). The papers in this volume use both terms.

3 Filming the Camps: From Hollywood to Nuremberg: John Ford, Samuel Fuller, George Stevens: (Mémorial de la Shoah: musée, centre de documentation, March 10–August 31, 2010 curated by film historian Christian Delage).

4 The work the Hollywood team did in filming the concentration camps and war in general was carried over in their documentary techniques into later fiction films that became American classics such as *The Grapes of Wrath* (Zanuck, & Ford, 1940), *Shane* (Stevens, 1953), and *The Big Red One* (Corman & Fuller, 1980)—films that fictionalized aspects of the directors' actual war experiences.

5 These scenes also are reflected in films made by the directors later such as the scenes of the Joad family entering the migrant camp in California in John Ford's *Grapes of Wrath* (Zanuck, & Ford, 1940) where the camera moves slowly forward focusing less on the details of the camp than on the expression of its inmates.

6 Interestingly enough, a prior film about the struggles of the Sonderkommando to blow up the crematoria at Auschwitz that actually occurred near the end of the war, failed to receive much attention. This film entitled *The Grey Zone* (Koffler, Lerner, Lerner, & Nelson, 2001), and based on actual events, also revolves around a quest of one member of the Sonderkommando, who when he finds a young female still breathing as he cleans out the gas chamber is reawakened to the sanctity and dignity of human life. His attempt to save her transgresses the rules of the Lager, leading to her execution and that of the entire group. It is possible that this former film was released when there was an inability to think in terms of the "gray zone."

References

Abraham, E., & Dzieciol, P. (Producers), & Pawlikowski, P. (Director). (2013). *Ida* [Motion Picture]. Poland: Solopan.

Adorno, T. (1955). Cultural criticism and society. In *Prisms* (pp. 17–34). Cambridge, MA: MIT Press.

Adorno, T. (1962). Commitment. In A. Arato & E. Gebhardt (Eds.), *The Essential Frankfurt School Reader* (pp. 497–511). Oxford: Blackwell.

Arendt, H. (2006). *Eichmann in Jerusalem: A Report on the Banality of Evil.* New York: Penguin Books.

Bromberg, P. M. (1996). Standing in the spaces: The multiplicity of self and the psychoanalytic relationship. *Contemporary Psychoanalysis, 32*, 509–535.

Bromkemper, B., & Rexin, J. (Producers), & von Trotta, M. (Director). (2012). *Hannah Arendt* [Motion Picture]. United States: Zeitgeist Films.

Caruth, C. (1996). *Unclaimed Experience: Trauma, Narrative, and History.* Baltimore, MD: Johns Hopkins University Press.

Cavani, L. (Director), & Edwards, R. G., & De Simone, E. (Producers). (1974). *The Night Porter* [Motion Picture]. United States: Embassy Pictures.

Chare, N., & Williams, D. (2015). *Matters of Testimony: Interpreting the Scrolls of Auschwitz.* New York: Berghahn Books.

Cowie, E. (2005). Seeing and hearing for ourselves: the spectacle of reality in the Holocaust documentary. In T. Haggith & J. Newman (Eds.), *Holocaust and the Moving Image: Representations in Film and Television since 1933* (pp. 182–192). London: Wallflower Press.

Danieli, Y. (1981). On the achievement of integration in aging survivors of the Nazi Holocaust. *Journal of Geriatric Psychiatry, 14*(2), 191–210.

Danieli, Y. (1985). The treatment and prevention of long-term effects and intergenerational transmission of victimization: A lesson from Holocaust survivors and their children. *Trauma and its Wake, 1*, 295–313. Also in C. R. Figley (Ed.), *Trauma and its Wake* (pp. 295–313). New York: Brunner/Mazel.

Danieli, Y. (Ed.). (1998). *International Handbook of Multigenerational Legacies of Trauma.* Berlin: Springer Science & Business Media.

Dauman, A., Halfon, S., Kamenka, S., & Shirakawa, K (Producers) & Resnais, A. (Director). (1959). *Hiroshima Mon Amour* [Motion Picture]. France: Dajei Stdios, Argos Films, Como Films, Pathe Entertainment, Pathe Overseas.

Dauman, A., Halfon, S., & Lifchitz, P. (Producers), & Resnais, A. (Director). (1955). *Night and Fog* [Motion Picture]. Paris: Cocinor Films.

Delage, C. (2010). Filming the Camps: From Hollywood to Nuremberg: John Ford, Samuel Fuller, George Stevens: Mémorial de la Shoah: musée, centre de documentation, March 10–August 31, 2010.

Fisher, D. (Director, Producer) (2011). *Six Million and One* [Motion Picture]. Israel. Fisher Features Ltd.

Freud, S. (1923). *The Id and the Ego. Standard Edition, 19*. London: Hogarth Press.

Goldfiner, A. (Producer & Director), & Kufus, T. (Producer). (2011). *The Flat* [Motion Picture]. Israel: Ruth Diskin Films.

Hamburger, A. (2017). Genocidal trauma. In Laub, M. D., & Hamburger, A. (Eds.). *Psychoanalysis and Holocaust Testimony: Unwanted Memories of Social Trauma* (pp. 66–91). London: Taylor & Francis.

Hohenadel, K. (2001, January 7). The grey zone: A Holocaust horror story without a Schindler. *New York Times*. Retrieved from www.nytimes.com/movie/review.

Insdorf, A. (2003). *Indelible Shadows: Film and the Holocaust*. Cambridge: Cambridge University Press.

Kerner, A. (2011). *Film and the Holocaust: New perspectives on Dramas, Documentaries, and Experimental Films*. London: A&C Black.

Kernberg, O. (2010). Some observations on the process of mourning. *The International Journal of Psychoanalysis, 91*(3), 601–619.

Kernberg, O. F. (2006). Identity: Recent findings and clinical implications. *The Psychoanalytic Quarterly, 75*(4), 969–1004.

Klein, M. (1935). A contribution to the psychogenesis of manic-depressive states. *The International Journal of Psycho-Analysis, 16*, 145.

Klein, M. (1997). *Envy and Gratitude: And Other Works, 1946–1963*. London: Random House.

Koffler, P., Lerner, A., & Lerner, D. (Producers), & Nelson, T. (Director, Producer). (2001). *The Grey Zone* [Motion Picture]. United States: Lions Gate Entertainment.

LaCapra, D. (1998). *History and Memory after Auschwitz*. Ithaca, NY: Cornell University Press.

Langer, P., & Lewis, R. (Producers), & Lumet, S. (Director). (1964). *The Pawnbroker* [Motion Picture]. United States: Allied Artists Pictures.

Lanzmann, C. (Producer & Director). (1985). *Shoah* [Motion Picture]. United States: New Yorker Films.

Lanzmann, C. (1985). *Shoah: An Oral history of the Holocaust.* New York: Pantheon Books.

Lanzmann, C. (1994). Why Spielberg has distorted the truth. *Guardian Weekly, 3*, 14.

Laub, D. (1992). An event without a witness: Truth, testimony and survival. *Testimony: Crises of Witnessing in Literature, Psychoanalysis, and History*, 75–92.

Laub, M. D., & Hamburger, A. (Eds.). (2017). *Psychoanalysis and Holocaust Testimony: Unwanted Memories of Social Trauma.* London: Taylor & Francis.

Laub, D., & Podell, D. (1995). Art and trauma. *The International Journal of Psycho-Analysis, 76*(5), 991.

Levi, P. (1986). *The Drowned and the Saved.* New York: Vintage Books.

Levi, P. (2015). *The Complete Works of Primo Levi.* New York: W. W. Norton & Company.

Liebman, S. (Ed.). (2007). *Claude Lanzmann's Shoah: Key Essays*. New York: Oxford University Press.

Nunberg, H. (1926). The sense of guilt and the need for punishment. *The International Journal of Psycho-Analysis*, *7*, 420.

Rajna, G., & Sipos, G. (Producers), & Nemes, L. (Director). (2015). *Son of Saul* [Motion Picture]. Hungary: Sony Classics.

Svarcová, I. (Producer), & Ludin, M. (Director). (2005). *Two or Three Things I Know About Him* [Motion Picture]. Germany: National Center for Jewish Film.

V-A-C Foundation. (2017, May 30). *Christian Delage Film as Evidence: From Nuremberg to the Khmer Rouge Trials* [Video File]. Retrieved from www.youtube.com/watch?v=RyfBoGe2TVMFairbairn, W. R. D. (1952). *Psychoanalytic Studies of the Personality*. London: Tavistock.

Wilder, B. (Director). (1945). *Death Mills* [Motion Picture]. United States: U.S. Army Signal Corps.

Winnicott, D. W. (1967). The location of cultural experience. *The International Journal of Psycho-Analysis*, *48*(3), 368.

Winnicott, D. W. (1971). *Playing and Reality*. London: Tavistock.

Winnicott, D. W. (1986). Transitional objects and transitional phenomena: A study of the first not-me possession. *Essential Papers on Object Relations*, 254.

Zanuck, D. F., & Ford, J. (1940). *The Grapes of Wrath* [Motion Picture].

Chapter 1

The art and angst of viewing Holocaust films

Bruce Sklarew

Holocaust films furnish vital portrayals of unimaginable and unspeakable horrors. They bear witness to tragic degrees of sadism and human suffering. As commemorative works of art, they confront us and bring us closer to absorbing the nightmarish reality of the Holocaust, but they remain only a facsimile of the horror.

To understand why these Holocaust films evoke such profound, threatening, and other affective reactions, we focus on the power of their indelible images and the milieu of their viewing. A devastating dream or nightmare stuns or overwhelms us abruptly, but relatively briefly, but Holocaust films like *Night and Fog* (Dauman, Halfon, Lifchitz, & Resnais, 1955) and *Son of Saul* (Rajna, Sipos, & Nimes, 2015) continue to disturb and haunt us for a long time. Our associations with a dream's visual and auditory content can unveil unconscious latent content. With film, one can search for the equivalent of these associations through juxtapositions, flashbacks, thematic relations, and in the director's oeuvre and life. Their weaving of fragmented perceptions through the dream work's visual representations and secondary revision is similar to film images arranged into a narrative structure through editing.

The impact of both dreams and film—as with literature, theater, and the other arts—relates to the viewer's particular history and ego functions including memory, reality testing, synthetic functions, fantasy, regulation of affects, and regression in the service of the ego.

Viewing a film, one is "plunged into a darkened, anonymous and indifferent tube which allows this festival of affects we call a film … an erotization of the space" (Barthes, 1981). Self-awareness, censorship, and the defenses are lulled, and suspension of disbelief allows access to primary process thinking. In this regressed and permeable state of weakened conscious control, one spawns associations in the form of memories, fantasies, affects, forbidden impulses, and primal scene imagery from conscious and preconscious reservoirs. In the ambiance of the dark theater, the film viewer's perception is imposed by the filmmaker. For both viewer and dreamer, stilled in a regressive, passive-receptive position, the lights go out and images appear. Since the dream intrudes into the passive state of sleep, the dreamer does not consciously seek the dream or the nightmare. In contrast, the film viewer can be hungry for the film experience. In this primitive state the viewer is fed, drinking like the infant at the breast. Lewin (1946/1973) suggests that the breast flattens onto a dream screen with which we merge as we drift into sleep and the dream emerges. "The dream picture is as if painted on or projected like a motion picture onto a screen." In *Persona* (Bergman, 1966) Bergman shows a literal screen with a boy watching two women. Bibi Andersson, a nurse and caretaker, merges with Liv Ullman, a rejecting mother, as her son searches and caresses the screen. Early childhood dreaming prepares us for the affective response and the style of the film experience. The infant's experience at the breast, the dream screen, and the actual screen at the theater coalesce.

In this state of confinement, the moviegoer is more attuned to the primary preverbal infantile experience of visual and auditory stimuli—facial expressions, gestures, or body movements—than to language. In *The Pawnbroker* (Langer, Lewis, & Lumet, 1965), the survivor (Rod Steiger) kneels silently at the body of his murdered assistant, a surrogate son. A viewer complimented Steiger for his blood-curdling scream—a tribute to silent image-making. Silence, Steiner (1967) suggests, is the best response to the unspeakable. The exquisite *Night and Fog* (Dauman, Halfon, Lifchitz, & Resnais, 1955) needs little narrative to move us as it exposes the "welcoming" in the shower room; we see torn concrete in a ceiling gouged from desperate fingernails,

> the camera tiptoeing in and out of the rooms of horrible human remains and possessions, almost having the quality of props, and that we can look but we cannot stay—it's too unbearable and ultimately, we are not truly invited because we weren't there.
>
> (Kaufman, 2017)

Steiner (1961) said explicit signification is unnecessary—"the kind of thing under which language breaks" (p. 352). Looking at photographs can lead from the still image to vibrant and relentless motion. The notorious photograph of the lone small boy raising his hands in horror before threatening Nazis can initiate in the viewer a continuing progression of images through space and time to his destiny in the gas chambers, like spawning a film. While prowling in the streets of Marseille, Henri Cartier-Bersson said, "I craved to seize the whole essence, in the confines of one single photograph, of some situation that was in the process of unrolling itself before my eyes" (Cartier-Bresson, 1952). Parallel to motion in time the photographic image presents a surface that invites the viewer's curiosity to plunge cognitively and affectively into the beyond, "what the reality must be like if it looks this way" (Sontag, 1977, p. 17).

Symbolic objects other than images and texts absorb the impact of the Holocaust, such as the piles of shoes and the cattle car in the United States Holocaust Museum and the coffin-like structures in the Berlin Holocaust Memorial that evoke a flow of visual and olfactory reactions. Another vehicle is the touch of proprioception, referring to the "archives of the feet," as experienced in walking on the killing fields in Lithuania (Sklarew, M., personal communication). The witness walks on the floor of loose, rattling ceramic faces of victims in the Berlin Jewish Museum. In the film *Ida* (Abraham, Dzieciol, & Pawlikowski, 2013), the novice who was left on the steps of the convent—with no knowledge that she was Jewish—visits the previously unknown death site of her parents and brother. Siblings visit their father's place of death in *Six Million and One* (Fisher, 2011). The protagonist in *Son of Soul* (Rajna, Sipos, & Nemes, 2015) desperately struggles to find a rabbi among the arriving inmates to preside over the burial of a preadolescent boy with the traditional prayers. Saul believes the boy is his son and thus wants to preserve his Jewish heritage. Elie Wiesel (1968) said that to remember is "a '*matzeva*,' an invisible tombstone, erected in the memory of the dead unburied."

With the exception of Holocaust deniers, people cognitively acknowledge its reality. Dealing with the horrific aspects of the Holocaust, however, necessitates a suspension of disbelief reinforced by what is actually seen and heard. Ilan Avisar (1988) wrote of Primo Levi's doubting literary expression in portraying the authentic horrors:

> Compared with words, the photographic image is a better means of objective representation and has a stronger immediate and sensuous

> impact on the viewer. Words have weight; photos have shock value. The extraordinary power of revealing and arresting photos rests on a complex mental process whereby the visual perception is associated with the knowledge that what is seen is the result of objective recording, and hence the content of the picture is immediately recognized as a piece of authentic actuality (p. 4).

Roland Barthes (1981) said the photograph evidences that what he saw has indeed existed.

> Always the photograph astonished me, with an astonishment which endures and reviews itself, inexhaustibly. Perhaps this astonishment, this persistence reaches down into the religious substance out of which I am molded; nothing for it: photography has something to do with resurrection ... what I see is not a memory, an imagination, but a reconstitution, a piece of Maya, such as art lavishes upon us, but reality in a past state: at once the past and the real (p. 82).

The reality of the Holocaust is so unimaginable and extraordinary that it defies our basic notions of empirical reality, the raw material of every realistic art (Langer, 1975). It was an "experience under circumstances in which death is more 'real,' a more accurate measure of existence—gruesome as that may sound—than life." Langer concludes that "the moment one speaks of the 'reality of the Holocaust,' one is compelled to include its 'unreality,' since the two fundamentally coexist."

The immobilized, chained prisoners in Plato's cave see only shadows of reality projected onto a wall, as the film viewer and dreamer see only illusions, mere reflections of reality, but reflections of a visual and auditory narrative, which may be perceived as real. When awakening from a vibrant and disturbing dream, we ask ourselves, is it real? Sometimes we emerge from a Holocaust film uncertain that the events portrayed really happened, wondering if this horrendous event can have occurred.

Many struggle with the overwhelming emotional impact summoning resistance, using defense mechanisms such as isolation of affect, avoidance, and denial. Even sophisticated filmgoers will not see or rewatch a film like the gritty *Son of Saul* (Rajna, Sipos, & Nemes, 2015) because they fear the emotional toll of confronting the gas chambers and incinerators used in the mass murders of Jews, especially when carried out by

Jewish inmates propelled by the Nazis. The Sonderkommandos, who were ordered to complete the exterminations, ironically become victims.

Many also avoid Liliana Cavani's *The Night Porter* (Edwards, De Simone, & Cavani, 1974) because of the complicity of the victim in sadomasochism; however, it is not gratuitous but a "tribute" to the continuing vulnerability to re-enact sadomasochistic behavior decades later, even if culminating in death. In the final scene Dirk Bogard, a former Nazi camp photographer, and Charlotte Rampling, who at age 15 was "rescued" by him, walk across a desolate bridge late at night to be assassinated by Nazis.

Annette Insdorf in her remarkably comprehensive book *Indelible Shadows: Film and the Holocaust* (2003) refers to Siegfried Kracauer (1960) recounting the myth of the Gorgon Medusa "whose face, with its huge teeth and protruding tongue, was so horrible that the sheer sight of it turned man and beast into stone" (Insdorf, Introduction, xvii). Athena warned Perseus never to look at the face itself but only at its mirrored reflection in the polished shield she had given him.

> Perseus cut off Medusa's head ... the reflection of happenings which would petrify us were we to encounter them in real life. The film screen is Athena's polished shield. ... In experiencing ... the litter of tortured human bodies in the films made of the Nazi concentration camps, we redeem horror from its invisibility behind the veils of panic and imagination.
>
> (Kracauer quoted in Insdorf, 2003, Introduction, p. xvii–xviii)

Some watch Holocaust films out of curiosity or duty, or perhaps even to unexpectedly find sadistic gratification in identifying with the Nazis. Reading, being read to, listening to speakers, proprioceptive reactions, still photos, visiting museums or memorials or other avenues can offer us knowledge or an array of meaningful images, but none provide the perturbing experience of watching a finely textured film that can stir unsettling feelings and help us mourn and commemorate through its haunting artistry.

References

Abraham, E., & Dzieciol, P. (Producers), & Pawlikowski, P. (Director). (2013). *Ida* [Motion Picture]. Poland: Solopan.

Avisar, I. (1988). *Screening the Holocaust: Cinema's Images of the Unimaginable.* Bloomington and Indianapolis: Indiana University Press.

Barthes, R. (1981). *Camera Lucida* (Trans. Richard Howard). New York: Hill & Wang.

Bergman, I. (Producer & Director). (1866). *Persona* [Motion Picture]. Sweden: Svensk Filmindustri.

Cartier-Bresson, H. (1952). *The Decisive Moment.* New York: Simon & Schuster.

Dauman, A., Halfon, S., & Lifchitz, P. (Producers), & Resnais, A. (Director). (1955). *Night and Fog* [Motion Picture]. Paris: Cocinor Films.

Fisher, D. (Producer & Director). (2011). *Six Million and One* [Motion Picture]. Israel: Fisher Features Ltd.

Insdorf, A. (2003). *Indelible Shadows: Film and the Holocaust.* Cambridge: Cambridge University Press.

Kaufman, B. (2017). Personal communication.

Kracauer, S. (1960). *Theory of Film: The Redemption of Physical Reality.* New York: Oxford University Press.

Langer, P., & Lewis, R. (Producers), & Lumet, S. (Director). (1965). *The Pawnbroker* [Motion Picture]. United States: Allied Artists Pictures.

Lewin, B. (1973). Sleep, the mouth, and the dream screen. In J. Arlow (Ed.), *Selected writings of bertram d. lewin.* Hoboken, NJ: Psychoanlytic Quarterly. (Original work published 1946).

Rajna, G., & Sipos, G. (Producers), & Nemes, L. (Director). (2015). *Son of Saul* [Motion Picture]. Hungary: Sony Classics.

Sklarew, M. Personal communication.

Sontag, S. (1977). *On Photography.* New York: Farrar, Straus and Giroux.

Steiner, G. (1967). *Language and Silence.* New York: Atheneum.

Steiner, G. (1961). *The Death of Tragedy.* New York: Alfred K. Knopf, p. 352.

Wiesel, E. (1968). *Legends of Our Time* (Trans. S. Donadio). New York: Holt, Rinehart and Winston, p. 8.

Chapter 2

Six Million and One

A documentary

Anna Ornstein

Introduction

An increasing number of Holocaust-related documentaries have been released during the last few years but few offer the insight into the extreme conditions that existed in concentration camps, and few reach the emotional depth, that *Six Million and One* (Fisher, 2011) does. This is the third documentary in the family trilogy by the award-winning Israeli film-maker, David Fisher. By revealing his own family relationships, Fisher raises questions of universal importance. In *Love Inventory* (2000) he tries to solve a family mystery and, in the process, he brings his family closer together. In *Moster Round Trip* (2011) he tackles the question of father–son relationships. In *Six Million and One* (2011), he challenges us think about the varied ways in which the Holocaust legacy may be transmitted to subsequent generations.

In my discussion, I will first place the documentary into its historical and geographical contexts and comment on the survivor-father to the degree that his personality is illuminated in the film. Second, I will offer some ideas about how each of the siblings may have experienced seeing the places where their father labored under the most inhuman conditions during the last year of World War II.

The place and the times

Mauthausen is a small town located in Upper Austria, about 20 kilometers from the city of Linz. The stone quarry adjacent to the town was established as a concentration camp shortly after Germany annexed Austria in 1938. The infamous staircase that leads from a granite cliff into the bowl of the quarry is called the "Stairway to Death." It was on these 186 narrow steps that the prisoners had to carry stones strapped to their backs that were heavier than their body weight. As they were made to walk up the stairs, the weak ones would fall backwards and the whole column behind them would tumble to their deaths. The cliff, about 100 feet above the quarry, was called "Parachute Leap" because inmates were either thrown down from here, or the lucky ones could parachute themselves to death.

Over time, the Mauthausen concentration camp complex became one of the largest camps in the Third Reich, made infamous because of its extensive tunnel system in the bowels of the Austrian Alps. The tunnel system began with the excavation and building of two relatively small tunnels, called "The Bergkristall," that were used for the manufacturing of machine gun parts and submachine guns; the labor was provided by the slave labor of the Mauthausen concentration camp.

The Mauthausen camp complex included Gusen I and Gusen II and had 101 subcamps. The growth of the complex was related to the

Figure 2.1 Knoten_A8_1.

Source: courtesy of Martin Scheiber and S Consult Management.

planning of a tunnel system, which was intended for the mass production of fighter jets. This was to be the largest underground manufacturing facility, measuring about 50,000 square meters. The project began relatively late in the war, in March 1944—importantly, and probably not accidently—with the German occupation of Hungary; the tunnel went into production in early 1945. By the end of the war, in May 1945, close to 1,000 fuselages were assembled here. Mauthausen and its 101 subcamps had quarries, munition and arm factories, mines, and over 200 fighter-plane assembly plants. Originally it was not considered an extermination camp, but in its crematoria, at its punishment wall, in the extensive tunnel systems where Jews and political prisoners worked on meager food rations, and in its granite stone quarry, people died here almost as efficiently as they did in extermination camps. The death toll remains unknown, but most sources place it close to 400,000. As we learn from one of the guides in the documentary, the life expectancy of a Jew working in the quarry, building and working in the tunnels, was expected to be one week.

The Mauthausen-Gusen concentration camp complex became not only one of the largest but also one of the most dreaded camps during WWII; even inmates of Auschwitz feared being sent there. It certainly became the largest cemetery for Hungarian Jewish men between the ages of 17 and 44.

The father of five children, Joseph Fisher, a Romanian Jew, was a slave laborer in Gusen II. He was liberated in Gunskirchen but he was not free: in his soul, says his son David, he remained a victim; he was successful in hiding his emotional pain by working hard and providing for his family in Israel where he arrived at the age of 17 before the establishment of the State in 1948. His effort to protect his family from knowing about his horrific experiences came with a heavy price: in some essential way, he remained emotionally isolated from his children.

At various points throughout the film, David quotes from his father's diary, which Joseph wrote two years before his death. It was the diary, which only David read before coming to this place, that was the incentive for this trip and for the making of the documentary. From the diary, we learn that there were times when Joseph wished he had not survived. In the few photos we see, he appears somber, with a distant look in his eyes.

Though Joseph did not *speak* about his experiences in the camps, he obviously wanted his children to *know* what he had endured and the pain he had lived with over the loss of his parents and siblings; his family had been deported and killed in Auschwitz while he was laboring in Gusen II. He wrote that the diary was to be his "gift" to his children; this was to be their inheritance (quoted in Fisher, 2011). As many survivors, Joseph Fisher considered his Holocaust memories to be just as precious as material wealth that people leave for their children upon their death.

While he did not speak about his experiences, in the diary Joseph wrote eloquently and in great detail about the humiliations and extreme hardships in Gusen II. The vividness of his descriptions of incidents of cruelty leaves the audience stunned and horrified. It was from the impact of these memories that Joseph tried to protect his children; he wanted to be a good father, a good provider, not one who burdens his children with stories of suffering. The silence was also a form of self-protection; the memories had to be kept in abeyance so he could attend to his daily tasks. Like other survivors of major traumatic experiences, Joseph could emotionally not afford to actively mourn his losses.

Not that his memories were not available to him: in his diary, Joseph describes witnessing a supervisor demanding that a young boy, about his age, beat his father as hard as he could. From the way he describes the scene, we can hear the father begging his son to hit him in order to save the boy from a beating he is sure to get if he fails to follow the order of the supervisor. Joseph wonders, what would he have done in the boy's place? A question we all have to ask ourselves. And he writes about the constant, unrelenting hunger. One of the most touching scenes in the film is watching David aiming his camera on a tiny crab in the river. In his father's diary, he read that his father managed to catch a tiny creature in the river and—with tremendous discipline—he put this delicacy in his pocket for his dinner, but the creature managed to escape. Memories of hunger when a tiny animal caught in the river may be the only meal for a day could not be shared without fearing that such memories would be dismissed as not believable. Even more difficult to share were memories of witnessing the slow deaths of a sister, a brother, or a father, or having to watch the execution of a friend for failing to salute an SS officer. Memories of this nature could only be shared with those whom survivors could expect to listen with respect and understanding; nothing was feared more than indifference, dismissal, or a quick reassurance. Many survivors of the Holocaust experienced an unbridgeable gulf between themselves and those who were not "there." Coming back from a place where they had witnessed scenes that others could not believe and comprehend, they felt as if they were now living in two different universes; communication was safe only with fellow survivors. For Joseph Fisher, that fellow survivor was his wife; the children were only dimly aware of conversations between their parents they knew that they were not supposed to hear.

Unable to share their memories and their grief, many survivors wrote memoires after the war. Writing memoires was a safe form of communication: they did not have to worry about the responses of the listeners and, at the same time, they could give expression to memories they felt to be unspeakable and unsharable. Writing, similar to a psychotherapeutic dialogue, liberates affect and facilitates mourning. This was beautifully expressed by an Israeli writer, David Grossman, whose son was killed in one of the Israeli wars:

> I write. In the wake of the death of my son Uri … the awareness of what happened has sunk into every cell of mine. The power of memory is indeed enormous and heavy, and at times has a paralyzing quality to it. Nevertheless, the act of writing itself at this time creates for me a kind of "space," a mental territory that I had never experienced before, where death is not the only absolute and one-dimensional negotiation of life. I write and I feel how the correct and precise use of words is like a remedy to an illness.
>
> (*The New York Times Magazine*, May 13, 2007)

After reading his father's diary, David traveled to Gusen in the middle of winter. The audience is treated to some extraordinary views of the snow-covered, hilly terrain where—with a little imagination—they can visualize the thousands and thousands of slave laborers as they were driven to cut the heavy granite stones loose from the mountainside. They can imagine what it must have been like to be wearing thin, striped pajamas or some threadbare clothing in this bone-chilling cold. If they tried, they could also see the men's emaciated bodies and they could look into their hollow eyes in their unshaven faces…

These images may become firmed up in our minds as we listen to a conversation between David and a woman involved in the historical preservation of WWII sites. The woman tells Fisher that the quarry where they are currently walking will be filled in because constructions of new homes are planned on this site. As they trudge through the ankle-deep snow, they are also discussing how many layers of socks one would need to keep one's feet warm in this kind of weather. But people who worked and died here only had their old, worn-out shoes; chances are they did not even have one pair of socks in their shoes. After all, they were sent here not to survive but to work until they either froze or starved to death.

After visiting the camp and experiencing the emotional impact the visit had on him, David decided to ask his siblings to come to this place so that they too could get to know an aspect of their father's life from which their father had tried to shield them. He hoped that the experience would rekindle the closeness and intimacy that they had enjoyed as children.

When David returned to Gusen with two of his brothers and his sister (leaving the youngest at home), it was summer and the beauty of this area made it even more difficult to envision the suffering and the cruelty that this place had witnessed. Their minivan passes through the picturesque small towns of Austria with their Gothic churches and neatly kept homes and gardens. Looking at the blooming orchards and the tranquil green pastures surrounded by snow-capped mountains, one can be overwhelmed by the irony of it all: could a place like this ever have been the site of concentration and extermination camps? Could extreme hunger, torture, and death ever have existed in an environment like this?

What is the meaning of the title *Six Million and One*?, wonders one of the brothers: "Who is the One?" he asks. David explains: "He is our father; he was among the last ones to be liberated. Six million had died and the one, our father, survived" (Fisher, 2011). After visiting the camp sites, and seeing the various places where their father lived, worked, and nearly died, the Fisher siblings realized that their father's survival was a miracle; with this realization, their own existence appears to be a miracle to them.

The siblings arrive in a small town, which, in the 1970s, was built on the site of one of the camps. They see the people engaged in everyday activities: washing cars, carrying grocery, sweeping the sidewalks. Do these people, living their daily lives without much reflection about the past, do they know that their homes are built on a place where the greatest crime of the twentieth century was committed? As the siblings walk the streets with their earphones, listening to the history of the town, they come upon a remarkable street scene. As if to enhance the absurdity of what they are experiencing, the camera focuses on this group of merrymakers wearing masks and circus-like costumes joyfully blowing their horns. Further along, they encounter young people playing on the street, an extraordinary effective way to bring together two different, totally discordant emotional universes! Watching the film, one wonders: Will these scenes relieve the heaviness in our hearts or will they only increase it? For me, the macabre nature of these street scenes highlighted the madness that was conceived of and perpetrated by one of the culturally richest countries in Europe.

The film is particularly successful in bringing together the past with the present. The impact of this integration is most effectively achieved with the periodic appearance of a young woman as she reads the causes of deaths in the camps. The woman reads the list in a matter-of-fact, monotonous voice without the expression of any emotions: death by malnutrition, death by execution, death by diarrhea, death by vascular disease, death by suicide. Nothing could bring home the cold-blooded manner in which death was hastened and torture afflicted on Jews, Gypsies, and assorted political prisoners than the emotionless monotone in which the woman is reading this carefully assembled list.

The film achieves further depth and a sense of completion with the inclusion of two American war veterans who participated in the liberation of the Mauthausen camp complex. With the Russian army approaching from the east, the inmates of the Gusen camps were put on a death march to Gunskirchen. As the end of the war was nearing, the inmates of Auschwitz, Bergen-Belsen, Ravensbruck, and Gross-Rosen also emptied their human cargo into Mauthausen and Gunskirchen. These camps were also the destination of many thousands of Hungarian Jewish men who were on a death march from various forced labor camps inside Hungary. They arrived here only weeks before liberation; starved and totally exhausted, most of them perished in a rapidly spreading typhus epidemic.

The Germans left the camp two and a half days before the arrival of the Americans. They gave the inmates a sugar cube and a loaf of bread for seven people. When food ran out completely, they herded the prisoners inside and locked the gate, expecting them to starve to death. The Americans had to shoot the lock off in order to liberate the inmates. In their rags, half-crazed from hunger, those who could stand surrounded the soldiers and begged for food. Unaware of the consequences, the soldiers gave them their food rations and then, in horror, witnessed how in their efforts to save the prisoners, the food ended up killing many of them.

In describing this scene to David, the two veterans appear to have difficulty finding the words to describe the extremity of the conditions they found in Gunskirchen: the stacks of bodies, the dead and, with the nearly dead on top of each other, the terrible smell. These conditions traumatized one of the veterans to a degree that, 60 years later, he still suffers from a severe case of PTSD. Turning to his fellow veteran, the old man cries and appears in great emotional pain as he recalls what these starved, foul-smelling men looked like: the picture refuses to leave his mind.

In his diary Joseph Fisher describes the scene vividly:

> I was very weak; I could hardly walk or stand up straight. Inside the camp, the people were huddled together on the muddy floor. There were no beds. Some of the people were dying, some already dead. There was no room for us. The people were much older than we were and had arrived several days before us, so they took over any free spots. I had to sleep outside, in the snow. After a few nights outside, I snuck in to one of the buildings and fell asleep alongside someone who let me cover myself with his blanket. You might guess why this person let me stay … You are correct.
>
> (Quoted in Fisher, 2011)

At the time of liberation on May 5, 1945 about 85,000 emaciated men and women were found in Gunskirchen, most of them sick or dying. Because of total absence of hygiene, terrible overcrowding, and starvation, most of these prisoners died of typhus. Mauthausen and Gunskirchen were the largest cemeteries for Hungarian Jewish men between the ages of 17 and 46.

Miraculously, Joseph Fisher was able to make his way to a nearby house where he ate his first, life-restoring soup. Just before leaving the camp site, his children celebrated this miracle by having a picnic in front of this house.

After the liberation of the camps, there was silence among the survivors. The silence of Holocaust survivors shortly after their ordeal was over, was a necessary silence; it was needed for recovery, for the creation of new families and preparation for a new life. Young people without families, without a home, they had to build a future, many of them in countries where they did not speak the language and where they may not have been welcome. This was not the time to succumb to grief that could have rendered them unable to "go on living." Disavowal, the mental mechanism protecting them from experiencing unbearable grief, had to be left in place for a long time after the war. Fisher's choice of work in Israel would indicate that routine, mechanical labor, which required attention to detail, may have helped him reinforce his active effort at repression and disavowal.

The impact of the trip on the Fisher siblings

David Fisher does not consider this to be a Holocaust film, rather a film about "sibling intimacy"; in his view, there is too much laughter here for this to qualify as a Holocaust movie. I would have to disagree with him on this point. What David calls "sibling intimacy" reveals some of the *differences* between the four siblings in the way they were experiencing and were responding to their parents' Holocaust past. For psychoanalysts, the documentary provides a limited but important insight into the question of *transmission of the "Holocaust trauma."* Specifically, we learn that even among siblings, there are great variations how the second generation experienced their parents' Holocaust history.

David's motivation for this trip and his experience of it was very different from those of his siblings. He obviously deeply appreciated his father's diary; he received the diary very much in the spirit in which it was written: as a legacy, an inheritance that had to be treasured. Being a film-maker, David understood the historical significance of the diary and the making of the documentary; he was eager to share this with his siblings and with a larger audience. He hoped that putting the content of his father's diary into the context of the actual site of his suffering would provide his siblings with a broader and deeper understanding of their father—and that this new insight would make them more forgiving and bring them closer together.

However, his siblings came reluctantly and from a very different emotional place; they questioned his motives for bringing them here. Sitting in the minivan as they were heading toward Mauthausen, the conversation ranged from openly expressed anger by Estee and humorous teasing of David by Ronel—both indicating anxiety in anticipating what they may experience at the camp sites. Estee attacked David without mercy:

> I don't need this trip to know where my parents were … it is already in me … I am one big wound … I bleed every day … You think you

> had to bring me to Mauthausen to make me feel it? I have never been there before but I knew what it looked like…
>
> (Fisher, 2011)

The shrillness of her voice barely conceals her fear of facing the extent of her father's suffering. We now have to feel sorry for Estee as she feels that she is the real victim of the Holocaust. Isn't every child entitled to have normal, loving parents? she asks. Estee is angry at fate for her having been parented by Holocaust survivors. Her outbursts occur early in the trip and we can witness, in the course of the film, how her voice gradually changes; anger slowly being replaced by compassion and understanding. The most striking change in her attitude occurs when the group walks in the tunnel. She "reminds" her siblings that it was their father who built this tunnel. I believe, in reality, she "reminded" herself who the actual victims were of this crime and that they, the children, have to accept their own emotional burden of this painful reality.

Ronel's response to the trip appears to have been more complex, harder to discern than Estee's. In the van, he is using humor, gentle teasing of David to hold off the inevitable: seeing the site of his father's suffering. Ronel recalls moments with his father when he did not think that his father really understood how he felt as a young child. Their father could not deal with emotions; he offered practical solutions to every problem. Ronel does not speak of his parents with anger, rather he appears to try to understand his father by placing the man he knew into this other-worldly setting. It is Ronel we see crying; he looks sad much of the time, especially when he says that anyone who went through so much suffering, should not go on living: "I don't like that battle for life … I think I would have died" (Fisher, 2011). He concludes that his father survived because he was "a tough bastard made out of iron" (Fisher, 2011). In the tunnel, Ronel makes a strange comment: he tells his siblings that it is here, in this tunnel, that his father came alive for him. Ronel's identification with his father appears to have come full circle: it is here, in the confines of the tunnel, that all four allow grief to penetrate.

Gideon, sitting in the back in the van appears somewhat aloof. When he speaks, he makes positive, appreciative comments about his parents, maybe to "correct" Estee's view of them. He appears to be less emotional than his siblings, as if he had reflected and accepted his parents'

Holocaust pasts before he embarked on this trip. But, he too changes in the course of the trip by becoming more visibly moved.

Recognizing the difference between the four siblings' reactions to this trip, the insight that the documentary provides regarding the transmission of the Holocaust trauma is this: generalizing on this phenomenon only blurs the individual way in which each member of the second generation lives with and has accepted this painful legacy.

The last scene of the documentary appears somewhat contrived. The Fishers are enjoying a picnic in front of the house where their father ate his first life-saving soup. This is an idyllic setting, it is all green and pleasant and the conversation is light-hearted; they appear affectionate toward each other. The message here appears to be that along with the pain and sorrow, there is also triumph in survival. The audience, however, has to wonder: Will the changes in their feelings toward their survivor-parents change for good? Will Estee return to the hurt and anger she had felt for not having been a properly loved child? Will Ronel use humor to overcome his identification with a remote and depressed father?

What we can predict is that David will continue to transform his experiences into the art of film-making. I am certainly glad he made this film, which, in my view, stands out among Holocaust documentaries because of its artful integration of spontaneous, highly revealing conversations among the siblings with information regarding the extent of cruelty that existed in concentration camps. The documentary also illuminates the National Socialist Government's resolve to pursue the war when the German military was already in full retreat. The documentary depicts a time in the war when the Germans were trying to save Berlin and were determined to complete the Final Solution by killing as many Jews as was possible in the rapidly shrinking territories they still occupied.

References

Fisher, D. (Director, Producer). (2011). *Six Million and One* [Motion Picture]. Israel. Fisher Features Ltd.

Grossman, D. (2007, May). Writing in the dark. *The New York Times Magazine.* Retrieved from www.nytimes.com/2007/05/13/magazine/13Israel-t.html.

Chapter 3

Between forgetting and remembering

Two films of Alain Resnais

Lissa Weinstein

Introduction

This chapter will examine two films by Alain Resnais, *Night and Fog* (Dauman, Halfon, Lifchitz, & Resnais, 1955) and *Hiroshima Mon Amour* (Dauman, Halfon, & Resnais, 1959). At first glance, both their subjects and their chosen genre (documentary versus fiction) appear disparate, yet a closer examination of both their form and content suggests that they are successive iterations of a singular trauma. This thinking is in line with recent efforts to reconsider the realist imperative and the "conservative doctrine of verisimilitude" (Kerner, 2011) that has formed the core of efforts to represent the Holocaust. In this wider line of thinking, all Holocaust films are "re-presentations" of an event; therefore even films that do not take the Holocaust as their overt subject, for example, Franju's documentary of the Parisian slaughterhouses, *Le Sang des Betes* (Legros & Franju, 1949), or *Hiroshima Mon Amour* (1959) might still be considered representations of the Holocaust based on their central themes of mass slaughter as well as the inclusion of iconic imagery associated with more direct representations of the Holocaust. Conceptualized in this way, the relationship between *Night and Fog* (Dauman, Halfon, Lifchitz & Resnais, 1955) and *Hiroshima Mon Amour* (Dauman, Halfon, Kamenka, Shirakawa & Resnais, 1959) can be used to examine questions about the construction of the trauma narrative and its veracity and utility as a therapeutic tool, both issues that have been addressed in the psychoanalytic literature as well (Laub, 1991; Laub & Auerhahn, 2017; Rosenblum, 2009*)*.

Originally, my intention had been to contrast filmic representations of trauma and discuss their relationship to the neuropsychology of memory. *Night and Fog* (Dauman, Halfon, Lifchitz, & Resnais, 1955) was seen as an exemplar of the documentary genre. Despite recent questioning of the supposed "truth value" of documentary film and even its viability as a category (Godmilow & Shapiro, 1997), it is a genre that has historically been defined by its indexical relationship to reality. There is an inherent supposition that an objective actuality exists, one that a subject can take hold of through an act of perception that will allow him or her to remain a removed observer, rather than being implicated in the events depicted or taking an active part in the construction of a narrative. The documentary filmmaker maintains fidelity to this idea through meticulous research and the maintenance of a distal perspective. Put simply, a documentary should leave the facts to speak for themselves. On the surface, *Night and Fog* (Dauman, Halfon, Lifchitz, & Resnais, 1955) meets these criterion; one can note its seemingly clear separation of past and present through the cinematic contrast of black-and-white archival footage with the Kodachrome colors that Resnais used to photograph the camps as they existed in 1955, a linear conception of time suggested by the sweep of the narrative beginning with the advent of National Socialism in the critical year of 1933 and ending with the Nuremberg trials, and Resnais' use of the long takes and distance shots common in documentary filmmaking. Further, the inclusion of newsreels, photographs, and other visual documents, as well as clips of films taken by the British, Americans, and Russians at the liberation of Bergen-Belsen, Mauthausen, and Auschwitz supports *Night and Fog*'s authenticity. In contrast, *Hiroshima Mon Amour* (Dauman, Halfon, & Resnais, 1959), a fictional film that uses scripted actors, has been examined in the light of a discourse of trauma that prioritizes repetition, condensation of past and present through the shattering of time, and the critical role of the witness in the need for reconstruction (e.g. Caruth, 1996; Hegarty, 2013; Shinebourne, 2006). Because it highlighted its protagonists' subjectivities as a narrative device, *Hiroshima Mon Amour* (Dauman, Halfon, & Resnais, 1959) was seen as diametrically opposed to the objectivity of *Night and Fog* (Dauman, Halfon, Lifchitz, & Resnais, 1955).

When working with art, it is necessary to let the other live inside you, just as it is with patients. As one becomes intimate with these two films, these heuristic distinctions that are so critical to theory become far less central in practice, much like the initial opposition drawn between remembering and repeating (Freud, 1914). Instead, a fundamental unity between the two works emerges upon repeated viewing, with *Hiroshima Mon Amour* (Dauman, Halfon, & Resnais, 1959) continuing to explore the same questions inevitably raised by the horrors depicted in *Night and*

Fog (Dauman, Halfon, Lifchitz, & Resnais, 1955), questions such as one's capacity to truly see, metaphorically to "know" the experiences of another's trauma, the veracity of memory and the questionable truth of the visual record, a concern with the distinctions between living and dead, body and object. In both *Night and Fog* (Dauman, Halfon, Lifchitz, & Resnais, 1955) and *Hiroshima Mon Amour* (Dauman, Halfon, & Resnais, 1959), Resnais will destabilize the position of the observer, leaving him or her unsure of what has transpired, and alter the usual linear and unidirectional relationship between past and present, thus encouraging a visceral connection to the visual material. The films are also connected by several technical devices—the use of quick cutting between different time periods without explanation and long tracking shots. In addition, they share numerous iconic images, among them bodily mutilations, shorn hair, skin, and ash, and eyes that do not see.

Night and Fog

"Nacht und Nebel," a term Himmler borrowed from Goethe to describe clandestine actions, referred to a German Army decree of December 1941 aimed at rooting out resistance in the occupied territories; suspects were taken to the camps in "night and fog." As a film title, it suggests a need to bring to light the *actual* events of the Holocaust; the idea for the film was suggested by the Comité d'historie de la Seconde Guerre Mondiale, a group of French historians studying WWII. Initially, Resnais was reluctant to make the film, as he believed a film about the camps should be made by someone who had experienced them, but agreed when Jules Cayrol, who had been a "Night and Fog" prisoner and whose parents had died in the camps, would write the script. As Grant and Sloniowski (1998) note, their different experiences of the Holocaust are woven into the film, contributing to the impression of a multi-voiced narrative, where the viewer must navigate between a more distal perspective and absorption in the imagery.

In this 32-minute film the facts appear to be the facts. Yet Resnais works continually to subvert the position of the observer. As Hebard (1997) suggests, the archival footage used is distressing "not so much from the images themselves, but rather from the use of the images mediated through montage and commentary" (p. 88). It is Resnais' purposeful juxtaposition of the archival material with the present-day footage and the desyncronization of the usually intertwined element of vision, narration, and music that makes the visual material so powerful, and works to "defamiliarize" the archive, thereby making the binding of affect and subsequent mastery of the trauma depicted more difficult. Even today, when many of the images are well known, *Night and Fog* (Dauman, Halfon, Lifchitz, & Resnais, 1955) shocks us, made even more alarming on repeated viewings; it remains for many *the* film of Nazi genocide (Insdorf, 2003; Nysenholc, cited in Wilson, 2005). Yet it is unusual for a film depicting horrific genocide to include an humorous/ironic narration recounting the architectural styles of the camp watchtowers—"Alpine, Garage, Japonaise, No Style"—while at other moments we hear a stark, neutral recounting of what was done with the skin, bones, hair, of the inmates of the camps. Far from a distant, neutral view, Resnais brings us into the camps as the film proceeds, literally into the belly of the beast, but as he does so, he erases not only the distinction between past and present, but also that of victim and victimizer and the living and the dead, upon which the film seems to be predicated. Despite its overt linear narrative, Resnais repeatedly sets up obstacles to "undisturbed vision" (Bersani & Dutoit, 1992, p. 19), that serve to "inhibit any account-giving, or any story-making on the part of the spectator" (ibid., p. 21).

The film begins with a placid view of the Polish countryside. As the camera slowly pans to the right, barbed wire rises into view from below, springing from the ground like tombstones in a horror movie cemetery as the narrator describes the "paysage tranquille" (calm landscape); abandoned observation towers join the scene. The soothing, slow rhythm of the left to right tracking shots (which Resnais will use repeatedly for the present-day footage) and the lilting song of the accompanying woodwinds is contradicted both by the visual of the barbed wire and the narration that tells us: "Even a road where cars and peasants and couples walk, even resort village with a steeple and a country fair can lead to a concentration camp." The narration reassures us: "No step can be heard but our own." Paradoxically, within seconds, there is a quick cut to newsreel footage, a scene from Leni Riefenshtals' *Triumph of the Will* (Riefenstahl, 1935), where the Nazis are seen marching from right to left. This directional shift, opposite to the original shots that established a complacent separation of past and present, now undoes the viewer's comfortable remove. The soldiers then march directly toward the viewer, as sounds of their goosesteps are accompanied by drum rolls, and then by mournful strings. Serenity destroyed.

The violence of the archival scenes is communicated directly through the rapid editing of the still footage; the frenetic pace of the group scenes contrasts with the bucolic present. There is also an effort to revivify those on their way to the camps, as still photographs from the archives are often followed by scenes of movement, as if these people, whom we know to be already dead, are still moving amongst us (Wilson, 2005). Related to this is Resnais' efforts to personalize the victims. Although he follows no particular individual's story, he notes that as the camps are being built, "Berger, a German worker, Stern, a Jewish student in Amsterdam, Schumlski and Annette a school girl in Amsterdam go about their daily lives, not knowing a place is being prepared for them." This naming of victims precedes and personalizes the archival footage of the group scenes of deportations shot at a distance with a high camera and the matter-of-fact recitation of the widely dispersed cities where they took place—Warsaw, Lodz, Prague, Brussels, Athens, Zagreb, Odessa, Rome. In one scene, the camera will linger on the face of a woman with a frozen catatonic stare, and later fixate on a girl staring through the doors of the cattle cars before they close. In another series of images, we see Resnais' efforts to communicate the humanity of the victims despite, or perhaps because of, the humiliation they suffer. A man pushes his mother, lying supine in a primitive wooden conveyance, to the cattle cars, a father holds the hands of his clearly terrified children. All of these shots work to build the viewer's identification with the victims.

Yet in other scenes the camera position forces us to simultaneously recognize, on a visceral level, our complicity with the perpetrators. One scene is filmed through the windows of an observation tower "from which soldiers stood watch, aiming at the prisoners on occasion killing them out of boredom." As audience we are both victim and Gestapo, seeing the camp as the guards would have, far from the faceless victims below. The calming nature of the present-day color scenes, the seductive beauty of the film, allows, or more accurately compels, us to see ourselves in the executioners. Thus, the shock is even greater when the next intrusive archival "flashback" scene is of a prisoner having electrocuted himself on the barbed wire, followed shortly by rows of naked men at roll-call attempting to cover their genitals.

Despite the overtly clear separation of past and present, there are moments in *Night and Fog* (Dauman, Halfon, Lifchitz, & Resnais, 1955) where it becomes ambiguous whether we are watching an archival segment or one that Resnais has reconstructed whose photographic texture is closer to that of the present-day scene (Bersani & Dutoit, 1993). The quick intercutting of archival footage of the trains leaving for the camps with the present-day view along the remains of the tracks is shot as though the viewer were looking out from the conductor's window in the front car. This view immediately cuts back again to archival footage of a night arrival. Lest one forget, as the present-day train slowly winds toward the camp, the narration brings us into the camps, informing us of what can be seen: "... the corpses that fell to the ground when the car doors opened ... those driven by gunpoint to the camps amid barking dogs and glaring searchlights, with the flames of the crematoria in the distance." Similarly, the scenes filmed in a sepia-like color form a compromise between color and black and white.

At several points, the color palettes representing past and present begin to interpenetrate. For example, the colors of the present fade as the camera pans along the bunks where the prisoners were housed. In another scene, perhaps the culminating image of *Night and Fog* (Dauman, Halfon, Lifchitz, & Resnais, 1955), Resnais brings us into the gas chamber, points the camera up at the ceiling from below, just the way the victims would have looked at it, to show the desperate scratches of their fingernails on the concrete as they tried to escape. Just as the viewer is experiencing being in the chamber, he cuts to a terrifying shot of a woman frozen in death (presumably from the gas) and for a moment the viewer experiences himself as lying next to that woman.

Perhaps what is most profoundly upsetting about *Night and Fog* (Dauman, Halfon, Lifchitz, & Resnais, 1955) is the depiction of the gradual loss of the humanity of the camp inmates; as the film progresses, they metamorphose into what Primo Levi (1947/2013) called Musselmen. These were inmates who while still alive were hard to distinguish from the dead, literally living corpses. When Resnais brings us inside the camp hospital, he concludes: "In the end each inmate resembles the next, a body of indeterminate age that dies with its eyes wide open." Watching the inmates lie moving almost imperceptibly on the hospital beds, the viewer enters what Masahiro Mori (1970), the Japanese roboticist, would later term the "Uncanny Valley," where the response to a humanlike robot shifts from empathy to fear and extreme distaste as the robot approaches human qualities while still failing to become fully lifelike. One could speculate that this unwilled uncanny response, a wish to turn away from the Musselmen, also places the viewer momentarily in identification with the Germans, who similarly wished "not to see" these people as fully human.

With the institution of the gas chambers the attempt to maintain the individual status of the inmates, all efforts at revivification, are defeated. The ovens can handle thousands of bodies a day. We see the transformation from living bodies into inanimate objects, no more than names on endless ledgers, no different from the materials used by Krupps, or Siemanns, or Henkels, all factories that employed inmates to make their products. At first, Resnais shows only the possessions of the inmates—combs, eyeglasses, shaving brushes. Then a shot of mountains of hair, but this fascinating image soon becomes an abstraction, shutting out momentarily an awareness of the thousands of heads that must have produced the hair and the neat rolls of cloth it turns into. The bones are similarly turned to fertilizer for organized rows of cabbage. Yet when describing the uses that the bodies were put to, the narration fails, leaving a few seconds of silence. What has been suggested earlier has come to pass—that there are no words: "The reality of these camps, despised by those who designed them and unfathomable to those who endured them. No description, no image can reveal their true dimension, endless uninterrupted fear." Heads, their expressions still visible, some with eyes open, lips pursed, fill a bucket. Separated, but nearby, their bodies line up like slaughtered cattle.

Resnais concludes the film with an interrogation: "Who is responsible?," reminding us of the moral imperative that forms the core of the film. Capos, guards, commandants, all deny their part. Yet Resnais implies that we too have watched from the perspective of the watchtower. Soothed by the passage of time and the concealing calm of the present one can become comfortable with an evil that is both banal and seductive. It is not a closed question, and Resnais omits the usual "Fin" at the end of the narrative.

On the surface, *Night and Fog* (Dauman, Halfon, Lifchitz, & Resnais, 1955) appears to be a film urging us not to forget something that is now fading from societal memory. But Resnais does much more, involving and implicating the viewer in the transpired events. Despite the screen of a linear narrative, instead of ordered events we find an alternation between a linear sense of time and a disjointed one, and between images of relative containment, narrative sense, and unexpected shock. Memory is detached and fragmented, with frequent intrusions of unwelcome images into the present, horror invading beauty. Because it is difficult to define a singular position of observation, there is a concomitant loss of distinction between victim and victimizer, the distinction further erased through shame and guilt, even at the mere observation of the trauma. The lack of integration is shown metaphorically through the disjunctions between the spoken narrative, the music, and the visual while the fragmentation of the self and loss of personal identity is shown in the increasing anonymity of the victims. Thus, in *Night and Fog* (Dauman, Halfon, Lifchitz, & Resnais, 1955), we find one iteration of traumatic remembering. On the continuum, "Forms of Knowing," proposed by Laub and Auerhahn (1993), *Night and Fog* (Dauman, Halfon, Lifchitz, & Resnais, 1955) would represent an early form of engagement, which they term "not knowing," as the ego's ability to formulate experience has been compromised by trauma. Thus, while there is an acknowledgment of the trauma, shown in the overt linear narrative, there is also simultaneous fragmentation and lack of integration of less conscious elements.

Hiroshima Mon Amour

Resnais was approached by the producers of *Night and Fog* (Dauman, Halfon, Lifchitz, & Resnais, 1955) to produce a documentary about Hiroshima. He refused, believing that excellent documentaries, which had not been distributed to the public, already existed. However, it may be that Resnais' refusal was also influenced by the fact that the creation of *Night and Fog* was itself distressing him, and as Laub (1991) notes, the close study of trauma is, in itself, traumatic. Resnais reported nightmares and disturbed sleep during the editing and said during an interview in 1994: "You can't imagine what it was like manipulating these kinds of images, editing them together … we all felt like were working in a strange atmosphere." Resnais concluded that he could only remake *Night and Fog* (Dauman, Halfon, Lifchitz, & Resnais, 1955), that despite the different circumstances, the actual subject, the memory of horror, would be the same (Moses, 1987). Meeting with Marguerite Duras, who eventually wrote the screenplay, they spoke only of how they could not write a documentary about Hiroshima. Resnais noted that "what has to be filmed," is "the impossibility of filming it—all you could do was suggest the horror and if you had to show the horror in film, the horror disappears" (*Hiroshima Mon Amour*, 2010). It is possible, perhaps imperative, to document the Holocaust—to show the mountains of shorn hair, piles of eyeglasses, skin turned to paper, bodies dumped into pits, heads severed—but how does one communicate what Nazism is, something far more elusive than the actions of the Nazis, an affective experience in which both victims and perpetrators participate—more than history and less than historical fact. What needs to be captured and bound is itself an absence, a gap in the experience both of time and identity; without the unity of affect and memory, there is only screen memory, a fetishistic attachment to fact that is used primarily to defend against the real. The documentary format was no longer sufficient to fulfill the imperative of memory, which is more than mere recall, but involves the reintegration of the experience, which has been excluded from any modification by association with the dominant mass of ideas in the ego, to borrow from Freud (1895). Duras and Resnais decided instead to make a fiction film. Perhaps as a compromise, the first 15 minutes of *Hiroshima Mon Amour* (Dauman, Halfon, & Resnais, 1959) include a "false" documentary, reminiscent of *Night and Fog*, detailing the tragedy of Hiroshima as seen from the outside, using a combination of archival news footage and pieces of other feature and documentary films interspersed with present-day scenes narrated by the film's female protagonist.

In *Hiroshima Mon Amour* (Dauman, Halfon, & Resnais, 1959), Resnais, hoping to better comprehend the nature of suffering, chose to explore the mind of a single individual struggling with that which cannot be contained psychically or represented, but must be enacted. Through exploring subjective, psychological time (Luchting, 1963), and its interaction with the present, Resnais offers a small and intimate study of suffering, one that traverses the distance between the unbounded nature of historical and cultural trauma and the claustrophobia of individual pain, each venue illuminating the other.

Yet, despite the change in venue, *Night and Fog* (Dauman, Halfon, Lifchitz, & Resnais, 1955) did not simply disappear. As noted earlier, Resnais' two films are linked both through formal filmic techniques, for example, the desynchrony of music, narration, and visual text, the long tracking shots and the interweaving of different time periods that bleed into each other. Moses (1987) and Ward (1968) additionally linked the two films by documenting the many visual images from *Night and Fog* (Dauman, Halfon, Lifchitz & Resnais, 1955) that are reprised in *Hiroshima Mon Amour* (Dauman, Halfon, & Resnais, 1959). Although these can be found throughout the film, they are most prominent in the prologue. They include the mountains of women's hair in the camps, reprised in the clumps of hair falling out from radiation exposure, the "human skin floating, surviving, still in the bloom of its agony" (Duras, 1961, p. 17) that also refers to the use of skin as drawing paper in the camps; the ashes that cover the bodies of the two lovers, reminiscent of ashes from the crematoria; the sightless eyes of a woman in the Hiroshima hospital staring passively, an unsettling reminder of the blank stares of the Musselmen; and finally, the displays of burnt or mutilated bodies in both films. Later, the images of desperate fingers digging into concrete in the gas chamber will reappear in *Hiroshima Mon Amour* (Dauman, Halfon, & Resnais, 1959), as the female character attempts to make her fingers bleed in order to connect to her lover's death while she is being kept in her parent's cellar. The barred window of her cellar prison is visually similar to the window camp inmates saw on the way to the gas chamber. Given these repetitive images, it is legitimate to view *Hiroshima Mon Amour* (Dauman, Halfon, & Resnais, 1959) as additionally representing a further reworking of Resnais' traumatic memories of the Holocaust, induced during the filming and editing of *Night and Fog* (Dauman, Halfon, Lifchitz, & Resnais, 1955). This supposition receives some textual support by the fact that Resnais put his own crew in the film, essentially filming himself filming a film about Hiroshima (Luchting, 1963). This inserted film functions essentially like a dream within a dream (Freud, 1905), expressing a piece of historical or emotional truth—in this case Resnais placing himself and his creative process inside the trauma. By connecting these intrusive traumatic images with a different external event, and through the active creation of a new narrative, rather than mere passive apprehension, the story begins to evolve into one that includes the self in action rather than just as an observer of external events. This represents an initial step toward integration.

The plot of *Hiroshima Mon Amour* (Dauman, Halfon, & Resnais, 1959) is uncomplicated. A nameless French woman (known only as She) is in Hiroshima acting in a film about peace. On the night before she is to return home to Paris, she begins a passionate affair with a Japanese man, who also remains nameless. In the context of their erotic relationship, which takes place over the course of one day and the ensuing night, she recaptures the memory of her love affair with a German soldier in occupied Nevers shortly before France was liberated, his death, and her subsequent punishment as a collaborator.

Upon this simple frame, Resnais creates a confusing, difficult film, a beautiful dreamlike narrative, open to multiple, shifting interpretations.

He will take us inside the mind of trauma through fracturing the temporal ordering of the film, offering what he will call "shattered time," a complete condensation of past and present, which has left the female protagonist mired in the tyranny of a present tense constructed from a fusion of the current context of Hiroshima and her disavowed memories that seek restitution through action. If time is an "undisciplined element [that] holds itself within bounds but precariously, thanks to unceasing cultivation, meticulous care, and a continuous regulation and correction of its excesses" (Schulz, 1997), Resnais will illustrate time's excesses, a subjective time, incongruous and bidirectional in its influence. Trauma belies our common or garden notions of past, present, future, bringing into question the ability so critical to identity of being able to distinguish what is internal, wished for, and hence remembered, from what is present and external and potentially apprehensible through our own actions. Yet it is not only the subjective experience of the female protagonist that makes this a difficult film. The lack of a sequential narrative induces a similar traumatic state in the viewer, at the same time as the film's extraordinary visual beauty, particularly in the opening scenes, makes it hard to disengage from the story. Further, the film seems to be narrated from several different perspectives—often the voice-over suggests the internal experience of the female protagonist; but the accompanying visual material could as well be the imaginings of her Japanese lover; at other times, the distal camera suggests a third person perspective, as if the woman is watching herself, as one might in a dream. Or, alternately, as if her actions were being surveyed by an unseen observer. Images seen in the prologue (cats, bicycles, deformed hands, mutilated skin, and visions of disembodied feet) will be repeated in the course of the heroine's narratives about her past in Nevers, raising the question of whether what she describes truly represents memory, a construction, or some fusion of the two.

The prologue will raise all of the questions the film will approach through the interactions of the two lovers, the question of whether one can ever see or know the trauma of another, the problems of memory, and the nature of Eros in the time of such massive historical trauma. The film begins with a vision of anonymous bodies; covered either in "ashes, rain, dew or sweat" (Duras, 1961, p. 15). They are initially unrecognizable, glowing with the radioactive ash of the bomb, mutilated, like the bodies seen in *Night and Fog* (Dauman, Halfon, Lifchitz, & Resnais,

1955). The bodies, at first formless and unrecognizable, evolve. Slowly this scene of death becomes decipherable and transforms itself into something erotic. We hear only the protagonists' voices, but do not yet see them.

The first words in the film: The woman's lover says: "You saw nothing at Hiroshima. Nothing." His statement already raises the question of the veracity of what we take in through our vision. She responds with equally repetitive phrasing, insisting on her knowledge.

> Four times at the museum in Hiroshima. I saw the people walking around. The people walk around, lost in thought, among the photographs, the reconstructions, for want of something else, among the photographs, the photographs, the reconstructions, for want of something else, the explanations, for want of something else…
>
> (Duras, 1961, p. 17)

She continues, detailing the horrific sights and sensations. Still, he repeats: "You saw nothing in Hiroshima" (ibid., p. 18).

"The photographs, for want of something else, the reconstructions, for want of something else" function as a reference to the gap, the aporia that cannot be traversed. If in *Night and Fog* (Dauman, Halfon, Lifchitz, & Resnais, 1959) we see grass growing over the mass graves, in *Hiroshima Mon Amour* (Dauman, Halfon, & Resnais, 1959), the sutures are even more vile, the garish representations of planes encased in pearls, the decrepit Hiroshima gift shop, the importation of American culture, the New Hiroshima hotel, a cheerful bus tour of the ruins. "For want of anything else" speaks as well to the absence of symbolization. Like all repetitions, it refers to a bodily tension, an idea that can neither be represented nor delayed, an urge emanating from the body, and yet stymied before it reaches the containing other. For his part, the Japanese man makes it clear that it is impossible to know the trauma of another. To be told about it, to read about it will never convey the experience. She asks him, "Were you at Hiroshima?" and then, realizing the ridiculous nature of the question, laughs. Hiroshima, much like the Holocaust, is an absence … unrepresentable in the usual forms; its memory exists only in the potential for action, or in conversion, written on the body as mutilation, as deformity.

Yet in this first scene, gravid with its dissolves and condensations, there are intimations of a rousing transformative desire, a desire that makes the possibility of a fruitful repetition through the implantation of signifiers produced by the relationship with an other (Green, 2000). The pairing of their erotic bodies with the scenes of the suffering bodies in the hospital will link Eros and death, allowing the possibility for one to modify the other. We hear intimations of this in the woman's recitation, "Hiroshima was blanketed with flowers. There were cornflowers and gladiolas everywhere, and morning glories and day lilies that rose again from the ashes with an extraordinary vigor, quite unheard of for flowers till then." Yet juxtaposed with these fertile descriptions of growth are visual images of charred flesh, piles of contaminated fish reminiscent of the bodies in Auschwitz, crippled dogs and decimated landscapes, an ineluctable mixture of hope and death.

Toward the end of a long tracking shot through the city that was "made to the size of love" (Duras, 1961, p. 25), we glimpse again the intensity of the as-yet ambivalent and unintegrated presence of Eros and Thanatos. The woman says,

> How could I have known that you were made to the size of my body. You're great. How wonderful. You're great ... You destroy me. You're so good for me. You destroy me ... plenty of time. Please. Take me. Deform me, make me ugly. Why not you?

In her sing-song testimony, words are used more as soothing chant then an effort to communicate: "I like you ... how unlikely" (ibid., p. 25). Suddenly, 16 minutes into the film we glimpse the faces of two lovers, the woman's surprised "you" suggesting that she has been responding primarily to an internal experience. The camera switches to the woman's subjective perspective.

The woman has done this before, had brief affairs with men she does not know, but there is something about the nature of the Japanese man's trauma, of his having lost his entire family, his "memory of shadow and stone" that makes her believe that he might be a similar-enough Other to awaken desire in her (Gorton, 2008), and in doing so lead her back to the trauma she has been trying to both remember and forget. The first hint comes as an intrusive flashback. Standing in the doorway to the terrace of her lover's apartment, she notices his hand curled in sleep, twitching slightly in sleep. She frowns. In place of the Japanese man, there suddenly appears another body in the same position, with nearly identical strong and virile hands. But he is immobile, dead. On top of the man, is a woman, kissing his blood-covered face; his blood is smeared across her mouth. However, the scene does not function as the usual film flashback, offering an explanatory insight into the heroine's motivations and actions. Instead it is gone as quickly as it arrived, an intrusive memory that can only be understood in the future, and whose occurrence disturbs the present. Despite their apparent pleasure in each other, the woman is adamant in her refusal to see the man again. He pursues her, finding her while an "enlightening" film is being shot at Peace Square, complete with actors made up as if burned from the bombing. Many of the images from the prologue are reprised. They leave, return to his apartment, and after they make love again she begins to tell him of her affair with a German soldier during the war in Nevers where she grew up, and her growing "mad with hate" (ibid., p. 35) when he is killed. As she talks, the scenes dissolve, past fading into the present; again, little is explained and we do not know if we are watching her memories or his visualization of her narrative. Their scene is shot in close-up, but when we watch her bicycling to meet her lover in Nevers, it is shot at a distance; impossibly, her German lover is also seen watching her. The theme music that has marked the eroticism of the woman and her Japanese lover is played while she lies with her German lover, bridging the two eras.

Whatever has been aroused by her narrative frightens her; she asks to leave and they go to a café, a modernized, half empty café where they sit cheek to cheek. Their clasped hands cover their watches; time fades. She drinks; he asks her questions about Nevers. "Would you have been cold in that cellar at Nevers if we had loved each other there?" and "When you are in the cellar, am I dead?" (ibid., p. 54). To our knowledge as viewers, the cellar had not been mentioned. These are questions he could not have known to ask. Grammatically as well, the Japanese lover has taken the place of her German lover; their identities have begun to lose their individual specificity, to literally dissolve into the other, as she begins to talk in the present tense. By joining the two affairs, Resnais underscores the related collapse both of individuality and temporality (Baker, 1999).

We also see the woman with her hair shorn for being a collaborator, before she has told that part of the story. According to Duras' directions: "Both of them act as though they are possessed by Nevers" (ibid., p. 55). He asks (in the present tense) "Do you scream?" and she replies "I call you softly" and he replies "But I am dead" (ibid., p. 56). She has made the transference of the experience onto him. She tells him that one day she screams his "German name, her one memory left," after which her disgraced parents put her in the cellar. With her shorn hair, she resembles one of the victims of the camps, her affect catatonic and she scratches her fingers along the cellar walls, recalling the images of the inmates in the gas chamber in *Night and Fog* (Dauman, Halfon, Lifchitz, & Resnais, 1955). A cat, reminiscent of a cat seen earlier in the day while filming, joins her in the cellar. As she is describing the cellar, a man puts a record of French *bal musette* music on the jukebox. The sights and sounds of Nevers come to dominate and begin to incorporate the tea room in Hiroshima as the woman continues her narrative, telling how her German lover was killed on the day they were to flee together and how she lay on top of him unable to "feel the slightest difference between this dead body and mine" (ibid., p. 63).

She is shouting "He was my first love…" The Japanese man slaps her; the slap brings her back to reality. She resumes her normal voice—the memory of the death and the accompanying affect has been recovered and to a degree integrated. She begins to separate past from present, "fourteen years have passed." The man hugs her when she tells him that she has never told anyone, not even her husband, the story of her German lover and her incarceration. There is a momentary relief, but now the parting, the forgetting, the loss of the state of love, of which she has been so afraid, begins. The woman returns briefly to her hotel. As she stares at herself in the mirror, she speaks to her German lover, alternately speaking of herself in the first and third person:

> …In Nevers she had a German love when she was young … We'll go to Bavaria my love, and there we'll marry … She never went to Bavaria … You were not yet quite dead. I told our story. I was unfaithful to you tonight with this stranger. I told our story. It was, you see, a story that could be told. For 14 years I hadn't found … the taste of an impossible love again … Look how I'm forgetting you. Look how I've forgotten you.
>
> (Ibid., p. 73)

Leaving the hotel, she wanders through the night. Scenes of Nevers are intercut with those of Hiroshima taken from exactly the same angle.

As she struggles with her loss, she considers the possibility of staying in Hiroshima forever. Her monologue from the prologue is reprised ("You were made to the size of my body. Who are you? You destroy me"), but now there is an awareness of her desire to recreate memory through repetition, her patient search for an identity in perception ("I was hungry. Hungry for infidelity, for adultery, for lies, hungry to die. I always have been. I always expected that one day you would descend on me. I waited for you calmly with infinite patience") (ibid., p. 77). The woman realizes that even the memory of their desire and connection will fade from memory, that ultimately she will give up her relation to the trauma, for so long her love object. She sees the inevitability of her rejection of her former "shorn hair" self, bequeathing her "to oblivion," along with her Japanese lover who will "little by little ... become a song." In a final scene, they bid each other goodbye.

> SHE: Hi-ro-shi-ma. Hi-ro-shi-ma. That's your name. (They look at each other without seeing each other.)
> HE: Yes. Your name is Nevers. Ne-vers in France.

This ambiguous parting gives evidence of only partial resolution, as she still loves the city of her trauma, not the man who will continue to remain nameless.

* * *

Hiroshima Mon Amour (Dauman, Halfon, & Resnais, 1959) offers a portrait of a trauma narrative, predating by almost 50 years the structural distinctions in the temporal aspects of PTSD narratives found by O'Kearney and Perrott (2006), a shifting from past to present tense, a significantly higher frequency of present-tense verbs in flashback memories, a high percentage of sensory words and the increased use of repetition. Anderst (2011) while noting the centrality of forgetting (of historical trauma, of personal tragedy, of the experience of pain and love) to *Hiroshima Mon Amour* (Dauman, Halfon, & Resnais, 1959), also notes the ambivalence Resnais portrays about the value of putting these disavowed remembrances into narrative, altering and changing them as they are communicated in language to another. Resnais will leave us no clear prescriptions about the benefits of giving testimony; if anything he makes us aware of the conflicts of ambivalence that surround the mourning that inevitably accompanies the memory of her lover's death, as the woman notes, "my life that goes on ... your death that goes on." The woman, having told her story, faces the true loss of her lover; in keeping the event private, she had kept him alive as an internal presence, safe from the ravages of forgetting. Thus testimony has advantages—it brings one back to the shared temporal order, but to its disadvantages as well, as further needs to reintegrate the self identity inevitably follow. The incomplete nature of the narrative remembering and the woman's reiteration of her connection to the trauma ("Hiroshima, that's your name") leave the impression that the narrative is but one step in an ongoing and never complete effort to symbolize, as the two lovers never gain identities of their own, apart from the traumas they have endured.

Conclusion

Hiroshima Mon Amour (Dauman, Halfon, & Resnais, 1959) and *Night and Fog* (Dauman, Halfon, Lifchitz, & Resnais, 1955) were initially conceptualized as reflecting different "sins" of memory (Schacter, 2001), which could be tied to diverse neuroanatomical sites associated with memorial function. Sins of transience, the tendency of memories to become less available over time and follow a forgetting curve (Ebbinghaus, 1913), particularly if they are not "used" or rehearsed. Areas in the left temporal lobe, the left parahippocampal gyrus as well as the left inferior frontal gyrus were implicated in fMRI studies of initial encoding of verbal material, with the level of activity in these two areas predicting subsequent recall for verbal material. The memory for nonverbal material was attributed to the activity (or lack thereof) in the parahippocampal regions of the right hemisphere as well as the inferior frontal regions of the right hemisphere. *Hiroshima Mon Amour* (Dauman, Halfon, & Resnais, 1959) was seen as tied to the sins of persistence, defined as the intrusion of unintegrated flashbacks and the loss of distinction between past and present. This "sin" is associated with the impairment of the limbic system, amygdala flooding, and the resultant obstruction in the integrative role of the orbitofrontal cortex that damages a capacity for coherent narrative organization as well as the malfunction of Broca's area, active in speech production, processing, and comprehension. These disrupted neuroanatomical pathways create a rupture between implicit and explicit memory systems that leads to the sense of speechless terror reported by survivors of trauma. However, as noted earlier, these distinctions did not hold up as repeated viewings of the two films established numerous similarities and continuities, both in method and specific content. While memory is disrupted in both films, the continuity of content and specific imagery suggests that the two films might be best conceptualized as subsequent iterations of a trauma. Like the heroine in *Hiroshima Mon Amour* (Dauman, Halfon, & Resnais, 1959), who uses her experience in Hiroshima to rework a past trauma of World War II, one can see Resnais, perhaps unconsciously, use the current tragedy of Hiroshima to creatively rework the trauma of creating *Night and Fog* (Dauman, Halfon, Lifchitz, & Resnais, 1955). Despite *Night and Fog*'s seeming linear narrative; the memory depicted is fragmented and unintegrated, the past intruding like a flashback into the present. In *Hiroshima Mon Amour* (Dauman, Halfon, & Resnais, 1959), the trauma memories, while also intrusive, are starting to be worked over in the context of a present relationship as the woman attempts to reintegrate herself into the stream of life. Her effort is to create a continuous experience, mediated through the desire aroused by a similarly traumatized other.

To return briefly to the question of what constitutes a trauma narrative. Perhaps, as the films suggest, there is no singular narrative, no final statement that allows us to leave a trauma behind, a perspective also noted by Hebard (1997) when discussing *Night and Fog* (Dauman, Halfon, Lifchitz, & Resnais, 1955). Herbert suggests instead a model of remembering based not on repression, but on the notion of the uncanny, which involves a return of the forgotten in a manner that disrupts the present with an uncomfortable familiarity, that reminds us of an inner compulsion to repeat. Thus remembering would never be complete and never offer closure, but would involve continuing transformation, the development of a theme with increasing variation, and ever more elaborate iterations of the original material, touched by objects of desire that support the capacity to change.

References

Anderst, L. (2011). Cinematic free indirect style: Represented memory in *Hiroshima Mon Amour*. *Narrative*, *19*(3), 358–382.

Baker, G. (1999). The predication of violence, the violence of predication: Reconstructing Hiroshima with Duras and Resnais. *Dialectical Anthropology*, *24*, 387–406.

Bersani, L., & Dutoit, U. (1992). Sadism and film: Freud and Resnais. *Qui Parle, 6*(1), 1–34.

Breuer, J. and Freud, S. (1893). On the psychical mechanism of hysterical phenomena. In *The Standard Edition of the Complete Psychological Works of Sigmund Freud, Volume II (1893–1895)* (pp. 1–17). Leipzig: F. Deuticke.

Caruth, C. (1996), Literature and the enactment of memory. In *Unclaimed Experience: Trauma, Narrative, History* (pp. 25–56). Baltimore: John Hopkins University Press.

Dauman, A., Halfon, S., & Lifchitz, P. (Producers), & Resnais, A. (Director). (1955). *Night and Fog* [Motion Picture]. Paris: Cocinor Films.

Dauman, A., Halfon, S. (Producers), & Resnais, A. (Director). (1959). *Hiroshima Mon Amour* [Motion Picture]. France: Dajei Stdios, Argos Films, Como Films, Pathe Entertainment, Pathe Overseas.

Duras, M. (1961). *Hiroshima Mon Amour* (text for the film by Alain Resnais). Grove Press: New York.

Ebbinghaus, H. (1913). *Memory: A Contribution to Experimental Psychology* (Trans., H. A. Ruger & C. E. Bussenius). New York: Teachers College Press, Columbia University. (Original work published 1885; reprint of translation published by Dover, New York, 1964.)

Freud, S. (1914). Remembering, repeating and working-through (further recommendations on the technique of psycho-analysis II). In *The Standard Edition of the Complete Psychological Works of Sigmund Freud, Volume XII*. London: Vintage, Hogarth Press.

Freud, S. (1900). The interpretation of dreams. In *The Standard Edition of the Complete Psychological Works of Sigmund Freud. Volume IV* (1900). London: Vintage, Hogarth Press.

Godmilow, J., & Shapiro, A. (1997). How real is the reality in documentary film? *History and Theory, 36*(4), 80–101.

Gorton, K. (2008). Desire, Duras and melancholia: Theorizing after the "affective turn." *Feminist Review, 89*, 16–33.

Grant, B., & Sloniowski, J. (1998). *Documenting the Documentary: Close Readings of Documentary Film and Video.* Detroit, MI: Wayne State University Press.

Green, A. (2000). The intrapsychic and intersubjective in psychoanalysis. *Psychoanalytic Quarterly, 69*(1), 1–39.

Hebard, S. (1997). Disruptive histories: Toward a radical politics of remembrance in Alain Resnais' *Night and Fog. New German Critique, 71*, 87–113.

Hegarty, L. (2013). Not passed over in silence. *DIVISION/Rev., 8*, 7–9.

Hiroshima Mon Amour (1959). Directed by Alain Resnais. Screenplay by Marguerite Duras. New York: Criterion Collection, 2003. DVD.

Insdorf, A. (2003) *Indelible Shadows: Film and the Holocaust.* Cambridge: Cambridge University Press.

Kerner, A. (2011). *Film and the Holocaust: New Perspectives on Dramas, Documentaries and Experimental Films*. London and New York: Continuum International Publishing Corp.

Laub, D. (1991). Truth and testimony: The process and the struggle. *American Imago, 48*, 75–91.

Laub, D., & Auerhahn, N. C. (1993). Knowing and not knowing massive psychic trauma: Forms of traumatic memory. *International Journal of Psychoanalysis, 74*, 287.

Legros, P. (Producer) and Franju, G. (Director). (1949). *Les Sang des Betes* [Motion Picture]. France: Forces et Voix de la France.

Luchting, W. (1963). "Hiroshima, Mon Amour," time and Proust. *The Journal of Aesthetics and Art Criticism, 21*(3), 299–313.

Mori, M. (1970). The uncanny valley. *Energy, 7*(4), 33–35.

Moses, J. W. (1987) Vision denied in "Night and Fog" and "Hiroshima Mon Amour." *Literature Film Quarterly, 15*(3), 159–163.

O'Kearney, R., & Perrott, K. (2006). Trauma narratives in posttraumatic stress disorder: A review. *Journal of Traumatic Stress, 19*(1), 81–93.

Resnais, A. (Director). (2010). *Hiroshima Mon Amour* [Motion Picture]. United States: Criterion Collection.

Riefenstahl, L. (Director & Producer). (1935). *The Triumph of the Will.* [Motion Picture]. Germany: Reichparteitag – Film.

Rosenblum, R. (2009). Postponing trauma: the dangers of telling. *International Journal of Psychoanalysis, 90*, 1319–1340.

Schacter, D. (2001). *The Seven Sins of Memory: How the Mind Forgets and Remembers.* New York: Houghton Mifflin.

Schulz, B. (1997). *Sanatorium under the Sign of the Hourglass*. New York: Houghton Mifflin.

Shinebourne, P. (2006) Trauma and culture: On Freud's writing about trauma and its resonances in contemporary cultural discourse. *British Journal of Psychotherapy, 22*(3), 335–345.

Ward, J. (1968). *Alain Resnais, or the Theme of Time.* London: Martin Secker & Warburg.

Wilson, E. (2006). *Alain Resnais.* Manchester, UK: Manchester University Press.

Wilson, E. (2005). Material remains: Night and Fog. *October, 112*: 89–110.

Chapter 4

The Pawnbroker

Robert Winer

Introduction

Some things transcend psychology. Elaine Scarry (1985) reflected on a passage in Elie Wiesel's *Night*:

> ... father and child on a train taking them to a concentration camp are in the presence of a woman who keeps seeing furnaces and fires. The others think her mad though she will turn out, of course, to have been a visionary. The moment when the actual furnaces are seen and the destiny of everyone is clear would, in the normal structure of experience, be the moment revealing the ironic position of the visionary and all those who misjudged her; but beside the fact of the furnace itself, it seems irrelevant in what way the end was or was not anticipated. Beside the horrible central fact, there are no peripheral facts, no relation between periphery and center, no irony, because in every direction there is only irony.
>
> (p. 330)

This is the difficulty in discussing a film that is in part about the Holocaust. Elie Wiesel wrote in the *New York Times* in 1989:

> Wittgenstein said it: whereof one cannot speak, one must not speak. The unspeakable draws its force and its mystery from its own silence. A 19th-century Hasidic teacher put it his own way: the cry unuttered is the loudest ... The truth of Auschwitz remains hidden in its ashes. Only those who lived it in their flesh and in their minds can possibly transform their experience into knowledge. Others, despite their best intentions, can never do so ... The Holocaust has become a fashionable

> subject, so film and theater producers and television networks have set out to exploit it, often in the most vulgar sense of the word.

Although Wiesel has implied that any representation of the Holocaust trivializes it, he has not, on that account, argued that filmmakers should not try. Summarizing an interview with Wiesel, Jarvis (1988) wrote: "The best movies on the subject—such as 'The Pawnbroker' or 'Sophie's Choice'—do not show you the horror so much as they show you the effect. They suggest the evil and let you try to imagine it." Of course, any presentation of an event, whether historical or artistic, will be reductionistic—at best a part truth, immediately on the edge of diminishing it. Wiesel considered the television docudrama series "Holocaust" exploitative, in the vulgar sense, a commercialization of the events. And historian Sharon Rivo said that when it was shown in Germany the impact was profound—it led directly to the German legislature extending the statute of limitations on prosecuting war criminals. Ironically, it was thought that this film, made in 1978, had had more effect on the (contemporary) German citizenry than the Holocaust itself.

We understand that any artistic treatment of a subject (or any historical treatment, for that matter) uses the material as a vehicle for developing a set of ideas that are in the mind of the creator. Perhaps the best criterion for judging the work is whether we find the ideas worth thinking about and their treatment *persuasive*. For all its apparent straightforwardness, the film *Night and Fog* (1955) is not a chronicle. It is Alain Resnais's statement about accountability, what we are capable of, what we must know about ourselves. Meanwhile we hold our films to a standard of literalness that we'd never use as a measure for novels or paintings. This is not by accident—the essence of Hollywood narrative structuring and Hollywood editing has been to present film as a seamless representation of reality. All the artifice is hidden behind Cary Grant's comfortable smile. "Trust us," Hollywood tells us, and we do.

Hollywood and the Holocaust

Hollywood had a complicated attitude toward the Nazi ascendancy and the events that followed, a process tracked by the 2004 documentary *Imaginary Witness: Hollywood and the Holocaust* (Anker & Baumel, 2004) which is my main source for the following account. By the late

1920s, Germany had become 10 percent of Hollywood's foreign market. The industry wanted to protect that source of revenue, even after Hitler took power in 1933. The newsreels produced by the major studios mainly accepted the cheeky accounts provided by the National Socialists of such events as the book burnings. Most of the studios complied with the Nazis' demand that they fire their Jewish staff working in Germany. More than profits were at stake. Many of Hollywood's executives were Jewish immigrants from Eastern Europe. They were worried that Hollywood might be seen as a Jewish industry, faced with the danger of an anti-Semitic response (and in fact they would have to deal with Ku Klux Klan and Black Legion threats). The Production Code had been set up by the filmmakers not only to police film morality, but also to protect the industry's wallets. The political content of films was censored to avoid giving offence,

After *Kristallnacht* in November 1938 everything changed. Executives tried to rescue their European relatives, they found jobs for refugees, some spoke out against Nazism, and many were active in Hollywood's Anti-Nazi League. But these efforts were all off-screen. Despite the showing of a handful of anti-Nazi films in the late 30s, it was not until 1940 and Charlie Chaplin's self-financed film, *The Great Dictator*, that director Sidney Lumet remembers finally hearing the word "Jew" in a movie. "Non-Aryan" had been the preferred industry term and Hollywood was determined to walk this tightrope. U.K. Ambassador Joseph P. Kennedy intimidated film executives by warning them that they shouldn't press for entry into the war, because it would then be seen as *their* war. And so it would be Chaplin's independent film that first asserted that Hitler was interested in killing people, not just acquiring territory. Even as a million Jews were being shot by Nazi firing squads in 1941, it was only the "B" movies made by refugee directors that confronted Nazism.

After America entered the war, some major directors began making documentaries for the Army Signal Corps Motion Pictures Unit. Dwight Eisenhower took 16 producers to see Europe after the war, and their tour ended with a day at Dachau. Eisenhower wanted them to bear witness, and the experience was excruciating. But America was also eager to quickly rehabilitate Germany, to make it receptive to American ideals and goods, and in our economic self-interest we were to set the past aside. Survivors wanted to find new lives and they were often ashamed to tell their stories. In the 50s, the House Un-American Activities

Committee maliciously linked Jews, communism, and Hollywood; the film industry was not about to deal with Jewish themes. Director George Stevens was determined that his 1959 film, *The Diary of Anne Frank*, would not make his audiences too uncomfortable, and he framed it as a coming-of-age story, with universal truths. He did not follow her to Bergen-Belsen. Finally, *Judgment at Nuremberg* (1961), released in the same year, included newsreel footage of the atrocities in the camps. The producers agreed to cut the word "gas" from the film, under pressure from one of its sponsors, the American Gas Company, and predictably this became the topic of interest for the media. And then, for four weeks in 1961, America watched the trial of Adolf Eichmann.

Steven Spielberg made *Schindler's List* (1993) in black and white, because he felt that color would make it too beautiful. But in one scene he has a small girl in a red coat. He said that he had in mind that she represented the United States, Britain, and Russia, who had all turned away from what they had to know was happening in the camps. Her red coat represented that which could be seen if you just looked, and it was the blood on their hands. Hollywood turned its head, but everyone turned their heads, and the Final Solution ground on, unabated.

The Pawnbroker, Hollywood, and the Holocaust

And then the cultural climate shifted. The civil rights movement was demanding attention and getting it, and the universal normativity of the 50s was yielding to the interest in particularities, and especially ethnicities, of the 60s—a good time for the story line of *The Pawnbroker* (Langer, Lewis, & Lumet, 1965), with its interest in the street life of East Harlem, the blacks and Puerto Ricans, and a Jewish merchant, a Holocaust survivor. In an essay in *American Jewish History*, Leonard J. Leff (1996) describes the difficulties the producers encountered in trying to get the film made. An independent producer, Roger Lewis, tried to interest a couple of major studios in the project. Arnold Picker, the head of the United Artists executive committee, was tough on Jewish films. "People don't want to see pictures about concentration camps," he told Lewis, "There're other injustices." MGM's Bill Zimmerman was bothered by the "business of Sol's Jewishness." Also, he thought the script "badly" needed some comic relief and that it should end with a moment of intimacy between the pawnbroker and his social worker acquaintance.

"At least they should figuratively touch hands in some manner." Lewis couldn't find someone willing to direct the film (perhaps they thought it wouldn't be a great career move), and its "realistic" content had discouraged investors. Finally Ely Landau, an independent producer and financier took an interest, and bought 80 percent of the film. Landau was trying to make two films at this point—*The Heart is a Lonely Hunter* (1968) as well as *The Pawnbroker* (Langer, Lewis, & Lumet, 1965). He'd signed on Sidney Lumet to direct the first and Arthur Hiller the second. But when Landau couldn't get insurance for the erratic Montgomery Clift for *Lonely Hunter*, he gave up on the film, and shifted Lumet to *The Pawnbroker*, which by now had been cast. Yet another piece of the Jewish resistance to this film was expressed by a Los Angeles rabbi who watched it and responded to the protagonist's misanthropy: "All [the Jews] talk about is the Holocaust and all the sufferings. The goddam fools don't realize that the more you tell gentiles that nobody likes us, the more they say there must be a reason for it."

There is yet one more story to tell about the making of this film, which is indirectly a consequence of its Holocaust content. The writing of the film included a crucial nude scene, in which a prostitute bares her breasts to the pawnbroker in an effort to get him to give her more money. For the pawnbroker, this dislodged an agonizing memory of being forced to look at his naked wife, who was waiting in a room for the Nazi who would rape her. The context completely preempted the viewer's desire. The administrators of the Motion Picture Association of America's Production Code rejected the scene, as did the Catholic Legion of Decency, which gave it a "C" (condemned) rating. Yet the National Council of Churches would later give it their award for best picture of the year. New York censors licensed the film without the cuts and a subsequent appeal to the MPAA led to a 6–3 vote permitting the scene, as an "exception" in this "special and unique case." While this was precisely not intended to be a precedent, within just a few years the Code was dead, replaced by the current film rating system. And so, for some in Hollywood, *The Pawnbroker* (Langer, Lewis, & Lumet) is most significantly remembered, ironically, as the film that ended censorship, thanks to its link to the Holocaust.

The film

Act I: memory, the Holocaust, and the pawnshop

The film opens on a sun-drenched pastoral scene, viewed in slow motion, against a wistful score, no dialogue. A lad and his younger sister chase a butterfly, their mother fills a pitcher at the lake, a grandfather wearing a yarmulke studies a chessboard while his wife spreads out a picnic. The children are scooped up by their father, one in each arm, he twirls them in the air. Then everything stops, the sky and the music darken, there's a menace, they can see it but we can't. The girl slips to the ground and the father cradles his son's head. The scene shifts to an overhead view of the camps, no, it's a Long Island suburb, and we've moved forward to the early 1960s. Sol Nazerman is trying to nap on a chaise-longue in the back yard, and we meet the family of his wife's sister, the wife who, we learn from his sister-in-law, died 25 years ago. Sol sees her in flash cuts from the opening sequence and we realize now that we were watching his memories. It takes us a moment to recognize that this is the same man, he has been so transformed by time, once vibrant, now water-logged. Given its cultural presence, I think it would be impossible to attend this film without knowing that it's about a survivor of the Holocaust. In fact, the film counts on your knowing that. Otherwise, for a time, you might be as lost as Nazerman is.

The scene shifts and we are with Sol in his car, driving through East Harlem, listening to Quincy Jones' jazzy score, taking in the people and the stores as the opening credits roll. We appreciate Lumet's passion for the city, for its vitality, for all the folks in the streets who are just hangin' out; we get why this social realist was up for making this film. As he walks from his car to his shop, there's a moment when Nazerman passes a window filled with a massive pile of used shoes, and for this moment we're in the collection rooms of the camps, then we're back on the sidewalk passing a vegetable street market, normality restored. We're in Nazerman's mind.

Once inside the shop, Sol dispassionately conducts his business. His customers arrive, each divests a part of himself or herself in the objects pawned. Sol offers them far less than they ask for, a dollar for a gold oratory award, two dollars for heirloom candlesticks. He cannot be bargained with and they accept the offer, feeling diminished by doing so. The transactions have become ritualized: "See you again, and that's for sure." That woman needed to be reminded to take her receipt and her money. We recognize the enormous gap between their hopelessness and his indifference. I sense that Nazerman is determined to not let any of them engage him, even for a moment, even those who this former professor from Leipzig might find interesting. We feel touched by them, he doesn't. Nazerman says that the only thing he cares about is money, but even that is complicated. Despite giving his customers so little, he won't make anything. We know they'll never redeem their possessions, which are also too personal to be salable. And we learn that this isn't even how Sol earns his living—the pawn business, no surprise, loses money. A powerful black racketeer, Rodriguez, has a financial connection with the shop and uses it to launder his vice profits, an arrangement that Sol finds sufficiently lucrative, allowing him to pay the mortgage for his sister-in-law and to support a survivor girlfriend of sorts and her father.

I've read that survivors, on the whole, are more sensitive to the false note, less tolerant of forged kindness. Sol Nazerman considers himself an authority on the question of what's real; he takes pride in that. He knows the imposters, the blind people with 20/20 vision, the deaf people who can hear the tumblers on his safe when he dials the combination. He knows what things are worth, he can tell diamond from cut glass, gold from brass. Sol has no illusions. The one line he repeats in the film is: "You must be joking." He's figured out what happened to the Jewish people: they became merchants to survive and lost the capacity to produce, and so they live as pawns, "pawns" as agents for others. The only truth that matters to him is the truth of the Holocaust, and his life has, through no conscious effort of his own, become a bearing of witness to that suffering. A river once flowed in him, he has now become a graveyard. Where desire lived, there was now only memory.

Memory intrudes on Sol, slapping him in the face. The film's editor, Ralph Rosenblum (Rosenblum & Karen, 1986), wrote, "We knew from personal experience that memories, especially unpleasant ones, are not engaged in by a voluntary swan dive into the past" (p. 152). The images assault us. They're flash cuts, some as short as four frames, a sixth of a second, too quick for us to read them, and they gradually lengthen, sometimes to two-thirds of a second, or longer. What's also distinctive here is the way the flashbacks are presented. We aren't looking through Sol's eyes in the moment before the flashback, which would be the conventional point of view for a subjective shot. Instead we are looking at Sol, and then see the intruding memory. This device allows us to experience the memories as Sol does, as alien, unconscious intrusions, not as felt associations. These are not daydreams or fantasies: repressed reality is appropriating his mind. Because Sol is unable to author these images, to make them part of self-experience, the *dissociated* self sculptures his life. His pawnshop, in its iconography and social practice, becomes the resurrection of the death camp: wires, cages, bars, piles of confiscated property, pandering, humiliation, pathos, betrayal. The film observes, in its own language, that when we cannot remember the past we repeat it. Sol's head was smashed on a window and he was forced to watch a camp officer rape his wife. He closes the glass door on Mendel and has passionless sex with the old man's daughter, the wife of a compatriot who died in the camp trying to escape. Mendel is forced to bear witness. Like the Nazis, Sol reassures Tessie that they have nothing to feel guilty about. The past unremembered is passed on to the generations that follow, something that we in the tinkering trade have thought a great deal about.

Another plot element needs mention. Sol has taken on as an assistant a jazzed-up ambitious young Puerto Rican, Jesus Ortiz, who lives with and flirts with his engaging mother. He's promised her he's giving up hustling and is going "strictly lee-git!" He responded to Sol's ad looking for "a bright willing-to-learn young man," and, against some resistance, is trying to force Sol to be his teacher. Sol relents a bit, and tutors him in the use of a touchstone. When Jesus then tries to advance the date on the tear-off calendar, Sol blocks him and sends him home.

And so, a quarter of the way into the movie we're getting a take on Sol. He's been extraordinarily traumatized by the camp experience, so much so that unlike many other survivors he can in no way find a new lease on life. His family died in the Holocaust, and by some error of fate he survived; he wanders through his days, waiting to die. He defends against any meaningful engagement with anyone, as though this would inevitably wound him more. And we sense that a crisis is amping up for him, the approach of the twenty-fifth anniversary, the date he can't bear having appear on his calendar. But the anniversary of what? His family didn't die in a single day. The anniversary of their capture? Something else? Traumatic flashbacks start to savage him.

Act II: power and impotence

Power is an obsessive presence in the film, from the early shot of the traditional three balls over the shop—they seem like massive, leaden, lifeless testicles, an emblem of the man inside. Scenes are shot from above and from below, to inflect power. In the stolen-lawnmower pawning scene, for example, we are the grass, looking up at the thugs and feeling their intimidating force. When Sol walks down the corridor at the apartment of the social worker who tried to befriend him, we view him from the ceiling and feel him diminished. Less conspicuously, virtually all conversations are shot on diagonals, slightly looking up or slightly angled down, each time to state the locus of power in the relationship. It has been argued that the Holocaust "feminized [all] European Jewish men, who were castigated as incapable of protecting their families and were therefore led sheepishly to the slaughter" (Kimmel, cited in Leff, 1996, p. 7).

We see Sol's paralysis in the camp as he helplessly watches his friend Reuben being captured as he's climbing a barbed wire fence, trying to escape. This memory was resurrected by walking past a playground scene, where he saw a Puerto Rican boy being gang-mauled on a fence. As determined as he is to not feel compassion, Sol is equally determined to never again feel powerless. He might be dead, but he will not be helpless. And so Sol has become the commandant of his own capitalist prison. After he tells Jesus that he doesn't believe in God, he snarls that he only believes in money: "Next to the speed of light, which Einstein says is the only absolute in the Universe, second only to that, I rank money." (Taken in another way, we can hear this as Nazerman saying that ahead of money he only ranks Albert Einstein, the great Jewish intellectual force of Sol's time, implicitly a claim on his own years at the university. In some universe, knowledge might still be power.) But his economics lecture to Ortiz has another, concealed, source. It's preceded by his response to a young pregnant girl's attempting to pawn what she believes is a diamond ring—a flashback to Nazis taking the rings off the fingers of their prisoners. While Sol doesn't include his wife in the image, surely he is taking in the transformation of symbols of connection into gems to be extracted and metals to be melted down, love transmogrified into profits. The Sol of the film's opening images will never trust love again.

Lumet plays off the power dynamics of the pawnshop against those of the East Harlem community, synoptically depicted in Rodriguez's relation to his fawning white manservant and his exploited prostitutes. The pawned oratory award had been won for the recitation of Poe's *The Raven*, the poem of Nevermore! I take Lumet's idea in making this film to be: Once again! Trying to shrivel up such an idea, film critic Andrew Sarris (1965) remarked: "The idea behind the production seemed to be that by combining the Jewish Problem with the Negro Problem the picture would be twice as profound because the audience would be twice as depressed." I don't think that Lumet is trying to take on either the Jewish Problem or the Negro Problem, as such. He is suggesting that we might learn something useful from reconsidering the Holocaust and its impact on us. His own retracing leads him to thoughts about the nature of power, authority, and authenticity. He has Jesus reach a small epiphany of self-discovery. Just before the attempted robbery later in the film, one of the thugs asks Jesus if he's worried about the Jew, and Jesus replies, "No … I'm worried about Jesus Ortiz."

The sharpest cut in the power dialogue is the young hophead's interchange with the radio he stole from his mother, which he is trying to pawn to get him his next fix. "Show the man your power, baby! … [the radio crackles] … Blast him, give him some of that tone! … [more crackling] … You radio, you mother, you turn CHICKEN on me, radio, huh?" Of course, more than by his radio, he is castrated by his addiction, the distemper of East Harlem's mean streets.

Act III: loss

A disillusioned Jesus Ortiz furiously embraces Sol's money mantra and contemplates inviting his thug friends to rob Nazerman's safe. (This is a weak point in the film. For me, there's no basis for thinking that he would turn on his boss in this way.) He knows it holds $5,000 that Rodriquez sent to Sol in the course of their laundering transactions. Jesus's girlfriend, afraid he's going to get himself in trouble, tries to find him some cash by pawning both a gold locket and her body to Sol. In the course of things, Nazerman learns that she is a prostitute in one of Rodriguez's whorehouses, which ignites flashbacks to being forced to watch the set-up for his wife's rape by the camp officer. Sol covers up the young woman, gives her some money, and turns away, in turn sad, trembling, enraged.

We shift to Rodriquez's townhouse, Sol telling him that he can no longer have anything to do with him, Rodriquez challenging him—

> Where do you think the money you've been living on comes from? ... Maybe you don't want to know about things! Are you that kind of a man, Professor, who doesn't want to know about things, feel about things? That makes you NOTHING!

After making this correct interpretation, Rodriquez squeezes Sol's terrified face, and Sol implodes—this is the most excruciating moment in the film. He walks all the way to Marilyn's apartment in the Lincoln Towers, looking for comfort, afraid to receive it. He tells her that he's been feeling afraid, that memories he thought he'd been able to push far away were rushing back at him. "Today is an anniversary ... I didn't die. Everything that I loved was taken away from me and I did not die. There was nothing I could do. Nothing." She reaches out her hand, he won't take it. She lowers her hand and he leaves.

Sol enters the subway car, thinks that people are staring at him. He's taken back to being on the transport car, half-asleep, his son David sleeping on his shoulder. This is the boy he had cradled in the opening scene when the troopers arrived. David starts to slip down Sol's back, Sol's wife yells, "Sol, don't let him fall!" Sol reaches desperately for David, screams, "I can't do anything! I can't do nothing." We see David on the floor. A moment later we recognize that he has died.

Now we understand. Today is the anniversary of *this* loss, of his failure to save his son. While this tragedy condenses his entire inability to protect his family in the face of the Nazi onslaught, we can also recognize that his son was most special to him, this failure the most inexcusable, most crippling. More than guilt, my sense is that he felt overwhelmingly ashamed of himself for letting his son fall. Telling Marilyn, "There was nothing I could do," expressing in this way a broader sense of helplessness, represents his (paradoxically) shrouding himself in impotence to obscure his shame about this particular failure. We can now make sense of his relationship with Ortiz, both wanting to father this young man and being terrified of the consequences, all masked by studied indifference.

It is commonplace when considering the impact of the Holocaust on its victims to read it in broad terms—the repeated violations of human needs, the exploitations, the abuses, the tortures, the travesties, the accounting without end. The Holocaust authenticated the power of power and the devastation of helplessness—in our culture, it has come to represent the endpoint in the spectrum of evil. And we think about the survivor guilt it engendered. It is one of the great ironies of the Holocaust that the survivors, on the whole, seem to have felt more guilt than their persecutors. Survivor guilt is a universal experience, occurring in a whole variety of contexts, but it is likely to have more force for the Holocaust survivors for several reasons. They are guilty of having wanted to survive, perhaps of hoping that others would be marked for extermination instead, perhaps of protecting themselves at others' expense. They feel guilt and shame about their passivity, their choosing to remain inactive while others suffered, even though activity would have cost them their lives. Sol chose to preserve himself by not trying to rescue Reuben on the barbed wire fence. The identification with the aggressor is another source of guilt, because in taking on the values of the persecutor, the survivor betrays his own conscience. Sol has made an unconscious Faustian bargain with his conscience: he will be allowed to live as long as he agrees to remain dead. Thus, he can allow himself sexual release on the condition that he feels no passion. We have *our* read on the totalistic trauma of being in the Holocaust, but for the individual there will be particular meanings that may trump all the others. For Saul, it was his failure to keep hold of his son, failing in his own eyes and in the eyes of his wife. It was this failure that would be reprised in the final act.

Act IV: repetition

Sol returns to his shop from the subway shattered. Jesus meets him outside, solicitous: "Mr. Nazerman, are you all right? You … you don't look good. Is there anything I can …" Sol shushes him and they go inside. Money has lost meaning for Sol—he offers his supplicants mostly too much, sometimes way too little, it seems random. But a pained recovery of self is emerging through the rediscovery of subjectivity, Sol's growing awareness of his authorship. The first flashback from a partly subjective point of view (we are at Sol's back when the image appears) is a view of David trying to capture a butterfly in the field. The memory is prompted by Jesus's continuing worry about his boss: "Are you all right? You look … bad!" Jesus tells Sol, "You're my teacher, I'm a student to you." Sol finds his impulse toward fatherhood unbearable and violently rejects Jesus, telling him, "You're nothing to me." This encounter will lead directly to the tragic ending, but in that interval we will see the one flashback shot from a wholly subjective position: Sal, looking at a customer's pinned butterflies, seeing the field again, and now remembering their capture (the missing scene in the film's opening flashback).

Rejected by Sol, in a panic, Jesus flees to his gang friends and they put the robbery in motion. But before they get there, Rodriguez and his henchmen have arrived to retrieve the paper he's earlier refused to sign. They try to force the issue and he's adamant. "If I don't sign the paper, will you kill me? [Rodriquez nods.] So *kill* me. You have to *kill* me." Taunted, Rodriquez realizes that this is what the professor actually wants, and he refuses to oblige him and leaves. Then the gang shows up and demands that he open the safe. Its door is ajar and Nazerman closes it. One of them points a gun at him, which Nazerman ignores. Afraid that they'll shoot Sol, Jesus rushes to grab the gun and in the brief scuffle he's mortally wounded. Sol cradles his head as he dies. Back in the pawnshop, useless, he methodically impales his left hand on the receipt spindle, then wanders into the street, and the camera pulls back as he blends into the crowd.

Critic Bosley Crowther (1965) pointed out that Sol is, in one sense, the legendary Wandering Jew who taunted Jesus on the way to his crucifixion, and was then condemned to roam the world, a lonely outcast. Lumet frames the ending in a cascade of overwrought religious ironies. Jesus, the gentile, sacrifices his life to the transformation of Nazerman, the attempted salvation of Nazi-man as Nazarene, and we end with the infliction of the stigmata. This thrust, impalement on the pawnbroker's receipt spindle, was not part of the ending of the film's source, Edward Wallant's novel. But we can read the act in other ways: as representing the sense that he is himself no more than a worthless, unredeemable receipt; as a wish to atone for the murder, a mortification of the flesh; as both a defiance of feeling and as a wish to be able to feel, in the way that we cut our wrists to feel the blood flow. Rainer Maria Rilke (1922) wrote: "Killing is one of the forms of our wandering mourning."

But I think most significantly he is attacking the left hand that could not keep a grip on his son in the transport car, a failure repeated now in his inability to protect Jesus. I have the thought that when he told Jesus that he meant nothing to him, he was trying to drive Jesus away to protect him from himself. He could feel that he ruined everything he touched and perhaps this foster son could be spared. But Ortiz took after his teacher, identifying with the aggressor, and in the horrific way that the unconscious betrays us, he tried to do to Sol what he felt Sol had done to him, and he paid the price. And so Sol was not to be allowed a sparing death. For failing to protect his son, and beyond that, his family, he had sentenced himself to a living death, a life sentence if you will.

Arguably the central concern of this film is authenticity, the need to speak truth, that which the Holocaust could not exterminate, that which has been expressed in the efforts to bear witness. I was talking to a patient who had lost a young child. She said that it seemed clearer to her now what was important, what was worth paying attention to, what was true. Sol recreates the past not only because he can't forget or remember it. He holds onto it because it is the experience that gives his life meaning. It confirms him: this is who I am. To let go of that would mean feeling *truly* estranged. At the same time, recapturing the memory of his family's capture, and of his failure to hold onto his son, has brought him no relief. Perhaps we aren't entitled to expect that. As therapists we hope that the truth will set our patients free. While that hope sustains us in our work, and in our own lives, some casualties are beyond repair. That is also what this film has in mind. It will not have a Hollywood ending.

References

Anker, D. (Producer & Director), & Baumel, E. (Producer). (2004). *Imaginary Witness: Hollywood and the Holocaust* [Motion Picture]. United States: Koch Lorber Films.

Crowther, B. (1965). The Pawnbroker. *New York Times*, April 21. Retrieved from www.nytimes.com/1965/04/21/archives/screen-the-pawnbroker-opens-at-3-theaters-rod-steiger-creates-a.html

Jarvis, J. (1988). Picks and pans review: A conversation with Elie Wiesel. *People Magazine*, November.

Kimmel, M. (1996). *Manhood in America: A Cultural History*. New York: Oxford University Press.

Langer, P., & Lewis, R. (Producers), & Lumet, S. (Director). (1965). *The Pawnbroker* [Motion Picture]. United States: Allied Artists Pictures.

Leff, L. J. (1996). Hollywood and the Holocaust: Remembering the Pawnbroker. *American Jewish History*, *84*(4), 353–376.

Rilke, R. M. (1922). *Sonnets to Orpheus* (trans. M. D. Herter Norton). New York: W. W. Norton (1942).

Rosenblum, R., & Karen, R. (1986). *When the Shooting Stops ... The Cutting Begins: A Film Editor's Story*. New York: Da Capo Press.

Sarris, A. (1965). Films. *The Village Voice*, p. 11, July 15.

Scarry, E. (1985). *The Body in Pain*. Northvale, NJ: Jason Aronson.

Wiesel, E. (1989). Art and the Holocaust: Trivializing memory. *New York Times*, June 11. Retrieved from http://link.galegroup.com/apps/doc/A175727402/STND?u=nysl_sc_cornl&sid=STND&xid=258962b4

Chapter 5

Multiplicity, dissociation, and mentalization in *Hannah Arendt* by Pam Katz and Margarethe von Trotta

Diana Diamond and Elliot Jurist

Introduction

Hannah Arendt's life and work are texts that endlessly continue to fascinate, perplex, and enrage us. At a conference at Wesleyan University's Center for the Humanities to commemorate the fiftieth anniversary of the publication of *Eichmann in Jerusalem: A Report of the Banality of Evil*, a group of Arendt scholars and critics from the U.S., Germany, and Israel, representing diverse disciplines from political theory to legal and gender studies, offered multiple and sometimes competing versions of Arendt's masterwork; each claimed hegemony for his or her interpretation. Was Arendt deluded by Eichmann, who had an uncanny ability to tailor his narrative to the desires and fantasies of his audience? Or was he, as Arendt argued, a non-person, an automaton caught in the machinery of the Final Solution rather than one of its masterminds? "As sometimes happens in the world of ideas," commented one scholar, "it is those who think least of *Eichmann in Jerusalem* who keep it alive by dragging its author out for what is by now ritual trial and conviction. This is how the book survives" (Lilla, 2013, p. 55).

The film *Hannah Arendt* (Bromkemper, Rexin, & von Trotta, 2012), starring Barbara Sukowa, directed by German New Cinema filmmaker, Margarethe von Trotta, and written by Pamela Katz and von Trotta, attempts to offer a more balanced understanding of the controversy. Unlike the warring scholars at Wesleyan, Katz and von Trotta's film, through a weave of images and words and fictional and archival footage, tries to bridge the contradictions, the multiplicity, and the conscious and unconscious motivations that fueled Arendt's life and work. The film offers a fine-grained study of the process by which Arendt struggled to understand Eichmann and, through a study of the testimonies of the trial, the totality of what she called "the moral collapse the Nazis caused in respectable European society—not only in Germany but in almost all countries, not only among the persecutors but also among the victims" (Arendt, 2006, pp. 123–124).

Arendt's major conclusion was that Eichmann and many like him were "neither perverted nor sadistic, that they were, and still are, terribly and terrifyingly normal" (Arendt, 2006, p. 280). She saw Eichmann as a thoughtless bureaucrat whose greatest failure was his "inability to think" (Arendt, 2006, p. 50). In her view, although he was a player in the horrific evil of the Holocaust, there was no demonic greatness about Eichmann; rather, it was his failure to think, which she elaborates in terms of his "reluctance to ever imagine what the other person is experiencing" (Arendt, 2006, p. 187). These conclusions, which we will try to explicate, have forever redefined our understanding of the relationship between state-sanctioned genocide and individual will, thinking, and judgment. In this chapter, we will take up the issue of how Arendt's view of thinking evolved through her coverage of the Eichmann trial, and show how it anticipates the concept of mentalization in contemporary psychoanalysis (Fonagy et al., 2002; Fonagy, Bateman, and Luyten, 2012; Fonagy and Allison, 2014; Bateman and Fonagy, 2015; Jurist, 2018). Indeed, in *Hannah Arendt* (2012), Katz and von Trotta's stated quest was to show the thought process—the struggle to reflect and understand—that Arendt engaged in during the years when she covered the trial and faced down her critics in its aftermath. The film also hints at the dissociative mechanisms, perhaps stemming from traumatic aspects of Arendt's own history, in which she was reimmersed during the trial that may have infused her thinking and interpretations of the events. As Laub (1992b) argues, listening itself can be traumatic, and the process of witnessing being witnessed is a crucial dimension to keep in mind when confronting the Holocaust. Katz and Von Trotta's film creates the space for the viewer to witness the witnessing.

In focusing the film on Arendt's coverage of the Eichmann trial, *Hannah Arendt* reminds us that films have become an optimal repository for images of some of the most compelling and cataclysmic events of our time—images that portray the complex and conflictual dynamics of individual lives unfolding against the often traumatogenic social and historical forces of the twentieth century. With its ability to combine fictional and documentary footage, and with its multiple registers of image and sound, which condense time and move fluidly between different mental states, internal and external, past and present, fantasy and reality, film may be an optimal medium for rendering the ineffable and complex nature of trauma, both individual and historical. Trauma is often encoded in imagistic rather than lexical modes of thought, in that an image encapsulates both victim and victimizer in a single trope encompassing aspects of self and other and their interaction, so that they are not as well differentiated as they might be in lexical recounting of traumatic events (Bruner, 1964; Diamond & Blatt, 1994). In this regard, *Hannah Arendt* provides us with a portrait of Arendt's psychic reality—that mélange of historical (both individual and collective) experience and fantasy, memory, wish and desire, past and present that lies at the heart of both cinematic and psychoanalytic narrative.

In watching Arendt, who narrowly escaped the Holocaust herself, struggle to apprehend the near incomprehensible human and social cataclysm of the Holocaust through understanding Eichmann, we also see her come face to face with her own unconscious terrors and longings. We see her defying simple answers or facile explanation. In short, we see her thinking—and thinking about thinking, or mentalizing—that process by which we reflect on our own mental states (e.g. desires, thoughts, feelings, and motivations) and imagine those of others (Fonagy et al., 2002). In Arendt's view, thinking grows out of one's own experience, and first and foremost involves the capacity to think from the perspective of the other.

As she put it in *The Last Interview* (2013): "I do not believe that there is any thought process possible without personal experience. Every thought is an afterthought, that is, a reflection on some matter or event. Isn't that so?" (Kindle edition, location 435). Thoughtlessness on the other hand, involves "the headless recklessness or hopeless confusion or complacent repetition of 'truths' which have become trivial and empty" (Arendt, 1958, Kindle edition, loc. 346).

In Arendt's view it was Eichmann's thoughtlessness, expressed in slavish and meticulous adherence to the genocidal policies of the Nazi regime, that rendered him a banal bureaucrat with a blunted moral sense that rendered him unable to tell right from wrong, good from evil, rather than a monstrous killer dedicated to evil. Further, she believed that this moral corruption also extended to the Nazi-appointed Jewish councils or Judenräte, who were complicit even if unwittingly in the expulsion, internment, and extermination of their own people by cooperating with the Nazis in organizing the Jewish community, in documenting their numbers and whereabouts, and in systematic selections of Jews for deportation. The collaboration of the Jewish councils was, for Arendt, "the darkest chapter of the whole dark story" (Arendt, 2006, p. 115), in that it sacrificed the first principle of morality—that it is better to suffer wrong than to do wrong. Justifying her position, Arendt stated later, "wrongs done by my own people naturally grieve me more than the wrong done by other people" (quoted in Young-Breuhl, 2004, p. 344), a comment that expressed the fierce emotions that were stirred up by the testimony of the victims at the trial. However, these emotions were also reflected in what some have seen as her harsh judgments and lack of empathy for the victims (Benhabib, 2000).

Indeed, in the scene when her editor William Shawn tentatively suggests that these statements might be inflammatory, Arendt defended her right to call attention to "facts" of their complicity, affirmed in chilling testimony by members of the Judenräte, such as the Hungarian Jewish leader Pinhas Freudiger, a member of the central organization of five persons who were appointed by the Nazis as spokesman for Hungarian Jewry. When asked by the prosecutor, "To what extent did you report to the communities and the provinces—those who were deported?" he replied,

> There was no such possibility because by the time we obtained the information and by the time we realized what Auschwitz was, the eastern part of Hungary and the northeastern part—this comprised 300,000 people, and they had received news from us they had known their fate, but what could we have done, what could we have done?
>
> (Quoted in Brokemper, Rexin, & von Trotta, 2012)

Again, Arendt's ideas were oracular, since recent films and writings on the Holocaust like *Son of Saul* (Rajina, Sipos, & Nemes, 2015) have focused on what Primo Levi (1986) called "the gray zone" (p. 2418) of layers of victimization, guilt, and complicity in the camps. As Primo Levi wrote of the leader of the Judenräte in Lodz, "an infernal order such as National Socialism exercises a frightening power of corruption against which it is hard to guard oneself ... to resist it requires a truly solid moral armature" (Levi, 1986, p. 68). Finally, Arendt believed that the trial itself had a shaky judicial basis, since Eichmann was kidnapped in Argentina but tried in Jerusalem, in a show trial that focused more on the experience of the victims than the crimes of the perpetrators.

These conclusions sparked what Irving Howe called "a civil war" not only among New York intellectuals, but among scholars and activists of all persuasions—a war that Howe predicted might "die down, simmer, but will perennially erupt again" (Berkowitz, 2013a). Recent "eruptions" occurred with the publication of new research on Eichmann's rabid and unrepentant anti-Semitism (Stangneth, 2014), and with further revelations regarding Martin Heidegger. The information on Heidegger regarded both Arendt's relationship with him, as her former lover and professor (Maier-Katkin, 2010), and the extent of his involvement with and support of the Nazi party. Recently, Eichmann has been in the media again with the publication of a letter to the President of Israel that he wrote in 1962 after he was convicted and sentenced to death, pleading for a pardon, and complaining about being a victim of a lack of empathy and an overestimation of his responsibility. Tellingly, Eichmann makes a case for his having acted on emotion, but does not affirm an ability to think (Eichmann, 2016). Mirroring Arendt's intellectual creativity and boldness, Katz and von Trotta intrepidly take on these controversies, focusing on the years during which she covered the trial and the repercussions of her ideas.

Thinking without bannisters

Von Trotta has said that she wanted to make films about women who think—and *Hannah Arendt* (Brokemper, Rexin, & von Trotta, 2012) is a film about one woman whose goal, as she put it, was to "think without banisters" (Bernstein, 2013, 2013; Kohn, 2013, 2018). The German phrase for this is *denken ohne Geländer*, that is, a form of thinking in which one is precariously balanced "moving deliberately up and down … a stairway without banisters, with the abyss of the past yawning on one side, and the on-rushing limitlessness of the future on the other" (Kohn, 2013). Such an original and reflective thinking process is not so easy to depict on-screen, but it was the imperative of its heroine, who said that writing for her was secondary, and what was important was "the thought process itself" (Arendt, 2013, Kindle edition, Location 86).

The film challenges the spectator to think without banisters along with Arendt. For an example, let us look more closely at the opening scenes of the film, which feature a frightening and puzzling scenario. A gaunt, black-cloaked figure walks down a road, illuminated only by his flashlight, when suddenly a truck approaches, and the man is grabbed, struggling and moaning, by two helmeted soldiers, who force him into the back of the vehicle. The dropped flashlight creates a small cone of light, which in the next scene becomes the light of a match in a dark room—illuminating a woman smoking a cigarette, her brow furrowed in thought. We soon learn that the man is Adolph Eichmann, kidnapped by the Mossad in Argentina, and that the woman striking the match is Hannah Arendt, and that she will cover the Eichmann trial. Before we are plunged into the drama of the trial and its aftermath, the filmmaker invites us to take a moment to contemplate what we have witnessed. Is this a just trial, and what political purposes might it serve? By posing such questions through visual ambiguity, the film consolidates our identification with Hannah Arendt as an observer. As one critic put it, this scene introduces the idea that "Arendt is alive and thinking and people will be held accountable" (Smith, 2013). This first scene also presages the ways that Arendt will be held accountable for her interpretation of Eichmann as a thoughtless bureaucrat, a man who lost his humanity in the murderous wheel of the Holocaust, by which she means his capacity to think from the perspective of the other (Arendt, 2006). She here will depart radically from the common view of him, which was that of a ruthless anti-Semite who delighted in and masterminded the slaughter of Jews. Indeed, from her viewpoint, Eichmann is all the more terrifying by having been judged as terrifyingly normal.

To create a nuanced portrait of Arendt's life and mind, Katz and von Trotta intersperse fictional film footage with archival footage of the Eichmann trial; and historically accurate scenes with scenes in which characters and places have been combined or transposed to heighten the dramatic impact. For example, the scene of Eichmann's kidnapping by the Mossad in Buenos Aires foreshadows a scene much later in the film, which takes place after Arendt's article series has appeared in *The New Yorker* (1960). Three Israeli agents, including her former fellow Zionist comrade Siegfried Moses, track Arendt down in the country retreat where she has sequestered herself in the face of the controversy, and attempt to intimidate her into retracting the book from publication, threatening that the book will be banned in Israel. Though obviously frightened, Arendt stands her ground, pointing out the ominous implications of censorship and sarcastically remarking that the Jewish State must be flourishing if they can afford the plane fare to send three men for the sole purposes of intimidating her. This scene is, in fact, fictional (though Moses did visit Arendt in Basel to try to dissuade her from publishing the book), but its inclusion here underscores Arendt's refusal to rely on stock formulations of perpetrators and victims based solely on categories of national or ethnic identity in order to establish guilt or innocence. Israelis, too, could behave in morally dubious ways—they, too, could be "thoughtless" out of self-righteousness or cowardice. During his visit to her in Basel, Moses warned her that her statements about the complicity of the Judenräte reflected her opinion or interpretation of events rather than being demonstrable assertions, and hence would make her the target of criticism from the Jewish community. Her response was that she had a responsibility to talk about the shared guilt and complicity of the Jewish community that had been overlooked and even covered up at the trial—a theme that continues to haunt the second and third generations of survivors, and reverberates through contemporary films such as *Shoah* (Lanzmann, 1985) and *Son of Saul* (Rajna, Sipos, & Nemes, 2015).

The multiple selves of Hannah Arendt

Arendt's capacity to identify and tolerate the complexities of victim/victimizer dynamics, what Levi (1986) has called the "gray zone" in the Shoah, stems from the multiplicity of her identity forged in the crucible of World War II and its aftermath. From the beginning of the film we are introduced to Arendt as a Jewish scholar at the center of a group of cosmopolitan émigré intellectuals in exile that formed almost an extended family or tribe. Deeply engaged in her work as a philosopher and political theorist (the latter, her preferred definition for herself), Arendt was an inspiring and sought-after teacher and lecturer. Although she had refused tenured positions to allow her more freedom for her work as a journalist and writer, she was the first woman awarded full professor status at Princeton and other universities where the film shows her conducting seminars and delivering lectures.[1]

However, even as Arendt ascended to become one of the foremost public intellectuals of her time, a high priestess of "thinking," she maintained a deep and enduring investment in personal life and relationships, and a capacity for fervent connections to others. For Arendt, thinking was

Janus-faced, in that it stemmed not only from solitary self-reflection (reflected in the film in the scenes of her thinking while reclining on a couch/daybed thinking about thinking), but also reflecting, remembering, and fantasying as one would in a psychoanalytic process. Last but not least, it stemmed from lively, and even combative, dialogue with others.

The film traces how her fascination and even hypercathexis of thinking was first forged in her inspiring, erotically charged, but conflictual relationship with her mentor/lover Heidegger, whom she met in her first year of college, when she was 18 and he was 35. He was her professor, and married, but, notwithstanding, they soon began a three-year affair. In a flashback of Arendt as a novice philosophy student, she tremulously puts forth her theory of thinking for Heidegger: "We are so used to considering reason and passion as opposites that the idea of passionate thinking where thinking and being alive are one and the same thing is terrifying for me…" (Arendt, quoted in Brokemper, Rexin, & von Trotta, 2012).[2] For Arendt, creative thinking is not a purely intellectual activity, but a loamy amalgam of affect, reason, and passion, with tangled roots in a libidinal experience that blends primary and secondary process.

If the filmmakers suggest that her passion for thinking had its inception in the blend of eroticism and suffering of her relationship to Heidegger, it gives center stage to how her capacity for thinking took a dialogical and reflective turn in her relationship with her charismatic husband, Heinrich Blücher. With Blücher, a self-taught philosopher and political activist, Arendt found intellectual companionship and erotic fulfillment. After their perilous flights across continents (from Germany to France in 1933 to the United States, where they were stateless persons in exile until granted citizenship in 1951), they established a secure base together in New York. The film depicts how their thinking together functioned as "a kind of contrapuntal melody" (Nixon, 2015, p. 141), at times erotically charged, at times infused with tenderness, at times sparking fiery intellectual debates—a melody that in America broadened to reflect the plurality of perspectives of their multinational group of friends and colleagues. A particularly important figure in this cosmopolitan family in exile was Mary McCarthy, the flamboyant, impetuous novelist and literary critic. From the first scene of the film, in which the two women share confidences about each other's marriages, divorces, and lovers, to the later scenes when McCarthy defends Arendt from the firestorm of criticism unleashed by the publication of *Eichmann*, the filmmaker suggests that the depth and continuity of this friendship, with its shared repository of memory and experiences and shared struggles to ascend in their respective male-dominated fields, may have contributed to their becoming "towering figures."[3]

Such a multifaceted figure as Hannah Arendt must embody contradictions. Indeed, the filmmakers depict Arendt as an engaged and outspoken public intellectual, but an avowedly private person; as a devoted, passionate wife, who nonetheless maintained an autonomous professional life as well as a vast circle of friends, which included Heidegger with whom she reconciled after the war, despite his failure to publicly repent his involvement in the Nazi party or to acknowledge the Holocaust;[4] as a constant friend who reveled in witty, gossipy exchanges with her best friend Mary McCarthy, but who had unreachable depths; and as a German Jewish scholar who was arrested by the Nazis for documenting the extent of anti-Semitic actions and propaganda on behalf of a German Zionist organization in 1933, but who maintained an enduring, if sometimes conflicted, identification with her German heritage and with German intelligentsia, particularly with mentors and colleagues Karl Jaspers and Martin Heidegger.

This identification is shown in the film through scenes of Arendt speaking in German whenever possible and only reluctantly switching to English, thereby demonstrating her refusal, as she put it in *The Last Interview* (2013), "…to lose my mother tongue." She states, "I maintained a certain distance from French … as well as from … English, which I write today" because "after all it wasn't the German language that went crazy … and I do things in German that I would not permit myself to do in English…" (pp. 21–22). Such things included reciting German poetry and literature that had been committed to memory early in her life. Arendt (2013) wrote: "In German I know a rather large part of German poetry by heart; the poems are always somehow in the back of my mind" (p. 22). The multiple scenes in the film of Arendt shifting from German to English and back enable the spectator to hear in a single context or scene the voices of multiple self-states, each linked to different experiences or registers of thought and language not as opposing realities but as aspects of past and present selves mutually interacting and converging in the present moment.

The film depicts how Arendt's identity as a Jew evolved and took on different configurations that appeared to others as contradictory. Although she was from a prominent German Jewish family in which her grandfather was a leader in the Jewish community, the word Jew was rarely mentioned in her home and it was only through the anti-Semitic remarks of her peers that she became aware of being Jewish. In fact, she wrote to Jaspers in 1933: "For me Germany means my mother tongue, philosophy and literature" (Bernstein, 1996, p. 15). As she observed in a letter to another of her mentors, the Jewish Kabbalist and Zionist Gershom Scholem, if she could be said to come from anywhere, it was from the tradition of German Philosophy (Arendt, Scholem, 2017, location 4954, Kindle edition). Although she endorsed the project of creating a Jewish homeland, particularly as a refuge for Jews after the Holocaust, she favored the creation of a secular and bi-national federation of Jews and Arabs governing together. Despite her Zionism, she was critical of the idea of an explicitly Jewish state inseparable from religious orthodoxy that would deny full citizenship to Israeli Arabs. With considerable foresight, she wrote, "no code of morality can justify the persecution of one people in an attempt to relieve the persecution of the other" (Arendt, 2008, p. 369).

These contradictions are highlighted in the film scene in which the grief-stricken Arendt rushes to the deathbed of her treasured friend and mentor Kurt Blumenfeld, only to be confronted by him for her lack of empathy and identification with the Jewish people. "Have you no love for Israel? Have you no love for your own people?" Blumenfeld asks. Hannah replies, "…You know me, I've never loved any people. Why should I love the Jews? I love only my friends—that is the only love I'm capable of" (Brokemper, Rexin, & von Trotta, 2012). Arendt thus refuses to identify herself with any "people" in the abstract. This statement is a shortened version of her response to her mentor Scholem after he poses the same question during an epistolary exchange:

> You are quite right—I am not moved by any love of this sort, and for two reasons: I have never in my life "loved" any people or collective—neither the German people, nor the French, nor the American, nor the working class, or anything of that sort. I indeed, I love only my friends and the only kind of love I know of and believe in is the love of persons. Secondly, this love of the Jews would appear to me, since I myself am Jewish rather suspect.… I do not "love" the Jews, nor do I "believe" in them; I merely belong to them as a matter of course, beyond dispute or argument.
>
> (Arendt, Scholem, 2017, location 4967, Kindle edition)

The transposition of this dialogue to Blumenfeld's deathbed is an example of the film's privileging narrative truth over historical truth, in that it underscores Arendt's anguish about the calumny and near irreconcilable conflicts with treasured colleagues that ensued after the publication of *Eichmann in Jerusalem.*

It is possible that Arendt's refusal to ally herself unilaterally with the Jewish people reflects the depth of her lifelong identification with her German mentors and teachers, particularly with Heidegger and Jaspers (with whom she remained in close contact until the end of his life). It also perhaps reflects her disidentification with her own father, who died of syphilis when Arendt was seven. Indeed, she states:

> Where Jaspers comes forward and speaks all becomes luminous.... if I may say so, I grew up without a father—I was educated by it. I don't want to make him [Jaspers] responsible for me, for God's sake but if anyone succeeded in instilling some sense in me, it was he.
>
> (Arendt, 2013, p. 474)

It is noteworthy that the phrase "the banality of evil," which continues to resonate through the public discourse to this day, had its roots in an epistolary exchange between Arendt and Jaspers. Reflecting on the rise of Nazism, Jaspers wrote to Arendt in 1946: "It seems to me that we have to see these things in their *total banality*, in their *prosaic triviality*, because that's what truly characterizes them ... I regard any hint of myth and legend with horror" (Arendt et al., 1992, p. 62). From this quote, it is clear that her focus on the banality of evil showed an identification with Jaspers. We could surmise that such multiple identifications and disidentifications allowed her to keep her multiple selves in motion while forging a unique voice and identity.

Believing in the duty or imperative of the individual to think and judge for him or herself and to act accordingly, Arendt valorized reflective thinking or self-reflective inner dialogue, shown in the film by the many scenes in which she is reclining on a daybed (reminiscent of an analytic couch but without the analyst behind), thinking, reflecting, and remembering. In making the couch the locus of her thinking process, the filmmakers drew their inspiration from Mary McCarthy's memorial to her friend in the *New York Review of Books*, "Saying Goodbye to Hannah" (1976), in which she recalled,

> Hannah is the only person I have ever watched *think*. She lay motionless on a sofa or a day bed, arms folded behind her head, eyes shut but occasionally opening to stare upward. This lasted—I don't know—from ten minutes to half an hour. Everyone tiptoed past if we had to come into the room in which she lay oblivious.
>
> (McCarthy quoted in Kiernan, 2000, p. 653)

Although her valorization of self-reflective inner dialogue was akin to self-analysis, Arendt was critical of psychoanalysis, which she felt does no more than discover the "ever changing moods, the ups and downs of our psychic life: and whose results and discoveries are neither particularly appealing nor very meaningful in themselves" (Kristeva, 2001, p. 179). The film shows how Arendt's multiple and sometimes seemingly contradictory selves, past and present, German and Jewish, public and private, reflect the powerful and often conflictual historical currents of the twentieth century, including the Holocaust and the formation of Israel. In turn, it was her multiple selves that enabled her to straddle the

Figure 5.1 Hannah Arendt watching the Eichmann trial from the press room.

Source: courtesy of Bettina Brokemper and HEIMATFILM GMBH + CO KG.

powerful historical divides that these events entailed, while maintaining that vibrancy of being, that steadfast adherence to sustaining ideals, and to a worldview that infused her work and life with meaning, and that commitment to love and work that is indicative of strong, integrated, if multifaceted and complex, identity.

Multiplicity and dissociation

In constructing such a portrait of Hannah Arendt, the filmmaker perhaps unwittingly herself straddles the divide in psychoanalytic thought between concepts of identity as unitary and as multiple. While portraying Arendt as a woman whose vital experience of wholeness, continuity, and self-cohesion bear all the hallmarks of a strong and integrated identity (Kernberg, 2006), it also shows her as an individual with multiple selves that coexist within this overarching, synthetic structure of identity. As Bromberg (1996) observes, when "we look within the psyche of well-put-together individuals, we actually see a 'multiplicity of selves' or versions of the self coexisting within certain contours and patterns that, in sum, produce a sense of individuality." In this view, "health is the ability to stand in the spaces between realities without losing any of them—the capacity to feel like one self while being many" (Bromberg, 1996, p. 166). Standing in spaces, according to Bromberg (1996), involves the capacity to experience a sense of continuity in the self despite disparate experiences of various self-states, and to tolerate the recognition of realities that do not necessarily map onto one's previous history, preconceptions, or current experiences of self.

Dissociation can be a crucial mechanism to facilitate such integration, especially when there is trauma or loss; it may temporarily sequester split-off memories, experiences, and self-states until they can be reflected upon, mentalized, or integrated, and need not take a pathological turn. In fact, when dissociative defenses are marshaled in the face of trauma without rigidifying it into a protective fortress against pain, or without a splintering of sense of self and identity, they may function to preserve psychic integration over the long haul. "Standing in the spaces" thus refers to the capacity to tolerate the emergence of subjective realities that are not necessarily containable by the self-state that one experiences at the moment. The capacity to tolerate such disparate experiences of self without either fragmentation or loss of self-coherence is what, in the view of Bromberg and others, distinguishes creative living from retreat into fantasy and/or stultifying rigidity or concreteness. The shifting theory of identity as comprised of "multiple selves" and "part egos" (Freud, 1990) is paralleled in psychoanalytic thought by a shift in psychoanalytic understanding of the nature of unconscious mental processes—away from the idea of a conscious/preconscious/unconscious distinction per se, and toward "a view of the self as decentered, and the mind as a configuration of shifting, nonlinear, discontinuous states of consciousness in an ongoing dialectic with the healthy illusion of unitary selfhood" (Bromberg, 1996, p. 511). This post-modern understanding of the self differs from the integration that ego psychologists imagined as possible.

In the film, the multiple selves of Hannah Arendt are depicted through a complex interplay of image and dialogue, black-and-white archival footage interspersed with fictional scenes in color, present-time narrative intercut with past flashbacks, with each register amplifying, commenting on, and even contradicting the others. Each cinematic dimension provides another layer of meaning to Arendt's reactions to, and account of, the trial. It is this multiplicity of perspectives conveyed through a variety of cinematic techniques that makes the film a work of the creative imagination—one that inexorably draws us into the workings of the passionate thinking, creative intellect, and even unconscious of its intrepid and multifaceted heroine as she covers the Eichmann trial.

Through a juxtaposition of words, images, and flashbacks, which weave together different levels of meaning and motivation, the conscious, preconscious, and unconscious, Katz and Von Trotta reveal why Arendt felt the imperative to cover the Eichmann trial even though it meant revisiting the horrors from which she had recently escaped. Her husband, Heinrich Blücher, initially opposed her decision, evoking their painful separation when Arendt was incarcerated at Gurs, the internment camp where she was detained by the French government simply for being a German citizen, even though the Nazis had previously arrested her for her illegal Zionist activities. Reminding her that had she not escaped she would have been deported to Auschwitz, as were the majority of the inmates at Gurs, Blücher asks her, "Do you really have to do this? … Remember how destroyed you were when we heard the news of Europe?" (Brokemper, Rexin, & von Trotta, 2012), by which he means the news of the death camps. It is telling that in this initial conversation even her husband, a tough-minded former communist labor organizer, cannot refer directly to the concentration camps. (He, himself, had been arrested during the war, and only narrowly escaped transport to a death camp.) In this scene, we see Arendt relive the feelings of terror and hopelessness that she struggled against during her incarceration. She replies:

> You told everyone how smart and brave I was to escape from Gurs … Many women stayed because they were afraid husbands wouldn't find them … we hoped it would soon be over … but then the waiting … more and more women let themselves go, stopped combing their hair, stopped washing themselves, lay on straw stacks … I tried to encourage them … and then one evening I suddenly lost my courage … I was so tired that I wanted to leave the world that I so loved. And in that instant, I saw you in front of me how you'd look for me and not find me. "Now do you understand why I don't want you to go," he replies.
>
> (Brokemper, Rexin, & von Trotta, 2012)

In this conversation, one has the impression that Arendt is revealing for the first time that the trauma of her incarceration was so great that she contemplated suicide (Katz, personal communication, 2014). Although the strength of her intellect and attachments, both internal and external, fueled her struggle to escape and survive, there are some indications that dissociated aspects of her experience were coming back into focus. Indeed, Arendt wrote, "to attend this trial is somehow I feel an obligation I owe to my past." She later described it as "a cura posterior"—by which she meant a retrospective cure effected through action and reflection (quoted in Young-Bruehl, 2004, p. 377).

In an early scene in the film, Arendt celebrates her assignment to cover the Eichmann trial with her circle of friends whom she refers to as her family in exile. Afterwards, Arendt withdraws to her study where she alternately contemplates Martin Heidegger's picture on her desk and her own reflection in the window of her apartment. This scene then cuts to a flashback of Arendt as a young woman, distraught after learning from her then classmate Hans Jonas about Heidegger's collaboration with the Nazi party. As she reads a newspaper article reporting on Heidegger's endorsement of the Nazi ideology of "the national awakening" in his inaugural speech as university rector in Freiburg, we see her relive the shock, even the trauma of learning about this betrayal by her revered teacher and former lover. By cutting between takes of her gazing at Heidegger's picture to flashbacks of learning that her professor has sworn allegiance to the Nazi party to shots of her looking at her own reflection, the filmmakers suggest that now she will bridge that divide in herself to confront aspects of her own dissociated experience. Indeed, one of the film's flashbacks shows her postwar confrontation of the still ardent but evasive Heidegger about his collaboration with the Nazi regime and his betrayal of Jewish colleagues, including his own teacher Husserl, during his time as rector of the University of Freiberg and after. She tells him that she has come to meet him at his cottage in the Black Forest to try to understand why the man who taught her to think behaved like a "fool." He justifies his actions as based on a combination of political ambition, naïveté, and misguided nationalistic fervor: "I'm like the lad who dreams and knows not what he does/I have no talent or experience of politics," (Heidegger, quoted in Brokemper, Rexin, & von Trotta, 2012) he tells the perplexed and skeptical Arendt. Nonetheless, she renews their relationship on the basis of forgiveness and reconciliation.

These scenes show how unconscious processes continually infuse conscious and preconscious dimensions; indeed, there is an ongoing dynamic relationship among these levels of thought. Classically seen as the repository of drives, wishes, traumas, and conflicts rooted in distinct memories that have been repressed or dissociated, the unconscious is continually being generated in current affects, thoughts, and actions that integrate all aspects of brain/mind functioning (sensory, motor, emotional, cognitive, and behavioral) (Ginot, 2015). We see how Arendt's quest to confront the Nazi Eichmann in the flesh is also sparked by her quest to understand Heidegger's complicity with the Nazi regime, portrayed through flashbacks as percolating in the background, infusing both conscious and unconscious aspects of her current psychological and intellectual functioning.

Arendt tells *The New Yorker* editor William Shawn that she is determined to cover the trial because she has never seen a Nazi "in the flesh" and wants to "confront the evil face to face" (Brokemper, Rexin, & von Trotta, 2012). Since we know that she had, in fact, been arrested and held for questioning for several hours by a Nazi officer when she was working on behalf of the Zionist cause, Arendt's statement perhaps signals both the extent of her denial and a readiness to confront aspects of her war experiences that had heretofore been intolerable to contemplate. Indeed, it is possible that Arendt's impassioned and unilateral condemnation of the role of the Judenräte was linked to her own sense of personal betrayal at the hands of close friends and colleagues who became Nazi sympathizers, abandoning and even denouncing their Jewish colleagues and classmates. In *the Last Interview*, Arendt (2013) revealed that for her,

> … the problem, the personal problem, was not what our enemies might be doing but what our friends were doing. This wave of … cooperation, which was relatively voluntary—in any case not yet under the pressure of terror, compelled in the way it is during the reign of terror—as if an empty space formed around one.
>
> (p. 18)

In similar fashion, highlighting how traumatogenic knowledge of the death camps could be, she stated that some of her fellow refugees were so shocked on learning about the death camps that they forgot their German:

> … I have seen it in people as a result of shock. You know, what was decisive was not the year 1933, at least not for me. What was decisive was the day we learned about Auschwitz. That was in 1943. And at first, we didn't believe it—although my husband and I always said that we expected anything from that bunch. But we didn't believe this because militarily it was unnecessary and uncalled for.… And then a half-year later we believed it after all, because we had the proof. That was the real shock … this was different. It was really as if an abyss had opened. Because we had the idea that amends could somehow be made for everything else, as amends can be made for just about everything at some point in politics. But not for this. This [the concentration camps] ought not to have happened. And I don't mean just the number of victims. I mean the method, the fabrication of corpses and so on—I don't need to go into that. This should not have happened. Something happened there to which we cannot reconcile ourselves. None of us ever can … About everything else that happened I have to say that it was sometimes rather difficult: we were very poor, we were hunted down, we had to flee, by hook or by crook we somehow had to get through, and whatever. That's how it was. But we were young. I even had a little fun with it—I can't deny

it. But not this. This was something completely different. Personally, I could accept everything else.

(Arendt, 2013, pp. 22–23)

Eichmann in Jerusalem: the trial

The tension between Arendt's shock and horror about the death camps ("this should not have happened … everything else we could accept") and her distancing from full knowledge of the experience of them, is evident in the language in the passage above ("I don't have to go into all that…"). The repetition of the idea that "this" (the death camps) should not have happened, as well as the sense of confusion and disorientation in the discourse of the above passage, bespeaks a struggle to master an unresolved trauma. Arendt's determination, even compulsion, to cover the Eichmann trial could be seen as an attempt to bear witness to the Holocaust experiences of others that she so narrowly escaped, but in the process, she opened the door to retraumatization, and risked a descent into the black hole of trauma (Felman & Laub, 1992; Laub, 1997).

The trial went on for 14 months, and Arendt witnessed only a fraction (four months) of it. Much of the trial she watched from the press room, one step removed from the action and passion of the courtroom. The filmmaker weaves archival footage with fictional re-enactments of the trial. This combination of documentary and fictional scenes pulls the spectator into identification with Arendt's role as witness to historical events unfolding before one's eyes. Along with Arendt we are immersed in the cascade of Holocaust horrors. There is the testimony of Jewish survivors, who describe death camp experiences in horrifying detail, and who catalog unimaginable losses of children, spouses, parents, and extended family. There is the testimony of the Jewish leaders who collaborated with the Nazis, who attempt to exculpate themselves over the angry cries and shouts of the spectators. Perhaps most disturbing is the footage of Eichmann, testifying from inside a witness box with a sealed glass partition over the top half to protect him from attack, with his reptilian grin, his hollow canned phases contradicted by an expression of arrogant contempt, his sudden flights of fancy and flashes of mordant humor. The clips of Eichmann in the glass box highlight his role as a bureaucrat removed from direct murderous action or intent, whose overriding imperative was to fulfill the duties of his office.[5] Through it all, we are also watching Arendt watching the trial, her face alternately registering shock, horror, and empathy for the victims as well as a certain aloofness.

It is noteworthy that Barbara Sukowa, the German actress who plays Arendt in the film, watched the original footage of the Eichmann testimony for the first time while these scenes were being filmed in order to maximize her emotional reactions to the events (Katz, personal communication, 2014). There is the sense here that Arendt will chart her own intellectual and moral course, that she will not be caught up in the drama of what she believed was in part a show trial, that she will maintain her own focus, and reach her own conclusions about Eichmann; at the same time, there is the sense she is confronting more directly not just the grimacing face of a Nazi functionary up close, but also the abyss that consumed so many of her friends, colleagues, and family, and that she and her husband so narrowly missed. In short, it is possible that her retreat into the pressroom where, chain-smoking, she watched the trial on TV, also may have functioned to insulate her from the retraumatization that full immersion in the direct experience of the trial might have entailed.[6] As we watch Eichmann dodge responsibility for being anything other than a bureaucratic functionary following orders, it is as though we have been transported back more than half a century and are being asked to think and judge along with Arendt.

Yet it has been observed that for all its studied objectivity, *Eichmann in Jerusalem* reads as a highly personal, even traumatized work (Davoine & Gaudilliere, 2004). It is clearly an attempt to deal with her unmastered past, which she felt was something shared by both Germans and Jews (Arendt, 2013). In their book *History beyond Trauma: Whereof One Cannot Speak, Thereof one Cannot Stay Silent*, French psychoanalysts Davoine and Guadilliere (2004) observe, "the patients who come to speak to us, unreconciled despite the amnesties, constantly bring us back towards the fault lines opened by the totalitarianisms of the century" (p. 236). In their view, the radical dislocation of human beings from their social context by way of generational trauma necessitates bringing into focus foreclosed aspects of the individual's life and family history, including breaks in the social contract that cannot be symbolized at crucial moments both in life and in treatment. They observe that Arendt approached such historical trauma and its origins "as an historian and philosopher … She described the Real Other that we have kept on running into in her works [such as *The Origins of Totalitarianism* and *Eichmann in Jerusalem*]" (Davoine & Guadilliere, 2004, p. 236). By "real other" or "pieces of the real" they refer to "the traumatic breaks in the social link" (location 304 in Kindle edition) catalyzed by the historical traumas of war and genocide, resulting in a void of understanding. One senses that in witnessing Arendt's witnessing, we are gravitating to, on a much more visceral level, the restoration of the subject who has been exiled from aspects of herself by the totalitarian discourses to which she was subjected (Davoine & Guadilliere, 2004).

Although her valorization of such self-reflective inner dialogue was akin to self-analysis, it is no wonder that Arendt was critical of psychoanalysis, which, along with her mentor Jaspers, she felt does no more than discover the "ever changing moods, the ups and downs of our psychic life" and whose "results and discoveries are neither particularly appealing nor very meaningful in themselves" (Arendt quoted Kristeva, 2001, p. 179)—comments that reflect defensive aversion to and fear of aspects of psychic life. Ironically, it was the writer and psychoanalyst Charlotte Berdt, Arendt's friend and Blücher's mistress, who trenchantly identified how Arendt's defenses, particularly the dissociative mechanisms through which she may have coped with both her traumatic past and the post-*Eichmann* firestorm, might have led to a certain intellectual rigidity.

"She thinks her sarcasm will protect her it but only shows her vulnerability … she tries to detach herself from the story but ends up bringing it closer to her," Charlotte tells Blücher over dinner, after Hannah has retreated to the country to avoid the cascade of calumny from her friends as well as her foes. "Where is she when she writes about the Nazi and his crimes?" asks Charlotte. "She has a right to feel pain and to show it," Blücher replies. "That would be shameless and quite out of character," only to be warned by Charlotte, "You have to be aware that she represses so much pain … it will eventually overwhelm her and you too" (Brokemper, Rexin, & von Trotta, 2012).

It seems significant that the filmmakers have a psychoanalyst make these observations about the emotional costs of Arendt's defensive strategies, a psychoanalyst whose collection of dreams of German citizens (from 1932 to 1938) was published in a book entitled the *Third Reich of Dreams* (Beradt, 1985). Both Arendt and Blücher supported the publication of this compilation of dreams, many of which revealed the emergence of the totalitarian machine, despite their reservations about psychoanalysis. This indicates perhaps that they gave credence to the importance of recognizing and documenting the reverberations of the Holocaust in the unconscious as well as conscious dimensions of experience. Indeed, in their rejection of psychoanalysis we are reminded of Howell's (2008) observation that dissociative mechanisms "protect our sense of (illusory) unity when the ravages of traumatic stress are overwhelming" (p. 102).

Of course, dissociation in the face of historical trauma is not unique to Arendt, nor is it necessarily pathological per se. A number of psychoanalytic theorists, including Fairbairn (1944), Bromberg (1996), Winnicott (1971) and others have observed that in the well-functioning individual personality structure repression of intrapsychic conflict may coexist with wholesale dissociation of it in situations of individual and historical catastrophe. Indeed, Arendt observed in *The Last Interview* (2013) that "[t]he greatest experience when one returns to Germany—apart from the experience of recognition which is always the crux of the action in Greek tragedy—is one of violent emotion" (location 320 in Kindle edition). This suggests that such extreme reactions involve the sudden activation of a self-state or memory held in separate and discontinuous state of consciousness. In scenes that reveal her intrepid intellectual boldness as well as her extreme vulnerability in the face of the vicious attacks levied against her in person and in print, the filmmaker insinuates that perhaps Arendt was still somewhat defended against such "violent emotions." It is important to remember that in the 1950s Jews were still going through the greatest trauma in their entire history, that they were just emerging from the horrors of WWII and the Holocaust, and that survivors were reluctant to talk about their experiences. It should be noted that Arendt at the time minimized the trauma of her exile, even seeing it as an "adventure" or as Arendt put it reflecting on her escapes, "I even had a little fun with it" (Arendt, 2013, Location 304, Kindle edition). Yet violent emotion certainly was evident in the fury that greeted *Eichmann*, as well as in aspects of the text itself.[7]

In spite of her aversion to psychoanalysis, the project of writing *Eichmann in Jerusalem* ought to be understood in terms of an attempt by Arendt to use her own experience in order to create a new narrative about evil. In this view, evil may simply take the form of the thoughtless submission of normal people to state-sanctioned violence, with the orders delivered by bureaucrats disconnected from the bloodshed they cause. Her account not only countered the prevailing narrative of Eichmann as the embodiment of the vicious and monstrous anti-Semitism that continued to threaten the Jews, but also served to master aspects of the traumatic war experience that previously could not be represented. As she wrote: "The sheer naming of things, the creation of words, is the human way of *appropriating* and as it were disalienating the world into which, after all, each of us born as a newcomer and a stranger" (Arendt, 1978, p. 100). Her narrative about Eichmann as a banal bureaucrat may have allowed her also to come face-to-face with her own unconscious terrors and anxieties. How else to understand Arendt's rather surprising statement in a letter to McCarthy written in the midst of the controversy over her report of the Eichmann trial: "I wrote this book in a curious euphoria. And that ever since I did it I feel—after 20 years—light hearted about the whole matter" (Arendt, McCarthy, & Brightman, 1995; June 1994, p. 168).

In the end, whatever its psychological function and power for Arendt—and it has been observed that in *Eichmann in Jerusalem*, fact and interpretation, social and psychological factors blur—it is clear that her work has redefined our understanding of the nature of evil and genocide. It is true that further information has come to light depicting Eichmann as a vicious and ruthless anti-Semite, which in the view of some scholars invalidates Arendt's interpretation of Eichmann. Nonetheless, as noted above, we also know that Arendt was familiar with some of these documents, including the interview of Eichmann by the Dutch Nazi sympathizer Willem Sassen conducted in Argentina in the 1950s. In this interview, Eichmann reveals the bone-deep anti-Semitism that he so relentlessly denied at the trial, stating:

> The cautious bureaucrat ... yeah that was me ... but joined to this cautious bureaucrat was a fanatical fighter ... I must honestly tell you that had we ... killed 10.3 million Jews I would be satisfied and say, good, we've exterminated the enemy...
>
> (Quoted in Lilla, 2013, p. 5)

However, the originality of Arendt's narrative, its vivid portrait of an everyday citizen unreflectingly carrying out the type of regime-sanctioned mass killing that has become so characteristic of our time, continues to resonate. Elizabeth Young-Bruehl (2006) argues that her most important contribution may be in changing our way of thinking about genocide:

> … to understand who we are and what our human possibilities are in the After—by which Arendt meant not only after Nazism and Stalinism, or after the Second World War and the Holocaust, but after the advent of weapons with the capacity to destroy the human race—we have to think about what is *new* in these fundamental assaults upon the possibility of politics. To think about what is new, we cannot use old concepts—particularly not concepts that have been emptied of their meaning and their usefulness by the very assaults that brought about this break in human history.
>
> (p. 9)

In similar fashion, psychoanalytic thinking and reflection on the Holocaust necessitates a revision or expansion of concepts to encompass historical and intrapsychic realities unprecedented in human history. One can see Eichmann as a new type of person—as both a vicious sadist and anti-Semite who delighted in the extermination of Jews and at the same time an unreflective bureaucratic caught up in the Nazi killing machine. Perhaps what Arendt revealed to us is the new face of evil for our time. As she puts it in the film,

> the greatest evil in the world is the evil committed by nobodies, evil committed by men without motives, without wicked hearts or demonic wills by human beings who refuse to be persons … and it is this phenomena that I have called the banality of evil.
>
> (Brokemper, Rexin, & von Trotta, 2012)

Arendt thinking about thinking

However history shall judge Arendt and her theory of the banality of evil, the film provides a compelling portrait of a woman academic at work, with the couch a metaphor for her dedication to the life of the mind, and by association to the depth of passion and affect that infused her thinking. The film also shows the everyday texture and tone of her scholarship, including her thoughtfully organizing the vast array of file folders containing over three thousand pages of court transcripts and testimony in piles around the floor and desk of her study and on tables and surfaces all over the apartment—much to the consternation of her good-natured husband. But the message here is that her work was important enough to take over the living spaces. Then the film depicts the actual process of writing *Eichmann in Jerusalem* in multiple shots of her reading and thinking on a couch with cigarette in hand, hearing in her mind the voices of victims from the trial, and fending off phone calls from an increasingly impatient *The New Yorker* editor, William Shawn. In these contemplative scenes, she appears to be in dialogue with herself, her internal objects, past and present, and the victims of Eichmann. Then there are scenes of her typing in a controlled frenzy when she finally begins to write. All of this suggests that for Arendt, thinking is infused with intellectual passion stemming from its connection to her internal representational world and affective experience.

Arendt's argument in *Eichmann in Jerusalem* (2006), that Eichmann demonstrated an "inability to think," aroused public furor insofar as it was interpreted as letting Eichmann off the moral hook by minimizing his responsibility for his actions. Leaving aside the question for a moment whether Arendt was right or wrong about Eichmann, the assertion that he was unable to think was, in her mind, the strongest possible way to condemn him. In order to come to terms more deeply with Arendt's claim about Eichmann, it is necessary to investigate more closely what Arendt means by "thinking." In this section, we use the film as a jump-off point to delve more deeply into Arendt's theory of thinking and its relationship with the contemporary psychoanalytic theory of mentalization. Characteristically, Arendt's view is subtle and convoluted, not to mention easily misconstrued. As we will argue here, a helpful way to shed light on

Figure 5.2 Hannah Arendt thinking.

Source: courtesy of Bettina Brokemper and HEIMATFILM GMBH + CO KG.

Arendt on thinking is to establish its connection to mentalization, a recent developmental concept in contemporary psychoanalysis that has been applied to therapeutic change.

For Arendt, thinking is at the heart of the Western philosophical tradition. The founding father of this tradition, Socrates, was so passionate about thinking that he was willing to die rather than to agree to give it up, and as Arendt comments, he went so far as to consider everyday life as an interruption of thinking (Arendt, 1978, p. 166). Following Aristotle, Arendt observes that given the skepticism about common sense, philosophers readily assumed the identity of being strangers (Arendt, 1978, p. 53). Arendt points out that thinking was understood to require a withdrawal from the world of appearances; it must be pursued as an end in itself, producing no results. Ironically put, the goal of thinking would be to perpetuate thinking. It seems that Arendt accepts that philosophy entails removing oneself from the world; however, as we will see, she is not content to conclude that thinking cannot be brought back into the world.

Kant had an enormous influence on Arendt, and his distinction between reason (*Vernunft*) and intellect (*Verstand*), in particular, paves the way to understanding her view of thinking. The distinction was a way to differentiate between "thinking" as the activity of *Vernunft* and "knowing/cognition" as the activity of *Verstand* (Arendt, 1978, p. 57). While *Verstand* represents the urge to know and aims at truth, *Vernunft* can only be about meaning. As Arendt points out: "To expect truth to come from thinking signifies that we mistake the need to think with the urge to know" (Arendt, 1978, p. 61). Arendt admires rigorous, unfettered thinking that transcends knowledge, but she is also wary of conceptions of thinking that are too rarified.

In her youth, Arendt was enthusiastic about Heidegger's effort to articulate a vision of thinking, based on experience that is situated in, rather than away from, the world. However, Arendt became disillusioned with Heidegger for his postwar stance, when he refused to acknowledge his complicity with the Nazis, and self-servingly affirmed the notion of "listening to Being," implying that when thinking descends into the world, it could only become corrupted. Heidegger claimed that thinking must purify itself from the will, given that for him, the will is Nietzsche's "the will to power." Arendt rejects Heidegger's position that real thinking cannot be reconciled with politics, which she sees as cowardly because it fails to entertain the hope that thinking can be realized in the world through the activity of judging.

Thinking as action

Although Arendt did not live to complete her final work, *The Life of the Mind*, her aim was to connect thinking, willing, and judging, and she clearly wants to reject the notion that thinking must be divorced from action. Ultimately, Arendt wants to affirm that thinking has a moral dimension as conscience. In a striking phrase, Arendt describes thinking as a "soundless dialogue of the I with oneself" (Arendt, 1978, pp. 74–75). It requires solitude—as shown in the repeated scenes in the film of her on a couch, cigarette in hand—but that is hardly the same as being lonely. Indeed, Arendt suggests that thinking necessitates an experience of duality: being two in one, being both the one who asks and the one who answers (Arendt, 1978, p. 185). Again and again, Arendt (2003) emphasizes that thinking leads us to examine and to question. It is, by definition, skeptical: "Thinking … which subjects everything it gets hold of to doubt, has no … natural, matter-of-fact relation to reality" (Arendt, 1978, p. 52). It is outside of time, but also serves a vital link between past and future: "Thinking annihilates temporal as well as spatial distances. I can anticipate the future, think of it as though it were already present, and I can remember the past as though it had not disappeared" (Arendt, 1978, p. 85).

Arendt's take on thinking, or, to recall her phrase introduced earlier, "thinking without banisters" (Bernstein uses this phrase as a subtitle to his 2013 book *Violence*, a study of violence in our times), means that we embrace thinking as an uncertain, creative exercise. We cannot know where it will lead, but it is a way for us to face ourselves and ideally something to be applied back into the world. This perspective on thinking anticipates the concept of mentalization, which Fonagy and colleagues (Fonagy et al., 2002) have introduced into psychoanalysis. Mentalization is the capacity to read and understand mental states—one's own and others'—as mental states per se, to recognize that they are present, and that they require interpretation. Mentalization can be defined in terms of four distinct aspects: automatic and controlled, internal and external focus, self and other, and cognitive and affective (Fonagy, Bateman, & Luyten, 2012). Mentalizing involves an internal dialogue that is closely tied to the quality of being open-minded, receptive to others, and always prepared to revise one's beliefs in the fact of new evidence. Mentalizing pushes us to keep asking questions, and to avoid the lure of premature, definitive answers. Mentalization heralds a new paradigm for psychoanalysis based on communication: the aim of treatment shifts from a static kind of self-knowledge to equipping patients with an ongoing capacity to negotiate life with the end of well-being, promoting a fallibilistic kind of self-knowledge (Jurist, 2005, 2010, 2014, 2018).

As mentioned earlier, Arendt's view of thinking is strikingly similar to mentalization: an internal dialogue in which one is immersed in reflection as an end in itself. Mentalizing can help us to decide what we believe is right and/or what to do, but first and foremost it requires an active searching process. Although Arendt ties thinking to the self (or really to the notion of "*selbst-denken*"), she also observes that judging directs us to understand from the perspective of others. Thinking for one's self would not have to mean that thinking collaboratively is impossible, but Arendt's Kantianism keeps her from focusing attention on the experience of thinking together. Nor is Arendt curious about an ego psychological way of thinking about thinking—for example, she does not consider Rappaport's (1950) challenging notion that thinking is always shot through with primary process, which the film seems to hint at.

So, let us return to the question of what it means to claim that Eichmann had an inability to think. It would suggest that he was unmotivated to carry on an internal dialogue within himself, to face himself, and not to be merely self-justifying. It seems to us that evidence exists to support this—for example, the fact that Eichmann insisted in his testimony that he was involved with transport, but not with killing. Another example, which is used as the opening of Stangneth's (2014) book, is especially revealing. In explaining why he decided to go to Argentina, Eichmann says: "I knew that in this 'promised land' of South America I had a few good friends, to whom I could say openly, freely and proudly that I am Adolf Eichmann; former *SS Obersturmbannführer*" (p. 3). In one sense, what stands out here is Eichmann's unapologetic self-identification, not just under the Reich but also as an abiding commitment that transcends time and place. In another sense, it is hard to avoid the chilling denial and narcissism of this statement that fantasizes about his welcome in the context of being on the run. Above all, we see here a complete absence of self-reflection, an inability to fathom the reality of being doomed to live in exile.

Eichmann was undoubtedly more of a committed, self-motivated Nazi than Arendt imagined. Does this invalidate her point of view? We think not. But does it make sense to hold Eichmann to the standard of being a philosopher? Is his non-philosophical aptitude what is so disturbing about him? Arendt's interpretation of Eichmann, that he suffered from an inability to think, helps her to make the argument that he manifested a particularly new, modern phenomenon, which, of course, has by now repeated itself with multiple genocidal examples. Arendt deserves credit for helping us to appreciate that one can commit heinous acts not just because one is inherently evil, but because one has gone along with things without questioning oneself and without anticipating the consequences of one's actions, as Hedges (2015) has recently pointed out. In spite of Arendt's disinterest in psychoanalysis, she beautifully captures Eichmann's primitive identification.

So, we would conclude that it is illuminating to attribute to Eichmann an inability to think, but in the spirit of thinking/mentalizing, we would like to raise a question of whether this account is the most perspicuous way to see him. What stands out for us is his failure of empathy. In Arendt's terms, empathy would be part of judging; so, perhaps, her argument could be revised and explicated: Eichmann's inability to think would mean that his sense of judgment would be impaired, which we see in the dramatic lack of empathy for the victims of the Holocaust. It remains uncertain whether this would work for Arendt. As the film highlights, nothing is more important to Arendt than thinking, and so, as already mentioned, there could be no greater insult to Eichmann than her assertion that he could not think.

Summary and conclusion

Katz and Von Trotta make compelling cinematic drama from Arendt's passionate engagement with what it means to think, and her affirmation of the redemptive capacity of the life of the mind, evident in her statement, "if there is anything in thinking that can prevent men from doing evil, it must be some property inherent in the goodness of the activity of thought itself" (Arendt, 1978, p. 180). Perhaps Arendt and others were beguiled by the surface banality of characters such as Eichmann, whose seamless functioning in bureaucracies, hyper rationality, and fierce loyalty to malignant totalitarian leaders obscures their own grandiose malignancy, dehumanization of self and others, and monstrous lack of empathy. Arendt's failure to recognize and analyze "the doubling" in such individuals, indicative of severe character pathology and even perversion, stemmed from her lack of understanding of or interest in depth psychology as Wurmser (2015) point out. However, in trying to reconcile, as Arendt put it, "the shocking mediocrity of the man with the staggering nature of his deeds" (Brokemper, Rexin, & von Trotta, 2012), she approached an understanding of the radical splitting evident in severe personality pathology. Indeed, Eichmann himself said at his trial, when asked if he felt any conflict between his duty and his conscience: "One could call it a state of being split, where one could fall from one side to another … one's personal conscience had to be abandoned" (Eichmann, quoted in Brokemper, Rexin, & von Trotta, 2012). We see in this statement the distortion of moral functioning that can occur when under the sway of the regressive pull of ideologies, individual conscience and identity are submerged in a paranoid mass movement led by a malignant narcissistic leader who functions as the group's ego ideal, promising the restoration of supremacy and power, often at the expense of demonized outgroups (Kernberg, 2003).

In identifying Eichmann's failure to think in terms of his inability to imagine "what the other person is experiencing," Arendt anticipated the implications of failures of thinking/mentalization for perpetuating character pathology. Indeed, subsequent clinical and research investigations in contemporary psychoanalysis have shown that deficits in mentalization contribute to individual psychopathology, particularly character or personality pathology, by fostering the transgenerational transmission of relational trauma at both the individual and societal levels (Volkan, 2007; Steele & Steele, 2008; Kernberg, 2003; Wurmser & Jarrass, 2015). Conversely, mentalization (also known as RF, reflective functioning) has been found to mediate the impact of adversity on personality functioning and development in numerous studies (Chiesa & Fonagy, 2014).

We further suggest that Arendt's capacity for such creative thinking and reflection on the process of thinking itself stems in part from her outsider status, from being "other" in many aspects of her identity and personal life—from her status as a Jew; from her status as an exile who evaded the Nazi perils moving cannily across the chessboard of nation-states; from her status as a scholar who crossed and re-crossed many linguistic, disciplinary, and national divides; and from her status as a female academic who triumphed and flourished on the competitive male-defined and controlled intellectual terrain. Arendt's confrontation with Jonas, her cherished friend and colleague, after she presents her defense of Eichmann in Jerusalem to her students and colleagues, is a case in point. Jonas castigates her for being a self-hating Jew, a German leftist intellectual blind to the depth of Nazi destructiveness, reminding her that she had never accepted "that the Germans shamefully betrayed her" and that she also would have been transported to a death camp (on Eichmann's orders) had she not escaped from Gurs. He ends his scathing diatribe on an ad hominem note by telling her disparagingly that he is "through with Heidegger's favorite student," thereby reducing Arendt as an independent thinker to an acolyte of her former mentor. Arendt's fierce, eloquent defense of her ideas in a public lecture given to colleagues (predominantly male) and students is a scene reminiscent of the great film courtroom dramas such as *Judgment at Nuremburg* (1961) or *To Kill a Mockingbird* (Brokemper, Rexin, & von Trotta, 2012).

As the film illustrates, even in the face of calumny and ostracism, even by some of her closest friends as well as her critics, Arendt staunchly defended her ideas. In the end, the thesis of the banality of evil, however flawed, was rooted in her capacity to do precisely what Eichmann could not do, to think from the perspective of the other. This capacity for mentalization, although flawed at times, devolved from her multiple experiences as a German philosophy student, an inmate in a French internment camp, a stateless person tossed across continents by the geopolitics of post-World War II Europe, an émigré and denizen of American democracy, a reigning public intellectual, an ardent wife and fervent friend. The various aspects of her identity functioned as contrapuntal themes that ascended or descended at different points in her life, without any aspect of the multiple self-states linked to each, effacing or elevating any other. Her work on Eichmann could be seen as the crescendo of her tolerance for multiplicity, in others as well as in herself, rendering her ultimately a doyenne of diversity.

The film suggests that it was Arendt's capacity to tolerate, embrace, and reflect on her multiple selves with all their contradictions and inconsistencies that that sparked the extraordinary originality of her thinking and the boldness of her ideas—ideas that have left their footprint across two centuries. It implies that Arendt's capacity to survive in the face of the extreme denunciation and even persecution she experienced after the publication of *Eichmann* derived not only from her intellectual boldness, honed by fierce political convictions, but also in the strength and nature of her internal object world. As Klein (1940), Kernberg (2010), Riviere (1964) and many others remind us, it is the latter that sustains us in the face of the inevitable losses, deprivations, betrayals, disappointments, and historical cataclysms that Arendt referred to as "the Dark Times" (Arendt, 1970).

After reading a particularly vicious letter in which she is told that the ghosts of the six million dead will haunt her for the rest of her days, Arendt recounts to her student, assistant, and friend Lotte Kohler, that she has dreamt about her father, whom, between the ages of two and seven, she watched slowly die of syphilis. In this scene, she tells Kohler:

> When I was a child my father was very sick … He died when I was seven after a long fight. I only knew him as a sick man, but in the dream where he appears he is healthy … he is handsome … he looks at me and he says, "I love you."
>
> (Brokemper, Rexin, & von Trotta, 2012)

It is notable that after telling Lotte Kohler this dream, she cries for the first time in the film. This dream scene reflects a dream that Arendt actually recounted to Kohler (Katz, personal communication, 2014). Perhaps Katz and von Trotta offer this scene to provide a window into Arendt's unresolved conflicts, particularly the ways this early loss might have both fostered her fierce independence as a thinker and intellectual, at the same time that it propelled her to seek paternal figures in the form of mentors such as Heidegger, Blumenfeld, and Jaspers.

The dream thus raises a number of questions about the impact of this loss of her father, her longing for him, and her denial of his chronic, debilitating, and shameful illness. Indeed, in her biography of Arendt, Young-Breuhl (2004) comments that Arendt's mother was concerned that Arendt, whom she depicts as a strong-willed, even headstrong child, was not "more disturbed" in the face of the death of both her father and grandfather. Instead, she seemed to focus on comforting her mother, reassuring her that this happens to many women—a statement that shows an unusual degree of reflectiveness for a seven-year-old (Young-Breuhl, 2004). The dream may also be an indication of *Nachträglichkeit* (Freud, 1896) in that it involves the reactivation of an early experience, in this case a traumatic loss, that is understood and reworked retroactively. As she relates the dream, we see the reactivation of an interrupted mourning process and a resuscitation of an identification with a paternal object. A renewed anchoring of a link between the representation of self and the lost object internally follows the acknowledgment of the pain of his permanent absence and the reawakening of a dormant, stalled mourning process (Freud, 1917; Kernberg, 2010). In such scenes, the filmmakers suggest that Arendt's apotheosis of thinking/mentalization had roots in experiences of childhood traumatic loss, as well as in the historical traumas of the Shoah that she endured later. This scene perhaps also functions to counter or at least mitigate the ungenerous accusation levied against Arendt by Podhoretz: "that is Hannah Arendt—all arrogance and no feeling" (Podhoretz, 1963). But whatever the motivations of the filmmakers, or of Arendt herself, which we can only speculate about, as psychoanalysts we are grateful to have such a dream of loss, mourning, and redemption.

As Freud (1923) has commented, when imaginative writers depict their characters' dreams, they aim "at nothing else but to depict his [sic] hero's states of mind through their dreams" (p. 8). In so doing, imaginative artists create narratives in which the richness and complexity of their characters blend unconscious as well as conscious dimensions. In *Hannah Arendt* (Brokemper, Rexin, & von Trotta, 2012), Katz and Von Trotta have clearly succeeded in elucidating both the conscious and unconscious dimensions of Arendt's fascinating life, multifaceted, complex, if conflicted identity, and prophetic theory of thinking.

Notes

1 Arendt held prestigious chairs and visiting lecture positions at The New School, University of Chicago, Bard, and Wesleyan among other stellar institutions, and there are centers for Hannah Arendt studies at both Bard and the New School.

2 This quote in the film is based on the following passage from the article Arendt (1969) published in celebration of Heidegger's eightieth birthday: "We are so accustomed to the old opposition of reason and passion, of mind and life, that the idea of passionate thinking, in which passionate thinking and being alive become one, can be a bit startling."

3 The bonds of friendship with McCarthy and others in this group forged in various battles—to survive the Holocaust and World War II, to achieve parity and prevail in male dominated professions—approximated the Greek ideal of

philia, which refers to an unconditional bond, stronger than sexual love or filial bonds, forged among those who have faced combat together (see Davoine, F. & Gaudilliere, J., 2004 for a discussion of this concept).

4 It should be noted that although she was an ardent intellectual who delighted in female friendship, Arendt was somewhat ambivalent about feminism. Indeed, she states in *The Last Interview*:

> Yes of course; there is always the problem as such. I have actually been rather old-fashioned. I have always thought that there are certain occupations that are improper for women that do not become them, if I may put it that way. It just doesn't look good when a woman gives orders. She should try not to get into such a situation if she wants to remain feminine. Whether I am right about this or not I do not know. I myself have always lived in accordance with this more of less unconsciously—or let us rather say, more of less consciously. The problem itself played no role for me personally. To put it very simply, I have always done what I liked to do.
>
> (2013, Location 77 of Kindle Edition)

5 It should be noted that the German word for duty, "Pflicht," is stronger than the English word for duty.

6 Focusing on Arendt watching the trial on TV monitors allowed the film-makers to integrate the fiction footage of Arendt with the black-and-white archival footage. In fact, they learned later that Arendt spent so much time in the press room because she was allowed to smoke there, but it may also be because she needed the distance from the immediacy of the courtroom experience.

7 Another example of dissociation in the face of past trauma in a high functioning person is provided by the psychoanalyst Donald Meyers (Meyers, 2012). In a tribute written after his wife's death, he tells us that his wife, Helen Myers, also a prominent psychoanalyst whose family fled Vienna when the Nazi's took over, suddenly vomited in midair when she flew over her childhood home for the first time while en route to a psychoanalytic conference In his tribute entitled "Helen's Return," Meyers (2012) wrote:

> Helen had always claimed that the move from Austria to the U.S. was for her a non-traumatic "adventure." As we were approaching our destination, Helen was looking out of the plane window. "Oh look," she said ... pointing to a rather grand looking apartment house bordering the park, "that is where I lived." At this point without missing a beat she threw up immediately.... Helen was a genius at reading everyone else's unconscious but, under such loaded circumstances, denial was still paramount.... Thus on her return to her homeland Helen had managed to greet it by throwing up, and then in attempting to treat this, had temporarily put a halt to both seeing and eating.... Following this crucial abreaction ... Helen showed no other evidence of the traumatic neuroses which overcame her the day before ...
>
> (pp. 62–63)

References

Arendt, H. (1958). *The Human Condition.* Chicago, IL: The University of Chicago Press.

Arendt, H. (1963). Eichmann in Jerusalem. *New Yorker*, www.newyorker.com/magazine/1963/02/16/eichmann-in-jerusalem-i.

Arendt, H. (1970). *Men in Dark Times*. New York: Harcourt.

Arendt, H. (October 21, 1971). "Martin Heidegger at Eighty," trans. Albert Hofstadter *New York Review of Books* www.nybooks.com/articles/1971/10/21/martin-heidegger-at-eighty/.

Arendt, H. (1978). *The Life of the Mind.* New York: Harcourt.

Arendt, H. (2003). *Responsibility and Judgment*. (Ed. Jerome Kohn). New York: Schocken Books.

Arendt, H. (2006). *Eichmann in Jerusalem: A Report on the Banality of Evil.* New York: Penguin Books.

Arendt, H. (2008). Zionism reconsidered. In J. Kohn & R. H. Feldman (Eds.), *The Jewish Writings*. New York: Schocken Books.

Arendt, H. (2013). *Hannah Arendt: The Last Interview and Other Conversations.* Brooklyn, NY: Melville House Publishing.

Arendt, H., & Scholem, G. (2017). The Correspondence of Hannah Arendt and Gershom Scholem [Kindle edition]. Retrieved from Amazon.com

Arendt, H. (Kohn, J. Ed.). (2018) *Thinking without a Banister: Essays in Understanding: 1953–1975.* New York: Schocken Books.

Arendt, H., Jaspers, K., Köhler, L., & Saner, H. (1992). *Hannah Arendt/Karl Jaspers Correspondence, 1926–1969*. New York: Harcourt Brace Javanovich.

Arendt, H., McCarthy, M., & Brightman, C. (1995). *Between Friends: The Correspondence of Hannah Arendt and Mary McCarthy, 1949–1975.* San Diego, CA: Harvest Book-Harcourt Inc.

Bateman, A. and Fonagy, P. (2015). Borderline personality disorder and mood disorders: Mentalizing as a framework for integrated treatment. *Journal of Clinical Psychology: In Session, 71*(8), 792–804.

Benhabib, S. (2000). Arendt's "Eichmann in Jerusalem." In D. Villa (Ed.), *The Cambridge Companion to Hannah Arendt.* Cambridge: Cambridge University Press.

Beradt, C. (1985). *The Third Reich of Dreams.* Munich: Nymphenburger Verlagshandlung.

Bernstein, R. (2013). *Thought-Defying Evil.* Paper presented at the conference Exercising Judgment in Ethics, Politics, and the Law, Wesleyan University, Middletown, CT.

Bernstein, R. (2013). *Violence: Thinking without Banisters*. Cambridge: Polity.

Berkowitz, R. (2013a). Misreading "Eichmann in Jerusalem." *New York Times*, July 7.

Brokemper, B., & Rexin, J. (Producers), & von Trotta, M. (Director). (2012). *Hannah Arendt* [Motion Picture]. United States: Zeitgeist Films.

Bromberg, P. M. (1996). Standing in the spaces: The multiplicity of self and the psychoanalytic relationship. *Contemporary Psychoanalysis, 32*, 509–535.

Bruner, J. S. (1964). The course of cognitive growth. *American Psychologist, 19*, 1–15.

Chiesa, M., & Fonagy, P. (2014). Reflective function as a mediator between childhood adversity, personality disorder and symptom distress. *Personality and Mental Health, 8*(1), 52–66.

Davoine, F., & Gaudilliere, J. (2004). *History beyond Trauma.* New York: Other Press.

Dean, M. (2013). The formidable friendship of Mary McCarthy and Hannah Arendt. *The New Yorker*, June 4.

Diamond, D., & Blatt, S. J. (1994). Internal working models of attachment and psychoanalytic theories of the representational world: A comparison and critique. In M. Sperling & W. Berman (Eds.), *Attachment in Adults: Clinical and Developmental Perspectives* (pp. 72–97). New York: Guilford Press.

Eichmann, A. (2016). Letter by Adolf Eichmann to President Yitzhak Ben-Zvi of Israel. *New York Times*, January 27. Retrieved from www.nytimes.com/2016/01/28/world/middleeast/adolf-eichmann-letter-to-israel-president.html.

Fairbairn, W. R. D. (1944). Endopsychic structure considered in terms of object-relationships. *The International Journal of Psychoanalysis, 25*, 70–93.

Fonagy, P., & Allison, E. (2014). The role of mentalizing and epistemic trust in the therapeutic relationship. *Psychotherapy, 51*(3), 372–380.

Fonagy, P., Bateman, A. W., & Luyten, P. (2012). Introduction and overview. In A. W. Bateman & P. Fonagy (Eds.), *Handbook of Mentalizing in Mental Health Practice.* Arlington, VA: American Psychiatric Publishing.

Fonagy, P., Gergely, G., Jurist, E., & Target, M. (2002). *Affect Regulation, Mentalization, and the Development of the Self.* New York: Other Press.

Freud, S. (1986). Letter 52. (Extracts from the Fleiss Papers). In *Standard Edition, 1*, (p. 233). London: Hogarth Press.

Freud S. (1917). Mourning and melancholia. In *Standard Edition, 14* (pp. 243–258). London: Hogarth Press.

Freud, S. (1923). *Delusion and Dream.* Oxford, UK: Acheron Press.

Freud, S. (1990). The Ego and the Id. *The standard edition of the complete psychological works of Sigmund Freud.* The Standa.

Ginot, E. (2015). *The Neuropsychology of the Unconscious: Integrating the Brain and Mind in Psychotherapy.* New York: W. W. Norton & Company.

Hedges, C. (2015). Our mania for hope is a curse. *The Nation*, May 26.

Howell, E. F. (2008). *The Dissociative Mind.* New York: Routledge.

Jurist, E. (2018). *Minding Emotions: Cultivating Mentalization in Psychotherapy.* New York: Guilford.

Jurist, E. (2014). Whatever happened to the superego? *Psychoanalytic Psychology, 31*, 489–501.

Jurist, E. (2010). Mentalizing minds. *Psychoanalytic Inquiry, 30*, 289–300.

Jurist, E. (2005). Mentalized affectivity. *Psychoanalytic Psychology, 22*, 426–444.

Kernberg, O. F. (2003). Sanctioned social violence: A psychoanalytic view—Part I. *The International Journal of Psychoanalysis, 84*(3), 683–698.

Kernberg, O. F. (2006). Identity: Recent findings and clinical implications. *Psychoanalytic Quarterly, 75*, 969–1003.

Kernberg, O. (2010). Some observations on the process of mourning. *International Journal of Psycho-Analysis, 91*, 601–619.

Klein, M. (1940). Mourning and its relation to manic-depressive states. *International Journal of Psycho-Analysis, 21*, 125–153.

Kohn, J. (2013). *Representing Hannah Arendt's Eichmann in Jerusalem on the Screen. A Discussion with Arendt Scholars and Moral Philosophers.* Paper presented at the conference, Wesleyan University Exercising Judgment in Ethics, Politics, and the Law: Hannah Arendt's *Eichmann in Jerusalem: A Report on the Banality of Evil*, Fifty Years Later, Middletown, CT.

Knott, M. L., & Heredia, D. (Eds.). (2010). *Der Briefwechsel: Hannah Arendt, Gershom Scholem* (The Correspondence: Hannah Arendt, Gershom Scholem). Judischer Verlag im Suhrkamp Verlag.

Kristeva, J. (2001). *Hannah Arendt.* New York: Columbia University Press.

Laub, D. (1992a). Bearing witness or the vicissitudes of listening. In S. Felman & D. Laub (Eds.), *Testimony: Crises of Witnessing in Literature, Psychoanalysis, and History* (pp. 57–74). New York: Routledge.

Laub, D. (1992b). An event without a witness: Truth, testimony and survival. In S. Felman & D. Luab (Eds.), *Testimony: Crises of Witnessing in Literature, Psychoanalysis, and History* (pp. 75–92). New York: Routledge.

Levi, P. (1986). *The Drowned and the Saved.* New York: Vintage Books.

Levi, P. (2015). *The Complete Works of Primo Levi.* New York: W. W. Norton & Company.

Lilla, M. (2013). Arendt & Eichmann: The new truth. *The New York Review of Books*, November 21.

Maier-Katkin, D. (2010). *Stranger from Abroad: Hannah Arendt, Martin Heidegger, Friendship and Forgiveness.* New York: W. W. Norton & Co.

Meyers, D. (2010). Helen's Return. *Bulletin of the Association for Psychoanalytic Medicine, The Society of the Columbia Center for Psychoanalytic Training and Research. 45,* 61–64.

McCarthy, M. (1976). (January, 1976). Saying good-bye to Hannah, *New York Review of Books. www.nybooks.com/articles/1976/01/22/saying-good-by-to-hannah*

McCarthy, M., & Kiernan, F. (2000). *Seeing Mary Plain: A Life of Mary McCarthy*. New York: Norton.

Nixon, J. (2015). *Hannah Arendt and the Politics of Friendship*. London: Bloomsbury Publishing.

Podhoretz, N. (1963). Hannah Arendt on Eichmann: A study in the perversity of brilliance. *Commentary Magazine*, September 1. www.commentarymagazine.com/article/hannah-arendt-on-eichmanna-study-in-the-perversity-of-brilliance/.

Rapaport, D. (1950). On the psycho-analytic theory of thinking. *International Journal of Psycho-Analysis*, *31*, 161–170.

Riviere, J. (1964). *Love, Hate and Reparation*. New York: W. W. Norton & Company.

Smith, G. (2013). Film review: Hannah Arendt. A vivid, honest, unflinching portrait. *The Berkeley Daily Planet*, August 2.

Stangneth, B. (2014). *Eichmann before Jerusalem: The Unexamined Life of a Mass Murderer*. New York: Alfred A. Knopf.

Steele, H., & Steele, M. (Eds.). (2008). *Clinical Applications of the Adult Attachment Interview*. London: Guilford Press.

Volkan, V. D. (2007). Not letting go: From individual perennial mourners to societies with entitlement ideologies. In L. G. Fiorini (Ed.), *On Freud's "Mourning and melancholia"* (pp. 99–109). London: IPA.

Winnicott, D. W. (1971). *Playing and Reality*. London: Tavistock.

Wurmser, L. (2016, January). *"Radical Evil," Banality of Evil," and "Character Perversion."* Paper presented at the meeting of the American Psychoanalytic Association, New York.

Young-Bruehl, E. (2004). *Hannah Arendt: For Love of the World*. Binghampton, NY: Vail-Ballou Press.

Young-Bruehl, E. (2006). *Why Arendt Matters*. New Haven, CT: Yale University Press.

Bibliography

Arendt, H. (1978). *The Jew as Pariah: Jewish Identity and Politics in the Modern Age* (Ed. Ron H. Feldman). New York: Grove Press.

Bernstein, R. (1996). *Hannah Arendt and the Jewish Question*. Cambridge, MA: MIT Press.

Dean, M. (2013). The formidable friendship of Mary McCarthy and Hannah Arendt. *The New Yorker*, June 4.

Ettinger, E. (1997). *Hannah Arendt/Martin Heidegger*. New Haven: Yale University Press.

Chapter 6

From *Shoah* to *Son of Saul*

Cinematic traces and intergenerational dialogues

Catherine Portuges

Holocaust films and Hollywood

Born in Hollywood to a Viennese mother and Hungarian father who fled Hitler's Europe in 1939, I dedicate this chapter to the memory of my European family—those who left and those who were unable to escape their fate: my Viennese grandmother Helene, interned at Gurs in occupied France, and her mother, Rosa, deported from Vienna to Theresienstadt; my Hungarian aunt Vera, deported to Auschwitz from Budapest; my Hungarian cousins Panni and Gitta, and our grandmother Jenny, all survivors of the Budapest ghetto; and my French uncle Jean-Claude, poet and photographer for the French Forces of the Interior (FFI), killed in combat in Normandy, France, June 1944. Before, during, and after the fall of the Berlin Wall, as a delegate of the annual Hungarian Film Week in Budapest, I had the privilege of observing first hand the evolution of these formal strategies in films made during the complex and often traumatic transition process that became the subject of my book *Screen Memories: The Hungarian Cinema of Márta Mészáros* (1993). A fellowship from the National Endowment for the Humanities enabled me to continue research on "The Subjective Lens: Intergenerational Transmission of Trauma in Cinematic Representations of the Holocaust," and my volume *Cinemas in Transition in Central and Eastern Europe after 1989* (2013) addressed the dramatic period following the fall of the Berlin Wall. In Budapest, where the Jewish community is now the largest in Central Europe, I witnessed the unfolding of the seventieth anniversary commemorations against a backdrop of rising nationalism, anti-Semitism, and racism in many parts of Europe.

In late January 1979, the four-part American TV miniseries "Holocaust" (Green & Chomsky, 1978) aired on West German public television. Prior to its broadcast, the NBC production had provoked strong misgivings; its most prominent critic, Holocaust survivor Elie Wiesel, called it a "trivialization of the Holocaust" and a "soap opera." Yet the West German public exhibited a surprising degree of interest in the miniseries: ratings indicated that more than 20 million viewers had watched at least one of the four episodes about the fictional German-Jewish Weiss family, and producers lost no time in realizing the subject's box office potential.[1] More than 2 dozen Oscar-nominated films have represented Holocaust themes, 20 of which received at least one Academy Award: *The Diary of Anne Frank* (1959), *Schindler's List* (1993, nine Oscars, including Best Picture), *The Pianist* (2002, three), *Judgment at Nuremberg* (1961, two), and *Sophie's Choice* (1982).[2] Indeed, nearly 85 percent of all Holocaust-themed Oscar nominees since *The Diary of Anne Frank* have received at least one Academy Award. Six documentaries have earned Oscars: *Genocide* (1982), *Hotel Terminus* (1989), *Anne Frank Remembered* (1995), *The Long Way Home* (1997), *The Last Days* (1998), and *Into the Arms of Strangers: Stories of the Kindertransport* (2000); in fact, none of the six documentary nominees since *Genocide* had failed to obtain the award. Likewise, five foreign films have been so consecrated: *Shop on Main Street* (1965); *The Garden of the Finzi-Continis* (1971), and *Life Is Beautiful* (1998); *The Counterfeiters* (2007); and Pawel Pawlikowski's *Ida* (2013). The multi-layered *Ida*, shot in stunning black and white, follows an 18-year-old novice nun orphaned during the Nazi occupation as she embarks on a search for the truth about her past and the fate of her family in 1960s communist Poland, in a nuanced existential exploration of questions of faith, identity, and forgiveness that juxtaposes the young nun's naïveté with her aunt's cynicism (Hoberman, 2015).

Many other films have, of course, addressed the Holocaust: notwithstanding the mainstream reception of these productions, it was Claude Lanzmann who transformed Holocaust film representation with the release of his magisterial documentary, *Shoah*[3] (Lanzmann, 1985), commissioned in 1973 by Alouph Hareven, an official in the Israeli Ministry of Foreign Affairs, who suggested that Lanzmann make a film about the Holocaust from "the viewpoint of the Jews"—a film that is not "about the Shoah, but a film that *is* the Shoah." Lanzmann discovered that

> what was most important was missing: the gas chambers, death in the gas chambers, from which no one had returned to report. The day I

> realized this, I knew that the subject of the film would be death itself, death rather than survival, a radical contradiction since in a sense it attested to the impossibility of the project I was embarking on: the dead could not speak for the dead.... My film would have to take up the ultimate challenge; take the place of the non-existent images of death in the gas chambers.
>
> (Jeffries, 2011)

Rising to that challenge meant plumbing the depths of soul and psyche for all involved. Appearing himself in hundreds of hours of daring and controversial conversations with victims, perpetrators, and bystanders, filming with a hidden camera in life-threatening circumstances, Lanzmann courageously imposes his vision on what Sartre terms "*le néant*," revisiting the sites of what he has called "*les non-lieux de mémoire*," or non-sites of memory,[4] seeking to inscribe in viewers' perceptions the massive material and emotional realities whose physical traces had been deliberately and comprehensively effaced by the Nazis. This strategy echoes recent efforts in museological and photographic research to portray actual sites and material objects associated with trauma rather than the experience itself, such as images taken from trains bound for the death camps (Wieworka, 2000; Gersht, 2012–2013).

Claude Lanzmann and *Shoah*

To revisit *Shoah* (Lanzmann, 1985) 30 years after its release is to realize that, not unlike in the intimate relationship of analyst to analysand in the consulting room, the documentary filmmaker and his or her subject engage a cycle of transference and countertransference through the arc of a film's production, which in the case of *Shoah* lasted well beyond a decade. Lacan's formulation of "*le sujet supposé savoir*"—the subject supposed to know—offers one useful conceptual apparatus for understanding the dynamics of this highly nuanced connection, particularly when oral testimony by a subject is central to the film's meaning. If the analysand attributes to the analyst the power to make meaning of his or her words, gestures, and affect, so, too, is the documentary filmmaker—and perhaps to some extent as well, the feature director—the recipient of the interview subject's projections and fantasies. As Lacan (2001) would have it, "even the psychoanalyst put in question is credited at some point with a certain infallibility."[5] The analyst may be well aware that he or she does not "know," yet the illusion of knowing becomes part of the patient's attribution of primacy of the "*supposé*" over the "*savoir*." Accordingly, the mutual dynamic of transference as a way of knowing the world (in contradistinction to its function in the consulting room) and its negation that can occlude the space between filmmaker and interviewee/participant may thus also be seen as both an ethical and an emotional encounter in this form of representational practice. For the filmmaker confronts the challenge of considering how to integrate the pursuit of historical traces through testimony into a narrative inevitably focused on an absent subject—what Lanzmann had described as a "circle of flames," a limit which cannot be crossed because a certain absolute horror cannot be transmitted" (Lanzmann, 1994).[6]

Likewise, in Lanzmann's case as in others, a kind of affective bond develops in the necessary collaboration between filmmaker and subject. Here he is compelled to inspire his subjects to speak the unspeakable, at times forcing them beyond what some consider to be acceptable ethical boundaries, guaranteeing that the cost of such emotional risk will ultimately be redeemed by the importance of their participation. Entirely dependent as it is upon verbal testimony, *Shoah* (Lanzmann, 1985) is a work of reflexive filmmaking, devoid of archival footage, newsreels, or re-enactments, with thousands of hours of unused outtakes, parts of which were later re-edited into subsequent documentaries:[7] *A Visitor from the Living* (1999); *Sobibór, October 14, 1943, 4 p.m.* (2001); and *The Karski Report* (2010). In *The Last of the Unjust* (Frenkel, Krausz, Labadie, Stocker, & Lanzmann, 2013), an edited version of the 14 hours of interviews the director conducted in 1975 with his first subject, Benjamin Murmelstein, the 70-year-old former rabbi from Vienna who served as the last "Jewish Elder" (Judenälteste, in Nazi parlance) of the ghetto camp at Terezín, Czechoslovakia, Lanzmann's controlled demeanor is evident on camera as he revisits and films the original sites of mass murder; his own feelings of guilt, shame, and rage figure intermittently as trauma, narcissism, or aggression. Lanzmann grows visibly fond of Murmelstein, his complex and rebarbative subject, as the film progresses, and in the closing sequence they walk arm in arm under the Arch of Titus in Rome. Lanzmann seems to identify with Murmelstein, the first subject he shot for *Shoah* (Lanzmann, 1985), when he asks: "What would you have done in my place?" Consistent with their reputations as tough, implacable Jews—the Viennese Murmelstein, the Parisian Lanzmann—Lanzmann has stated that he felt unable to fit his subject into the epic *Shoah* (Lanzmann, 1985), convinced that he "needed his own film, representing the other side of the story … I don't betray him or myself, it was so very difficult and required courage to be myself in this film" (Lanzmann, interview, September 2013).

Claude Lanzmann has described the making of *Shoah* (Lanzmann, 1985) itself as a kind of hallucinatory voyage, positioning himself in the figure of a pioneer in the desolate ruins of the camps, "spellbound, in thrall to the truth being revealed to me … I was the first person to return to the scene of the crime, to those who had never spoken" (Shatz, 2012, pp. 11–12). He chooses to construct his films on the testimony of survivors, perpetrators, and bystanders, and it is their words that provide the primary account of the *univers concentrationnaire*: in one of many controversial statements, Lanzmann has denounced visual representations of the death camps as "sacrilegious," asserting that if he were to discover footage of Jews being asphyxiated in the gas chamber, he would destroy it (Shatz, 2012, pp. 11–12). *Shoah* nonetheless remains the most significant and celebrated intervention in modern cinematic Holocaust narrative[8] and a touchstone for subsequent filmmakers. Three decades prior to the release of *Shoah* (Lanzmann, 1985), one of the first cinematic reflections on the Holocaust, Alain Resnais' groundbreaking *Night and Fog* (Dauman, Halfon, Lifchitz, & Resnais, 1955), documents the grounds of Auschwitz by contrasting the stillness of the abandoned empty buildings with haunting wartime footage shot ten years after the liberation of the camps, while Marcel Ophüls' *The Sorrow and the Pity: Chronicle of a French City Under Occupation* (Part One, The Collapse; Part Two, The Choice, 1969) foregrounds interviews with a German officer and collaborators who comment on the collaboration between the Vichy government and Nazi Germany. The documentary was first shown on French television in 1981 after having been banned from that medium for many years.[9]

In the decades following the liberation of the camps, a number of international films positioned largely outside conventional distribution channels have not been favored with such critical attention. As discussions of the ethics and aesthetics of cinematic representability continue to preoccupy novelists, poets, film scholars, psychoanalysts, spectators, and filmmakers alike, new genres, formats, and narrative modes are programed in hundreds of film festivals around the world in which the Shoah reverberates prominently, defying assumptions that viewers must be suffering from a form of "Holocaust fatigue." These textual inscriptions of traumatic histories acquire particular urgency in the East-Central European cinematic landscape where topographies have been redrawn, political alliances renegotiated, and sealed archives opened since the fall of the Berlin Wall. In reaction to the practice of "organized forgetting" that prevailed during the socialist decades under the Kádár regime in Hungary when ethnic and religious identities were discouraged in favor of communist internationalism, large-scale co-productions featuring multigenerational narratives have been instrumental in drawing attention to the differences between western and eastern European experiences of the Holocaust.

Out of the past: transgenerational fictional representations

Perhaps not surprisingly in view of the silence in which the Holocaust was shrouded for almost a generation, fictional representations were among the first to emerge. István Szabó's *Sunshine* (Hamori, Lantos, & Szabó, 1999), an English-language film with a predominantly Anglo-American cast, was produced in Canada and filmed in Hungary. With a screenplay co-written by an American playwright and a Hungarian director renowned in the West for a film in German (the Oscar-winning *Mephisto*), it is a transnational epic with a decidedly Hungarian theme: the fate of the Jews in twentieth-century Europe and its sequellae for Hungarian identity after the Holocaust. The trajectory of the Sonnenschein family is followed over four generations, from the Hapsburg Empire through the years of fascism, WWII and communism; the dilemmas of assimilation find the family changing its name to the more Hungarian-sounding Sors (meaning fate) and ultimately reclaiming it in identification with the traumatic collective history of the family's Jewish ancestors (Portuges, 1998). Conversely, the subjectivity and interior monologue of a single narrator is the focus of Lajos Koltai's *Fateless* (Sorstalánság) (Barbalics, Hamori, Kemeny, Olsberg, & Koltai, 2005), based on Nobel Laureate István Kertész's autofictional account of his deportation to Auschwitz as an adolescent: "The experience that contributed to writing the novel was about solitude, a more difficult life … the need to step out of the mesmerizing crowd, out of history, which renders you faceless and fateless" (Kertész, 2002). The film transposes the novel's first-person singular voice of the protagonist, 14-year-old Gyuri Köves, who recounts his deportation from a Budapest city bus in the fall of 1944 to Auschwitz, and the carceral isolation that ensues. Gyuri knows nothing of concentration camps nor of Nazism: indeed, his knowledge of the Jewish origins for which he is condemned is at once superficial and inexpressible. Kertész has suggested that he did not know even as a child what to make of the Jewishness that had been thrust upon him: "What kind of Jew is one who did not have a religious upbringing, speaks no Hebrew, is not familiar with the basic texts of Jewish culture, and lives not in Israel but in Europe?" (Himka & Michlic, 2013, p. 298). *Fateless* (Barbalics, Hamori, Kemeny, Olsberg, & Koltai, 2005) shifts the locus of cinematic discourse to a quasi-autobiographical mode with documentary undertones, suggesting—however momentarily—a greater receptivity toward confronting and perhaps even integrating parts of the experience, notwithstanding Kertész's belief that Hungary has yet to face its role in the Holocaust.

Cinema/psychoanalysis/*Shoah*

That, among these works of Kertész, *Fatelessness* (Barbalics, Hamori, Kemeny, Olsberg, & Koltai, 2005) was adapted for the cinema marks a moment in Holocaust representation in East European cinema that drew upon literary and semi-autobiographical sources rendered in a globalized Hollywood style, one that would soon give way to different forms of artistic practice. Auto-fictional modalities associated with the second post-WWII generation suggest that individual and cultural memory, while inherently uncertain and unreliable, can serve both as primary material and a critical source for understanding past events and experiences, as well as a basis for further artistic expression and inquiry. What, then, can we learn today from the films of artists whose work concerns memorialization, reconstitution, re-enactment, reconstruction, and repression? In what ways do filmmakers of these different generations avoid or reckon with the traumas of history? Countering the ethos of "organized forgetting" that characterized official policy in the former East Bloc, how can we read these often disguised conversations between contemporary filmmakers and their counterparts in the postwar and socialist eras?

As traumatic memories of the contested terrain of familial and personal history are revisited, re-evaluated, and at times reconciled in the interplay between spectator and moving image, new visual, textual, and emotional understandings may emerge. The use of first-person voice-over, home movie-style imagery, and a proclivity for archival images—in contrast to Lanzmann's rigorous exclusion of such footage—extend the boundaries and conventions of artistic practice.[10]

Transference and documentary filmmaking

Documentary films, many of which, as I have suggested, are inevitably influenced by or in some way in conversation with *Shoah* (Lanzmann, 1985), occupy a consequential position at least equal to that of fiction in Holocaust reconstruction and memorialization. Second-generation filmmaker Gyula Gazdag's groundbreaking documentary *Package Tour* (Társasutazás) (Gazdag, 1985) gestures toward Lanzmann's *Shoah* via the trope of a temporal and spatial journey to revisit the site of earlier trauma. In the East European socialist context of the time, the Holocaust could only be evoked in indirect language, resorting to circumlocutions such as "persecution" rather than speaking of genocide, extermination, or murder. In its refusal of this official vocabulary, Gazdag's film was a courageous and liberating point of departure from the constraints of official discourse. As a group of former inmates and their sons and daughters embark on a tour to Auschwitz and Birkenau, *Package Tour* (Gazdag, 1985) asks why they have come back—to remember, to try to understand the magnitude of what they experienced, how it could have happened, or whether it might happen again? While the camera's presence can seem intrusive in the face of such grief, an interview with a survivor unable to make the journey due to post-traumatic illness exposes her discreet recollection of the arbitrary nature of life and death in the camp. The intimate complicity between interviewer and subject, indispensable to such documentaries, casts into bold relief the need to speak for oneself, and the sense of responsibility for doing so, in spite of the extreme suffering it may arouse in the speaker.[11]

Package Tour (Gazdag, 1985) was one of the first films to document early-stage initiatives to revive Jewish spaces through restoration, restitution, memorializing, and tourism. Two decades after Gazdag's groundbreaking film, in *Szomszédok Voltak* (*Once They Were Neighbors*)

(Wizner & Geller-Varga, 2005), Zsuzsanna Geller-Varga interrogates neighbors of Jews who had been deported 60 years earlier from Kőszeg, a picturesque town surrounded by mountains on the Austrian border of Hungary: what do they remember, she asks, of the town's ghetto, its brick factory, the train station, the mass graves, in the heart of the very community in which they continued to live? What did they do and what could have been done? What did the bystanders see and what do they believe they saw in their small community during the last days of World War II? As in *Shoah* (Lanzmann, 1985) and *Package Tour* (Gazdag, 1985), the camera gazes unflinchingly at the facial and gestural discomfort of those who were present at the site of suffering and death. Geller Varga continues her investigation of the shadow screen memories cast by the failure to face the past in *Zsinagógát Vegyenek/Synagogue for Sale* (Wizner & Geller-Varga, 2007), as her camera confronts the citizens of the same town of Köszeg where the dilapidated 150-year-old synagogue—long abandoned, overgrown by weeds, its gates locked, officially under landmark protection—still stands in the town center. Sixty years earlier they had been neighbors, while today—as elsewhere in the countryside—there are few if any Jewish inhabitants. The citizens of Kőszeg participating in the interviews are surprisingly willing to share their memories, yet clearly distance themselves from any personal, emotional connection, while every word and gesture attests to evidence of their silent assent to—or active collusion with—the deportation and ultimate death of their fellow Jewish citizens.[12] Denial again emerges as a potent force in scenes from Judit Elek's *Elie Wiesel Goes Home* (*Mondani a mondhatlant: Elie Wiesel üzenete)* (Elek, Marmiesse, Ozorai, Simó, 1997), a documentary retracing Wiesel's haunting journey, the first in 20 years, to the neighborhood where he played as a child in his birthplace—Sighet, Transylvania—where his deportation to Auschwitz took place in 1944, and where he lost his parents, sisters, family, neighbors, and his entire Jewish community in the gas chambers. Only one significant feature has changed: not a single Jew remains in the village.

The third generation

Diana Gróo (born in Budapest in 1973) claimed in an interview I conducted with her in the Seventh District, the first and most important Jewish quarter in Pest:

> We are the third generation after World War II. Our parents' generation could talk about communism and they were closer to their parents' war experience. For us to talk about the past is very unusual. The Prime Minister has said that only those who follow the Christian-Hungarian tradition and are proud of the state's foundation are true Hungarians … our generation is searching for an identity and for topics that will appeal to a broad audience. We no longer have a common landscape. Our style has to be different from [that of a] Szabó, Makk, Jancsó, Elek, or (film composer Miklós) Rózsa.[13]
>
> (Gróo, 2012–2014)

Gróo's *Regina* (Angelusz, Gróo, Reich, Weisz, & Wittenberg, 2013, Lia Award for Jewish Heritage, 30th Jerusalem Film Festival), a poetic documentary based on a single surviving photograph of Regina Jonas (1902–1944), is constructed entirely from archival materials—papers, letters, diplomas and documents, interviews—from the life of the first woman rabbi to be ordained in 1930s Berlin. The film evokes the city's atmosphere through black-and-white images and multi-vocal narrative voices that seem to speak across generations as if in a dreamlike condensation. Rabbi Jonas was arrested in 1942 and deported to Theresienstadt where her elderly mother was also imprisoned in the "model concentration camp" depicted in Nazi propaganda films of the time. Jonas spent two years there, providing pastoral care *in extremis* to deportees. In 1944 she was transferred to Auschwitz, where she perished at age 42.

Found images: Péter Forgács and the archaeological palimpsest

These documentary projects function as palimpsests, condensing spatial-temporal and emotional traces. Metaphor, allegory, and montage establish connections across space and time that invite—and at times compel—the spectator not so much in terms of an attachment to a particular event or moment but as a dynamic process of transference between and among intergenerational experiences. The cinematic *oeuvre* of Péter Forgács, a second-generation child of the Holocaust, and the first Hungarian filmmaker to be awarded the prestigious European Erasmus Prize,[14] weaves an innovative pattern of associations and resonances among different kinds and sources of personal and historical information, an intimate yet fragmented perspective on cataclysmic events through haunting images drawn from amateur film footage and home movies. A student of psychoanalysis when its practice was suppressed as subversive under communism,[15] Forgács filmed *Conversation on Psychoanalysis* (1993) in five parts: Freud and Vienna (53 min), Sándor Ferenczi and the Budapest School of Psychoanalysis (53 min), The Psychoanalytic View of Man (55 min), Psychoanalysis & Society (53 min), and Psychoanalysis as Therapy (58 min). The provocative artistic method inaugurated in that work urges the uneasy and even reluctant spectator to examine the intimate spaces of memory that one might rather avoid.[16] His groundbreaking series, *Privát Magyarország/Private Hungary* (Forgács, 1988–2002), uses prewar amateur family film footage to evoke the annihilation of a once-thriving milieu, a reminder that twentieth-century history is layered with cinematic images, not only those shot by filmmakers, newsreel cameramen, and photojournalists, but also by amateurs. And it is from these private, often overlooked images that Forgács draws to inscribe the lost world of Europe—not the official version, but history as it was lived: "I am not a historian," Forgács has said. "I am interested in the psychoanalysis of history." Just as for Freud, dreams, jokes, and slips of the tongue could reveal the unconscious life of the mind, for Forgács, the sequences produced by amateur filmmakers reveal the complexities and slippages that recorded history may mask or elide. Forgács has referred to his work as "re-orchestrating history," taking up the large events of twentieth-century Europe but presenting them anew, from the point of view of daily life rather than the actions of famous and powerful figures (Portuges, 2011, pp. 159–176).

The Maelstrom: A Family Chronicle (Messemaker & Forgács, 1997) follows the Peerebooms, a Jewish Dutch family, through the 1930s and into the 1940s via the home movies filmed by one of the sons, Max. Like many Jewish families, the Peerebooms go on living at first unknowingly in the shadow of the Holocaust, only gradually coming to understand the full measure of the fate that awaits them. A more lucid awareness guides *A Bibó Reader: Private Hungary 13, the Bishop and the Philosopher* (Forgács, 2001)[17] in a portrayal of the philosopher and historian István Bibó—arrested in 1944 by the (fascist) Arrow Cross, sentenced to life imprisonment, and later released under amnesty. The opening intertitle of *Free Fall* (Forgács, 1996)—"Apparently everything is normal"—gestures toward the film's tragic dénouement: the daily life of a Jewish family in

Szeged during World War II, when, inescapably, the anti-Jewish laws are put into effect and ultimately doom the family's existence. *Class Lot* (*Private Hungary 11*) (Forgács, 1997) reveals that the story of *Free Fall* (Forgács, 1996) does not end at the close of World War II: György Petö and his wife Eva have survived the death camps; György takes up his previous life in the lottery shop; and everything does indeed seem "normal" until 1949, when the communists confiscate whatever property the Nazis had not already seized from the family.

Expanding his historical investigation, Forgács designed *The Danube Exodus: The Rippling Currents of the River* (Forgács, 2002) under the auspices of the Labyrinth Project at the University of Southern California's Annenberg Center for Communication for exhibition at the Getty Center in Los Angeles.[18] A multimedia installation designed to engage museum visitors in simultaneous interactive narratives projected in three adjoining galleries, it incorporates found footage of two historic voyages along the Danube River and includes amateur film footage by Captain Nándor Andrásovits who ferried Eastern European Jewish refugees along the Danube from Slovakia to the Black Sea (and eventually Palestine) in 1939. The "found images" include original 8mm footage obtained by the filmmaker from the captain's widow, together with outtakes from the Jewish voyage donated to Forgács by historian-archivist János Varga, who originally inherited the material from Andrásovits' close friend, Captain Zalán Petneházy. (It was Varga, coauthor of Forgács's Jewish exodus story on the Danube, who first suggested the idea for a multimedia gallery installation) (Alexander & Kinder, 2002). This narrative is paralleled by a "reverse" exodus the following year when Andrásovits' ship transported Bessarabian Germans fleeing to the Third Reich to escape the Soviet annexation of Bessarabia. A touchscreen interface allowed visitors to navigate through the orchestration of found footage projected on multiple screens, thereby allowing for a simulated personal engagement with these historical subjects. The immersive experience was enhanced by an audio mix that included ambient sounds of the river and harbor, the mechanical rhythms of ships' engines, regional music from the period, songs and prayers of the refugees, voice-overs of the captain and his passengers, and the haunting minimalist music of composer Tibor Szemző, the filmmaker's collaborator on the project.

Forgács's video installation, *Letters to Afar* (Forgács, 2013)[19] was based on home movies made by New York City's Jewish immigrants returning to visit Poland during the 1920s and 30s, primarily 6mm and 8mm amateur films of Polish Jewish communities made between World Wars I and II and held in the YIVO archives. Entering the exhibition, one is immediately surrounded by—and at times overwhelmed by—multiple images of past lives reflected in film fragments that capture intimate moments in communities that have long since ceased to exist, positioning us as if we were part of those once-lively streets and families. Through a fragmented triptych construction of screens in the gallery, both vertical and horizontal, the viewer is at once physically located in the present while simultaneously surrounded by sensory visual and auditory signifiers of the now-distant past. An amateur film from the traditional Jewish neighborhood of Kazimierz in Krakow, for example, is accompanied by scenes from *The Dybbuk* (*Der Dibuk*, Poland, 1937), the classic Yiddish-language feature film directed by Michal Waszynski and set in an Hassidic *shtetl*.

Projected on nine intermittently reconfigured screens, the images are variously doubled, frozen, mirrored, slowed down, or staggered, their shadowy presence underscored by a minimalist musical accompaniment and occasional bits of ambient sound by The Klezmatics, the multilingual American band whose artistic practice fuses Klezmer music with elements of jazz, rock, gospel, and other modern musical genres. As spectators we witness the lives of locals in the streets, markets, parks, schools, and synagogues, observing quotidian gestures and activities, while discreet commentary in the form of occasional seemingly spontaneous narration provides a counterpoint to the flow of impressions, thoughts, and sensations evoked by the fragmented and juxtaposed projections that require the viewer's gaze to ceaselessly travel in a futile attempt to encompass the captivating and absorbing images. Yet in place of a sentimental or elegiac reconstitution, Forgács's installation invites rediscovery and revision, rereading and re-experiencing of "letters" from the past, counterposing as "screen memories" both the footage recorded by interwar filmmakers and its artistic retransmission by the filmmaker in what one critic has called an example of the emergent genre of "Jewish material-memory film,"[20] an increasingly contemporary form whose contours are defined by the reworking of amateur movies by or about (mainly) European Jews and their New World descendants. Forgács has made a number of such material-movies, mainly for television, over the years, including *The Bartos Family* (1988), *Free Fall* (1996), *The Maelstrom* (1997), and *Miss*

Universe 1929 (2006), often drawing upon his own comprehensive private archive of amateur films.

Letters to Afar (2013) is reminiscent in some ways of the earliest films of Louis and Auguste Lumière, pioneers of the cinema in the 1890s, who shot footage of workers at their factory leaving at the end of the day. The filmmakers showed the resulting film, *La Sortie des ouvriers de l'usine Lumière* (*Workers Leaving the Lumière Factory*) at an industrial meeting in Paris in March 1895; it is considered to be the very first motion picture.[21] Like the Lumière brothers, filming sequences destined for their families back in America, the Polish amateur filmmakers recorded relatives and friends in their daily surroundings, capturing unique moments that allow the viewer to be at once elsewhere and present, to experience the illusion of transcending temporal and spatial limits. They recall as well the intimate amateur footage portraying Freud, his family and colleagues, and his chow Yofi, shot from 1930–1939 and narrated by Anna Freud who insists that her father "didn't like to be photographed." In one 1932 sequence, taken at home in Pötzleinsdorf, Vienna, Freud appears with his former school friend "who became an archeologist in Rome," both ostensibly unaware of the camera's presence (*Sigmund Freud: the Last Decade*).

Inviting the visitor to a rereading of these "letters" from the past, *Letters to Afar* (2013) avoids constructing an epic historical narrative like those of the multigenerational fictionalized sagas of the 1990s, but instead tries to penetrate the private, internal world of inhabitants from a different place and time. These filmic fragments portray prewar life not only in its documentary and historical aspect but also in its existential dimension, seeking to establish a connection between the world filmed and those to whom the films are addressed as if in a reciprocal memory-project.[22] One thinks, in following Forgács's trajectory as a filmmaker, of Lanzmann's formal dynamics—the shifting camera and the sense that one is participating in a "theater of memory" rather than a documentary (Liebman, 2014). Recalling Hannah Arendt's formulation of "pariah or parvenu," Péter Forgács says: "I'm a pariah. I know how to be an outsider. I learned distance surviving through the Soviet-era. Where do I belong? I belong in dialogue with the country" (Forgács, 2014). Occupying a space at the interstices of documentary, fiction, and experimental filmmaking, his films interpellate the spectator as witness in the absence of subjects who can speak for themselves. Forgács's latest installation,

"*Attribution of Meaning*," again reprocesses private archives, this time focusing a family narrative with, at the center, a maternal figure—his own mother, who worked as an intelligence agent in Hungary from 1975–1985, a fact she concealed from her children. *Mrs. Pápai and her Sons* traces the life events of this artistic family through official reports and Forgács's personal diary entries in a photo archive of over 400 images. In a video begun in 1982 and finished in 2015, based on a letter Kafka wrote to his lover, Felice Bauer, the artist portrays family members and friends whose uninhibited behavior testifies to their trust in the camera operator, in much the same way that documentary filmmakers examined above establish mutual confidence with their subjects (Portuges, 2009; Forgács, 2016).

Counter-narratives and transferential dialogues

The fall of communism has led to manifold changes in the representation of the Holocaust, in both Eastern and Western Europe. Access to archival sources in Central and Eastern Europe has altered the ways in which current generations apprehend and imagine the Shoah. In the forefront of such discoveries is a documentary on the creation and suppression of a film: as Allied troops liberated camps in what had been German-occupied Europe, Sidney Bernstein (head of the Film Section of the Psychological Warfare Division of the Supreme Allied Command) was commissioned to make a documentary that would provide incontrovertible evidence of the Nazis' crimes, *German Concentration Camps Factual Survey*, also entitled *Memory of the Camps*, for which Alfred Hitchcock served as advisor.

As they worked, reels of film arrived from British, American, and Soviet combat and newsreel cameramen from camps including Auschwitz, Buchenwald, Dachau, and Bergen-Belsen. Graphic footage of corpses, starving survivors, and human remains in ovens was deemed too sensitive to be screened for the public. Despite being hailed as a masterpiece of British documentary, *Memory of the Camps* was never completed, and remained abandoned and shelved; a truncated version was shown on *Frontline* in 1985, the year *Shoah* was released. The Imperial War Museum (London) completed a vital last reel of the film, and director and anthropologist André Singer has produced a documentary, *Night Will Fall* (2014), on the fate of Bernstein's project.[23] Predating this restoration project, in 2010, the French historian and film director

Christian Delage curated *Filming the Camps: from Hollywood to Nuremberg*, an exhibition documenting the work of Hollywood directors John Ford, George Stevens, and Samuel Fuller for the U.S. Armed Forces and Secret Services as they filmed the realities of war and the liberation of Nazi concentration camps.[24]

A mainstream commercial release, the fictionalized historical narrative *Woman in Gold* (USA/UK, 2015) enjoyed popular (if not unanimous critical) success for its presentation of Viennese-born survivor Maria Altmann, who successfully sued the Austrian government for the return of commissioned paintings by Gustav Klimt expropriated from her family by the Nazis and displayed for decades in Vienna's Belvedere Gallery. Filming in three countries and two languages, the British director, Simon Curtis,

> fell in love with the story. And I believe it brings the terrible events of the 20th century into contemporary America in a way that is very important at the time when anti-Semitism has risen again, … reminding us of some of the mistakes of the 20th century.
>
> (Altmann, personal communication, January 2010)

Like other exiles, Altmann considered herself fortunate, many of her relatives having survived, while mourning others "who had suffered far worse losses" (Altmann, personal communication, January 2010).[25] The confiscated portraits of Adele Bloch-Bauer, Altmann's aunt, at issue in the film, function as silent witnesses to the violation of their identity as intimate visual representations of a truncated family history. The film restores an iconic image not only materially confiscated but also deprived of its authenticity as a portrait of a Jewish woman. Like archival footage, the portrait exists as an artifact whose meaning requires reconstruction in order to resurrect from history the vicious struggle against its own restitution, a process that evokes as well the concomitant cultural repression and dissociation to which it was subjected. For her compassionate portrayal of Maria Altmann and for her role in educating the public about Nazi-looted art, Helen Mirren received the inaugural World Jewish Congress Recognition Award from Ronald S. Lauder in June 2015. Lauder, co-founder of the Neue Galerie in Manhattan, purchased Klimt's painting, *Portrait of Adele Bloch-Bauer I* (later known as "The Woman in Gold") in 2006 for the then-record price of $135 million.[26]

Son of Saul

As a counter-narrative to attempts to visualize the extermination camps discussed earlier, the début fiction feature, *Son of Saul* (Rajna, Sipos, & Nemes, 2015) brings to the screen a controversial chapter of Holocaust history: the role of the Sonderkommando (the special command unit known as *Geheimnisträger*, bearers of secrets), teams of Jewish prisoners forced to assist the SS in the gas chambers and crematoria, themselves in turn condemned to extermination. The 38-year-old Hungarian director, László Nemes, whose own family were Holocaust victims, was inspired by his discovery of the publication of hidden manuscripts written by Sonderkommandos buried in the grounds of the crematoria in 1944: from 1945–1980, eight sets of documents by five known authors were recovered[27] (Des Voix Sous La Cendre). Retrospectively known as the Scrolls of Auschwitz, they are of extraordinary immediacy, composed as they were within the *univers concentrationnaire*, and include witness accounts, letters, and lists in Yiddish, Greek, French, and Polish that raise critical questions with regard to the ethics, memory, and interpretation of Holocaust testimony.

The directors' efforts to secure international co-production partners were rejected due to the "risky" nature of the subject; the Hungarian National Film Fund fully supported the project, with additional support from the Claims Conference. The only first feature selected in the main competition category at the Cannes International Film Festival was awarded the Festival's Grand Prix, the first time in thirty years a Hungarian film has been thus acknowledged,[28] going on to win the Golden Globe for Best Foreign Language Film (2016) and the New York Film Critics Circle Award for Best First Film, the Independent Spirit Award, and the Oscar for best foreign film at the 88th Academy Awards (February 28, 2016).

It is October 1944, the Allies are approaching as the film unfolds over a day and a half in Auschwitz-Birkenau. Saul Ausländer (his family name translates as "foreigner" or "stranger") stumbles into focus in the square 40mm frame; the camera remains only inches away from him in the chaotic space of his forced labor, following him into a concrete block where the door closes behind them: only at this point do we realize we are in the antechamber of a gas chamber. Convoys arrive transporting deportees; as Saul rescues the corpse of a young boy he believes to be his own son, a fellow prisoner accuses him of having failed the living—the Sonderkommando, then engaged in rebellion against the camp commanders—for the dead. Saul (played by Géza Röhrig[29]) is forced to lead prisoners into the fictitious showers of the gas chambers; in over-the-shoulder point-of-view throughout, extended shots of his impassive face against a blurred background, and an immersive wall of chaotic sound design, Nemes creates a claustrophobic hell of confusion and incomprehension. Indeed, in opposition to Primo Levi's view of the Sonderkommando as numbed servants of the Nazis, the writers of the Scrolls engaged in acts of resistance of which the writings were an important part (Chare & Williams, 2016). Saul's moral dilemma—to participate in the extermination machine or join its victims—is a foregone conclusion. Because the Sonderkommando were summarily executed to remove evidence of Nazi atrocities, his own demise is simply a matter of time. In his influential 1986 essay, "The Gray Zone," Levi uses the Sonderkommando to instantiate the moral dilemmas of Jewish prisoners who "compromised themselves by collaborating," addressed in his book, *The Drowned and the Saved*:

> The arrival in the Lager was indeed a shock because of the surprise entailed. The world into which one was precipitated was terrible, yes, but also indecipherable: it did not conform to any model, the enemy was all around but also inside, the "we" lost its limits, the contenders were not two, one could not discern a single frontier but rather many confused, perhaps innumerable frontiers, which stretched between each of us.
>
> (Levi, 1988, p. 12)

As if apostrophizing Levi, Nemes explains his own conception of the film's visual representation:

> The camera is hand-held, we planned all the camera positions and the movement of the main actors in the background action, but as everything is moving, introduces a sort of chaos into the scene, this idea that it's unpredictable, and that you're in a place that is very well known to the public but at the same time we believed it was never shown the way it was. Having this chaos and organization at the same time—this frenzy, the voices, the languages, the lack of information—everything about that and the fact that much is left to

> the viewers' and their imagination, these things are put in place in the very first moments of the film.
>
> (Murphy, 2016)

Unlike in other Holocaust films motivated by a redemptive narrative, there is no savior here, no heroic or rescuing figure, only victims trapped in the killing zone. "I didn't want to make a film with a distant, detached point of view," says Nemes, instead seeking to "place the audience from the point-of-view of one person in the middle of the killing machine. Otherwise the Holocaust becomes an abstract concept and the audience can back away." This relentless use of close-ups, shallow focus, and long takes denies spectators the possibility of de-cathecting or distancing ourselves from Saul's experience, nor are we allowed the relative comfort of abstracting his existential fate. Through its insistence on a relentlessly personal, subjective perspective, subjectivity itself thus becomes in a sense the film's own subject while paradoxically denying the audience access to Saul's inner world. Yet *Son of Saul* conveys a sense of loss by virtue of these very cinematic strategies, distinguishing itself from the films referenced at the beginning of this chapter and, in so doing, radically reinventing film language for a subject at risk of losing resonance 70 years on.[30]
The director believes that:

> ... this film is an important step in our vision of the Holocaust. We might be ready now to forget the theatrical versions. My film never shows the horror in an open way, it's always very restricted to the main character, a very narrow focus that leaves most everything to the viewer's imagination ... so in the way that this film relies on the viewer I think it's an innovation, because now the viewer has to go through the journey of this film and it becomes personal because the imagination is at work ... we're showing the human face, it's actually the human face as a reference, that is what gives the film its importance. The Holocaust has become an abstraction, we forgot about the individual face ... it became too big to understand, but if you have one person it now becomes understandable in a very visceral way.[31]

Nonetheless, as a descendant, so to speak, of *Shoah*, *Son of Saul* is perhaps after all not a film about the Holocaust, seeking neither to denounce nor describe its horrors; rather, it places the spectator in the

Sonderkommando's cinematic body, evoking the sensation of seeing through his terrorized gaze, hearing strictly what he sees and hears. Every shot is tightly framed and often in close-up, accompanied by a disorienting sound mix of SS voices in Hungarian, German, Polish, Russian, and Yiddish, mixed with concentration-camp slang. The set, designed by Hungarian architect László Rajk, who was also responsible for designing the Hungarian exhibition at Auschwitz, is essential to the film's taut energy. Long takes, at times of as much as four minutes' duration, executed with a hand-held camera, required sets of complete rooms that could accommodate 360-degree takes for which Rajk recreated a Nazi crematorium in an abandoned 1912 warehouse on the outskirts of Budapest:

> When the set was ready, Mátyás [Erdély, the cinematographer] and László and I went through the set and I was explaining the connections. We were leaving the gas chamber and someone slammed the door on Mátyás. And immediately we open the door and there is this young man, completely pale. His grandfather's family was killed in Auschwitz. It was this really speechless moment where you stand there and you see the effects.... When it came time to think about the exhibition design, I started to think about the 6 million people that are missing—missing grandsons, missing descendants, this lack of people. I wanted to make visible what it means to be missing.[32]
>
> (Miranda, 2016)

Assigned to the gas chambers whose functioning he must oversee, Saul robotically scrubs the showers, removes cadavers, collects clothing and effects from those who have been gassed, loads the ovens, scatters ashes in the neighboring river, believing (or imagining) he recognizes his own son among the victims. The boy has not died in the gas chamber, and the doctor intends to administer a fatal injection. In a scene between Saul and the camp doctor, the following dialogue takes place:

> Saul: "Don't cut this boy. Leave him as he is." Doctor: "No. Is he one of yours? Even then." Saul: "You don't need it, but your boss does. Doctor: "Where are you from?" Saul: "Hungary." Doctor: "I'm a prisoner like you. You'll have five minutes alone with him tonight. But then he'll burn like the rest. What's your name?" Saul: "Ausländer. Saul."

It is at this point that Saul seems to realize that, in Röhrig's reading, "this boy belongs to him and he belongs to the boy. Even for a second the boy survived the gas chamber—he survives and then is killed by the Nazi doctor." This death, then, is different from the others, offering Saul a moment of emotion, of empathy and identification. Whether or not it is his own son—a question left ambiguous in the film—through Saul's seemingly random dedication to the fate of this one individual, can the viewer, too, engage authentically with the otherwise overwhelming reality of the Shoah? Desensitized and psychologically annihilated by his inhuman tasks as a Sonderkommando, Saul is suddenly galvanized, consumed by the desire to recover the child's body for burial and to identify a rabbi to recite the mourners' Kaddish.[33] The dénouement, criticized by some critics as a *reductio ad absurdum*, sees Saul swept up in the Sonderkommandos' attempted escape that takes him across a river, where the precious body he has "saved" drifts away in the current, and ultimately taking refuge in a shed in the forest where his fellow fugitives plan their next moves. Suddenly, a small blond (Polish, we imagine) boy appears, glimpses the men, and quickly runs off. The ambiguous conclusion may be read as a moment of transcendence for Saul, whose face grows beatific at the sight of him, perhaps imagining in his madness that his "son" is alive, or simply from the joy of seeing a living child.[34]

Unlike Spielberg's *Schindler's List* (1993), in refusing to depict the Holocaust as "décor"—a trivialization for which Lanzmann has strongly reproached Spielberg—Nemes proposes instead to limit himself to the raw reality of quotidian details while resisting the lure of voyeurism, instead de-coupling each frame from familiar or unquestioned representational modes. This is accomplished through Saul's gaze alone in images often blurred, out of focus, or oblique, and through the deafening, often unbearable diegetic noise heard off-screen. Resisting the kind of redemptive discourse prevalent in certain Holocaust films and rejected by Lanzmann, Saul's obstinately determined struggle may be read as leaving open the possibility of a hopeful gesture even from the depths of despair. Indeed, in a sense recapitulating the affective bond between filmmaker and subject referenced earlier, Lanzmann states:

> ... [László Nemes] is young, intelligent, handsome, and he has made a film about which I will never say anything negative ... *Son of Saul*

is the anti-Schindler's list. It doesn't portray death, but rather the lives of those who were forced to lead their own to death.

The French philosopher/art historian Georges Didi-Huberman, author of *Invention of Hysteria: Charcot and the Photographic Iconography of the Salpêtrière* (MIT Press, 2004), devoted a slim volume to *Son of Saul* in the form of an open letter addressed to László Nemes, published immediately following the film's Cannes premiere, commending an intelligence that justifies the film's brutal cinematic strategies:

> What a demanding test, this crush of images, this hell of sound that incessantly cadence your narrative! Yet what a necessary and fertile test! […] Your story (your fiction), out of the dark, itself 'carries' the secret [that of the Sonderkommandos], transporting it toward the light.[35]
>
> (Didi-Huberman, 2015, p. 1)

The protagonist is driven to expiate an ambiguous, perhaps fantasized "paternal" sorrow or guilt through the symbolic enactment of rescue, despite the fact that the object of his obsession is no longer among the living.[36] *Son of Saul* thus reframes the camp without engaging in the kind of "mirroring" or repetition of violence that has been the object of much critical debate Holocaust representation. Its boldly existential terms counter the more conventional narrative approach of a film such as *Fateless* a decade earlier (with its embrace of iconographic images of beauty despite horror) without betraying Lanzmann's ethical proscription of fictionalized portrayals of the *univers concentrationnaire*—indeed, of representation itself—as if cognizant of Adorno's proscription that "to write poetry after Auschwitz is barbaric" (Adorno, 1981). Says Nemes:

> We didn't want to stand back from the situation, to establish a historical distance. We can't put post-war emotions on it. We didn't want to make a beautiful film full of icons, or for it to be emotional in the conventional sense. Because after several months, these men are empty of conventional emotions.[37]
>
> (Shoard, 2015)

Nemes may be seen here to be indirectly addressing the direct testimony to Lanzmann by one of the major witnesses in *Shoah*, Abraham Bomba, the "barber of Treblinka" responsible for cutting the hair of women about to be exterminated in the gas chamber, and himself a member of the Sonderkommando: "You know … it's very hard to feel anything at all in the camps: imagine, working day and night among the dead, the cadavers, your feelings disappear. You were dead to feeling, dead to everything" (Lanzmann, 1985). Immersing the viewer in these grotesque gestures, the cinematography is structured primarily from Saul's point of view, his head occupying the frame; all action peripheral to the objects of his obsession remains resolutely beyond the frame. It is an extraordinarily original and bold concept, from the opening sequence that establishes the viewer's perspective, and Saul's: sensing what transpires out of focus, what we cannot bear to know and see, yet what we know is taking place, in Lacan's formulation of *le sujet supposé savoir*.

In press conferences at the film's Cannes premiere and often thereafter, the lead actor, Géza Röhrig, urged greater understanding of—and renewed debate on—the controversial role of the Sonderkommando. In *The Drowned and the Saved*, published in 1986, the year after *Shoah* was released, Primo Levi, inclined as he was to sympathize with those who had experienced such humiliation for so many months and years, remarked that those who had worked in the special squads could not be trusted to tell the truth about what they had been forced to do and their motives. These survivors, he wrote, would more likely utter "a lament, a curse, an expiation, an attempt to justify and rehabilitate oneself: a liberating outburst rather than a Medusa-faced truth." As a result of such characterizations and condemnations, in the aftermath of testimony by witnesses at early trials of Nazi criminals, most retreated into anonymity, haunted by what they had seen and done, and understandably fearful of attempts at retribution to which they were subjected[38] (Liebman, 2012). Claude Lanzmann continues to believe that this period should not be approached through the prism of fiction, insisting that: "Un certain absolu de l'horreur est intransmissible" (Lanzmann, 1994). Considering that cinema may always be regarded with suspicion with regard to the Holocaust, these debates continue to fuel controversy. As Lanzmann has noted, the autumn of 1944 was a particular moment in the chronology of Auschwitz when some 250 Jews assigned to the Sonderkommando unit organized a mutiny, succeeding in exploding crematorium No. IV and the adjacent gas chamber before being massacred by the Nazis. The revolt, a real historical event, is suggested in *Son of Saul* as background to the fictional narrative of a man seeking to bury a child with dignity (Bouchara, 2015).[39]

Conclusion: spectres of the *Shoah*

Thirty-seven years after the broadcast of *Holocaust* (Green & Chomsky, 1978) described in the opening of this chapter, a new French documentary series, *Jusqu'au dernier: la destruction des juifs d'Europe* (Dedio, Finger, & Karel, 2014–2015) gathers 50 internationally renowned historians to provide expert analysis, edited with supporting documents, photos, and archive films from every continent, as well as survivor testimonies and current images of memorial sites. This scrupulously documented multipart film, designed in a style accessible to a broad audience, is made all the more urgent by the rapid disappearance of first-generation survivors and witnesses. "La Destruction des juifs d'Europe," like other films discussed in this chapter, honors the determination of Holocaust victims to document their experience in writing by any means necessary, with full awareness that they would not survive to bear witness themselves.

Thirty years after the release of Claude Lanzmann's *Shoah*, a new documentary, *Claude Lanzmann: Spectres of the Shoah* (2015), written, directed, and produced by British filmmaker and journalist Adam Benzine, was scheduled for release on Holocaust Remembrance Day, 2016.[40] Benzine secured exclusive access to the director, who sat at length to discuss the making of *Shoah* (Lanzmann, 1985) in a riveting portrait of a tough, determined, and uncompromising man. Lanzmann movingly recalls his efforts to convince traumatized death camp survivors to relive their experiences, confessing to the life-threatening dangers he encountered while tracking down and secretly filming SS officers with a hidden camera. Now nearing 90, he speaks of his engagement in the French Resistance as an adolescent, his romance with Simone de Beauvoir, and his friendship with Jean-Paul Sartre, admitting that he deceived *Shoah*'s financiers, who expected a two-hour screening time. It is perhaps an act of poetic justice that Lanzmann, himself a voting member of the Academy who has never been nominated, attended the ceremony for the first time ever, witnessing the triumph of *Son of Saul* (Rajna, Sipos, & Nemes),[41] although *Lanzmann: Spectres of the Shoah* (Benzine, 2015) failed to win the Oscar in the short documentary competition.

In a remarkable countertransferential moment in the filmmaker/subject relationship, Benzine asks Lanzmann to narrate for the camera a dramatic episode during the production of *Shoah* (Lanzmann, 1985) in which he and an assistant conducted secret undercover filming of former Nazi Heinz Schubert using a hidden camera, the "Paluche," during which he, the director, was brutally attacked, sustaining physical injuries requiring hospitalization. Visibly reluctant and disturbed by this request, Lanzmann at first refuses, then relents when Benzine says: "Je sais que c'est difficile," echoing the words Lanzmann had used to urge Bomba, the barber, to confront the worst atrocity he had experienced when incarcerated in Treblinka: the sight of a fellow barber forced to cut the hair of his own wife and child in the gas chamber, a scene that has been the subject of voluminous debate on the part of film scholars, philosophers, and psychoanalysts.[42] "We must do it," Lanzmann insisted then, explicitly using the first-person plural. Lanzmann's primary consideration, then, is not to provide emotional support to his survivor witnesses, but rather to persuade them to give testimony in the very *lieux de mémoire* of exterminations, which some had to witness a second time when corpses were exhumed and burned in an effort to further disguise traces. Some of his questions cannot be answered: "You survived, but are you really alive?," thereby allowing no clear point of entry for empathy, denying the viewer the catharsis or sense of superiority that condemnation can elicit. As spectators, we are outsiders as we enter Lanzmann's film; yet even after reactivating the past over nine hours, we emerge understanding relatively little about the internal world of its subjects (Benzine, 2015).

Emphasizing the integrity of the present moment, Lanzmann incontrovertibly reinscribes the reality of the Shoah by prompting, even forcing, survivors such as Bomba to re-enact their most profound anguish as the traumatic past is alive in the present.[43] Shoshana Felman has described such moments of testimony, which she believes have become "... a crucial mode of our relation to events of our time" as they "... limit experiences whose overwhelming impact constantly puts to the test the limits of the witness and of witnessing, at the same time as it constantly unsettles and puts into question the very limits of reality" (Felman & Laub, 1992, p. 5). As viewers, we inescapably join the "now" of the film in its *longue durée*, which in turn becomes our own present tense; the strategy of filming and translating in real time gives the slowed-down space and time to reflect, imagine, and place ourselves in its narrative.

Composed of real-time testimonies by witnesses remembering and working through layers of resistance to excavate their memories, not unlike the psychoanalytic process itself, *Shoah* (Lanzmann, 1985) makes meaning of the unimaginable past in the present by its very refusal to resort to archival evidentiary substantiation. Unlike other films on the aftermath of genocide, it offers no reassurance nor catharsis, instead enduring as a monument to what has been lost, to a catastrophe whose sequellae continue in the present. Lanzmann thus retrospectively bears witness to his own epic struggle, enacting the "law" he established for himself during the making of *Shoah*: "... rester froid pour le film ... il ne fallait pas que ce soit facile."[44] Describing himself as having felt as if he were at total war with everything and everyone while making *Shoah*, his truest confidante and unfailing supporter, emotionally and financially, was Simone de Beauvoir: "I was proud of what I achieved, definitely, yes," confides Lanzmann, who was 87 during the filming of *Spectres of the Shoah*: "But it did not relieve me from anguish," acknowledging a "feeling of bereavement" on the day *Shoah* was finished: "I was swimming in the ocean in Jerusalem, nearly drowning from fatigue, and not happy to be saved [by a passing boat]; I rather wanted to commit suicide" (Benzine, 2015), arguably a reference to Primo Levi's death in 1987 at age 67. After falling down the stairwell of his apartment building in Turin, Italy, his fellow writer and survivor Elie Wiesel delivered an epigrammatic coroner's report: "Primo Levi died at Auschwitz forty years later."

Two generations later, Nemes acknowledges *Son of Saul* (Rajna, Sipos, & Nemes, 2015) as a direct descendant of *Shoah* (Lanzmann, 1985), the film that inspired him throughout his life. Abraham Bomba's testimony, and the film that immortalized it, are systematically evoked by László Nemes as one of the major sources of *Son of Saul.* To embody the daily life of an Auschwitz Sonderkommando, Nemes chose a hybrid representational mode, neither fully fiction nor documentary, inhabiting a "gray zone" in the interstices of the inferno:

> Even in the darkest hours of mankind, there might be a voice within us that allows us to remain human. That's the hope of this film. Nemes believes Hungarians have not dealt with the trauma of the Holocaust, during which during which some 600,000 Hungarian Jews perished, almost all after Nazi Germany invaded in March 1944. "Every kid should watch it," he said of the film, "not because the cinemas should be full, but that many of them lack empathy."
>
> (Murphy, 2016)

Like Spielberg, who approached the Holocaust via the true story of a thousand Jews rescued by a single German industrialist, Nemes tells the singular story of a man determined to bury a boy he believes to be his son. But the comparison ends there, according to Lanzmann, who famously reproached *Schindler's List* for using the Holocaust as "décor." He is interested in *Son of Saul* precisely as a Hungarian film, having devoted numerous scenes in *Shoah* to the deportation of Hungarian Jews in the spring of 1944, particularly through the testimony of Auschwitz survivors Rudolf Vrba and Alfred Wetzler. Lanzmann seems to have found in Nemes an heir worthy of him and of his memory work, having purportedly whispered to Nemes, in an oedipal moment on the Croisette in Cannes: "You are my son," declaring, in press interviews, *Son of Saul* to be "a film I will never denigrate" (Donadio, 2015). Thus does Lanzmann perhaps wish no longer to be the one who condemns, instead choosing for himself, *in extremis*, a classic mode of survival—a symbolic son, like the boy chosen by Saul. Although such an intergenerational bond, at once affective and artistic, may be traced through many of the works referenced here, it is, I believe, most powerfully present between Lanzmann and Nemes. Both have created works that incarnate terrifying reality, neither sparing us as viewers nor offering a comforting distancing or separation between present and past. Their images are fiercely embodied, as if wrenched directly from the nightmare, yet rendered with an audacity, urgency, and intimacy that nonetheless complicates prior representational strategies. Both compel us to think visually, through a radically personal and original point of view, in images that are themselves tantamount to originary experiences transformed cinematically into a continuous present tense. Seventy years after the end of WWII, under often precarious financial, political, and psychological circumstances, these filmmakers are reframing a legacy of guilt and sorrow into artistic projects that engage viewers in transformative encounters, reckoning with its long aftermath in dialogue with themselves and each other, and with the films that continue to resonate across generations (Imre, 2012).

Notes

1 According to the executive director of the National Center for Jewish Film, "[t]he series was high-profile, it was in English, it had star power, and it covered every possible survivor's story."

2 The only films not to have received an Oscar were four nominees in the foreign language category, including the 1983 Hungarian feature, *The Revolt of Job*. (Hoberman, 2016).

3 (the Hebrew word for catastrophe) *Shoah* (1985, French, Hebrew, Polish, English, Yiddish and German)). See also Richard Brody, "Witness: Claude Lanzmann and the making of "Shoah." *The New Yorker*, March 19, 2012. (At over nine hours, the film is approximately the same length as the miniseries *Holocaust*.)

4 In a reversal of the French historian Pierre Nora's formulation, elaborated in *Les Lieux de Mémoire*, three volumes that analyze the places and objects that are presumed to embody French national memory, perhaps also a play on the French legal term, 'non-lieu' (dismissal).

5 See also Shoshana Felman, *Jacques Lacan* and *the Adventure of Insight: Psychoanalysis in Contemporary Culture (*Cambridge: Harvard UP, 1987).

6 See also Lanzmann's objections to NBC's 1978 television miniseries in "From the Holocaust to the *Holocaust* (1979/80)" published in *Le Monde* (1994).

7 I was present for the film's premiere at the New York Film Festival where, in the Q&A that followed the screening, Lanzmann acknowledged: "There are a lot of staged scenes in the film. It is not a documentary," comparing his film subjects to theatrical characters on a stage.

8 Simone de Beauvoir, whose life Lanzmann shared for seven years, later called the film "a monument—one that for generations to come will enable everyone to understand one of the most sinister and enigmatic moments in history." From my conversation with Claude Lanzmann at Harvard University, Cambridge, MA, April 2009, following the launch of the English translation of his memoir, *The Patagonian Hare.*

9 *Nuit et Brouillard* (France, 1956, 32 min); *Le Chagrin et la pitié* (France, 1969, France/Switzerland/W. Germany, 251 min). Ophüls' film not only exposes the political repression and anti-Semitism in Vichy France and growing opposition to the regime, but also questions the postwar mythology created about Charles de Gaulle's Free French movement. Marcel Ophüls, the only son of film and stage director Max Ophüls and actress Hilde Wall, was born in Germany in 1927 and lived through some of the period covered by the documentary. Ophüls' family moved to France in 1933, where his father continued to direct films, served in the French army as a private from 1939–1940 and was also involved in producing anti-Nazi radio broadcasts. The family fled Paris in 1940, just days before German troops took over the city, traveling to Spain and then making their way to the U.S. in 1941.

10 In Hungary, a government decision to erect a monument portraying the country as a victim of the "German Occupation" provoked outrage from Jewish organizations, historians and ordinary citizens; Transylvania-born Holocaust survivor Elie Wiesel returned a Hungarian national award. Apart from protesting the participation of top Hungarian officials at a ceremony

honoring a famous writer who was also a Nazi sympathizer, Wiesel said at the time that he was rejecting the award also because "Horthy, who sent 500,000 Jews to Auschwitz in 1944, is becoming a heroic figure again in his country." Likewise, the eminent Hungarian-born Holocaust historian Randolph L. Braham returned his award to protest what he considers government efforts to rewrite history and exonerate the country from its role in the Holocaust.

11 Gyula Gazdag is professor emeritus at the UCLA School of Theater, Film and Television since 1993, artistic director of the Sundance Filmmakers Lab since 1997, creative advisor for the Maurits Binger Film Institute in Amsterdam since 2002, and at the Script Station of the Berlinale Talent Campus since 2006. His feature films include *Stand Off* (1988), Special Jury Prize, San Sebastian Festival; *Singing on the Treadmill* (1974), banned in Hungary for ten years, and *The Whistling Cobblestone* (1971), banned from foreign exhibition for 12 years; *A Hungarian Fairy Tale* (Hungary, 1987, 97 min, in Hungarian w/English subtitles), Special Jury Prize at the Locarno Film Festival, Best Feature Film of the Year of the Hungarian Film Critics, screened at Cannes Directors' Fortnight; for a clip on YouTube: www.youtube.com/watch?v=H5JHsmRwoQg.

Gazdag has also written and directed eight documentaries, including *The Resolution (*1972), named one of the 100 best documentaries of all time by the International Documentary Association, and has directed *Candide*, *The Tempest,* and *Tom Jones* for the stage. cf. Catherine Portuges, "Interview with Gyula Gazdag," special issue of *Kinokultura*: www.kinokultura.com/specials/7/hungarian.shtml.

12 In Hungary, the general view is that the war crimes were the Germans' responsibility, and Hungarians couldn't do anything about them. Yet historians' research makes clear that about 150 German soldiers (the "Eichmann commando") were in charge of the deportations from Hungary in the summer of 1944. Clearly, this group would have been incapable of carrying this out on their own; they had to rely on the cooperation of 200,000 Hungarian soldiers, gendarmes, police, transport personnel, bureaucrats, doctors, nurses and others. These people were us: our parents and grandparents had a hand in the deportation of their own neighbors. It is worth asking them how they saw things then and what they thought … Our film does not form a judgment; we ourselves have no idea what we would have done if we had been in their position, no matter how clearly we may know the ideal, the laudable and humane course of action.

(Varga, 2005)

13 For *Regina* (2013) non-professional actors include the director's own grandmother, an 87-year-old Holocaust survivor of four camps, and George Weisz, the film's producer, who voices Leo Baeck, the rabbi, scholar, and leader of

Progressive Judaism to whom Jonas appealed for ordination. The film's impact is all the more powerful in view of Gróo's own transference relationship, enacted without benefit of a living "other," indeed with little more than a single photograph as anchoring image. The director was inspired and supported by previous generations of filmmakers such as Judith Elek and Miklós Jancsó who also faced disinterest and even derision for their dedication to film projects depicting the silenced, forgotten and repressed narratives of the traumatic history of European Jews.

14 Born in Hungary in 1950, Forgács has made more than 30 films since beginning in 1978. In 1983, he established the Private Photo & Film Archives Foundation in Budapest, a collection of more than 300 hours of amateur film shot in Hungary. Forgács made his reputation with a series of films from this footage called Private Hungary, but his international profile has led him to make films using images from other countries as well. Again and again, Forgács returns to the central trauma of World War II, as his films seek to reclaim the record of life in modern Europe from the shadows of Nazism and Stalinism.

15 Awarded the Erasmus Prize in 2007 by a Dutch non-profit foundation (since 1958), he is cited for his "original contribution to the process of cultural memory and the transmission of culture, thereby furthering and deepening our understanding of the past" (Friedman, 2009).

16 In January 2014, he was awarded the Special Prize of the Hungarian Film-Critics Society in Budapest.

17 *A Bibó Reader*, Official selection, La Quinzaine des Réalisateurs, Cannes Film Festival 2001; Best Director Prize, Short & Experimental Film, Thirty-third Magyar Film Szemle, Budapest.

18 I had the privilege of attending the opening of this installation at the Getty Center in Los Angeles where I interviewed the artist, whose critical explanatory remarks are integrated into this section.

19 I spoke at length with the filmmaker at the opening; a portion of his earlier work focused on psychoanalysis and its relation to the filmic experience. My comments here are based in part on that conversation and on many previous interviews about his work in Budapest, London, and New York, 1998–2015. *Letters to Afar* was commissioned by the Museum of the History of Polish Jews in Warsaw and the YIVO Institute for Jewish Research in New York. Premiered on May 13, 2013 at the Museum of the History of Polish Jews in Warsaw, it traveled in November 2014 to the Museum of the City of New York.

20 During the course of a Q&A following screenings at the Center for Jewish History Forgács distanced himself from filmed oral history, suggesting that home movies deceptively suggest that summer holidays constitute the festive core of lives, leisure without struggle, marriage without divorce (Hoberman, 2014).

21 The Lumière brothers unveiled the Cinématographe in their first public screening on December 28, 1895, at the Grand Café on Paris' Boulevard des

Capucines. In early 1896, they would open Cinématographe theaters in London, Brussels, Belgium, and New York. After making more than 40 films that year, primarily scenes of everyday French life, but also the first newsreel (footage of the French Photographic Society conference) and the first documentaries (about the Lyon Fire Department), they began sending other cameramen-projectionists out into the world to record scenes of life and showcase their invention.

22 A Budapest-based independent filmmaker and video artist, Forgács's films and installations are created from archival amateur films and found footage shot in twentieth-century Europe. His primary focus is on the disparities and tensions between official and private history and between the historical and existential dimensions. He is best known for his "Private Hungary" series of award winning films based on home movies from the 1930s and 1960s, which document ordinary lives that were soon to be ruptured by an extraordinary historical trauma that occurs off screen. The Grammy Award-winning Klezmatics, a multilingual American music group based in New York City, fuse Klezmer music with elements of jazz, rock, gospel, and other modern musical genres.

23 Footage from the unfinished film, however, proved key to the prosecution of camp commandants at the Nuremberg and Lüneburg trials in 1945. Into the gap left in 1945 by the suppression of Bernstein's film came another documentary, made by exiled Austrian Jew Billy Wilder. Steven Spielberg chose Branko Lustig, a Croatian survivor of Belsen who was interviewed in the original documentary and later became a filmmaker, to be a producer for Schindler's List. www.theguardian.com/film/2015/jan/09/holocaust-film-too-shocking-to-show-night-will-fall-alfred-hitchcock. I thank Stuart Liebman for personal communication in connection with his presentation and discussion of *Memory of the Camps*, New York City, May 19, 2015.

24 The original installation opened at the Mémorial de la Shoah in Paris in 2010 and traveled to the Museum of Jewish Heritage, New York City in 2012 where I had the opportunity to view it. The Atlanta History Center commemorated the seventieth anniversary of Falkenau Liberation with the opening of "Filming the Camps: John, Ford, Samuel Fuller, George Stevens: From Hollywood to Nuremberg" May 6–November 20, 2015. The curator, Christian Delage, designed the exhibition with the narrative at the center of the display, allowing the visitor to experience content rather than extensive text, and to keep the atmosphere appropriate to the subject matter. "My main goal with the exhibit is to enable the audience to view the footage in its historical context and read the accompanying narratives written by the cameramen and writers, practically in real-time, as soon as they finished shooting for the day," said Delage. "This level of detail adds much to our comprehension of the conditions of the camps and the complex experience of liberation from both the liberators and the inmates' points of view."

25 A close personal friend of my Viennese-born mother, Lisl Lassner Furedi Steckler, for over 40 years, Maria Altmann generously helped many fellow refugees and émigrés in Los Angeles in the process of restitution from the Austrian and German governments. In the film, directed by Simon Curtis, Mirren plays Altmann as an elderly woman living in Los Angeles who enlists the grandson of Austrian composer Arnold Schoenberg, a California lawyer played by Ryan Reynolds, to accompany her back to Vienna to take on the Austrian authorities. Altmann finally won her battle in 2006 and died five years later aged 94.

26 Ronald S. Lauder states:

> The history of the "Woman in Gold" painting exemplifies the immense suffering, painful loss and, for a prolonged period, the injustice that many Jews were subjected to during the 20th century. With the opening of this new movie, audiences can learn about the second half of the Nazi-looted art story: the postwar art grab by governments and museums that willfully continued the Nazi theft, both by hiding the art from the rightful owners or their heirs and by fighting the victims in court to keep the artworks.
>
> (May 2015)

27 The following note was found buried in the Auschwitz crematoria, written by Zalman Gradowski, a member of the Sonderkommando who was killed in the October 7, 1944 revolt:

> Dear finder of these notes, I have one request of you, which is, in fact, the practical objective for my writing … that my days of Hell, that my hopeless tomorrow will find a purpose in the future. I am transmitting only a part of what happened in the Birkenau-Auschwitz Hell. You will realize what reality looked like … From all this you will have a picture of how our people perished.

28 *Son of Saul* was released in 48 countries at a time when its country of origin is plagued by anti-Semitism and xenophobia. The category was composed of 21 films from 19 countries. Hungary's first Oscar contender in 28 years, *Son of Saul* is the first Hungarian film to win an Oscar since István Szabó's *Mephisto* in 1982. The film has already become the most successful Hungarian production ever in the U.S., earning over $1 million in box-office revenue, while in Hungary, where mainstream movies rarely draw audiences of over 100,000, more than 140,000 have bought tickets to date, making it the highest grossing Hungarian film since the release of a comedy blockbuster in 2010.

29 In a television interview broadcast on Charlie Rose (WGBY-TV) on January 4, 2016, Röhrig stated:

> Overwhelmingly, the prisoners did not survive—two out of three Jews in Europe were murdered. A few weeks ago we met a Greek Jew, possibly

the last surviving Sonderkommando, in L.A. Elie Wiesel said I'm ready to put my name on the line for this film. I didn't have a chance to meet any of them before the shoot, he's a man who can still smile, there's a spark in his eyes.

30 Cited from Nemes's presentation at the Golden Globes Foreign Language Film Symposium, to which I was an invited participant, January 11, 2016, Egyptian Theater/American Cinematheque, Hollywood, California.
31 From Nemes's Q&A following the screening of *Son of Saul* at the 53rd New York Film Festival, Walter Reade Theater, New York City, October 5, 2015, and from my personal interview with the film's editor, Mathieu Taponnier, Paris, November 5, 2015.
32 The cinematographer Mátyas Érdély won the Spotlight Award for his work on *Son of Saul* at the 30th Annual American Society of Cinematographers Awards, Los Angeles, February 13, 2016. http://variety.com/2016/film/awards/asc-awards-announced-winners-list-1201706261/.

The set designer Lászlo Rajk was also responsible for designing the Hungarian national exhibition at Auschwitz, in 2014, which he first visited as a university student in the late 1960s, before restoration work and high-tech national exhibits had been added: "It was the poverty of communism," he says.

> All of these things were run down. In a way, the atmosphere was much closer to the atmosphere of a death camp.... The exhibition is in the barracks, in the blocks of the original camp, where prisoners lived. It's Number 18. I started to know not only the building, but also the detailed structures, how they looked. Most of those buildings were built by prisoners and their work is very professional. That is a very striking fact—that those people who are dying in three weeks or three months, they are meanwhile carrying out very professional carpentry and masonry.
>
> (Miranda, 2016)

33 In many commentaries on this point, Talmudic scholars and others have noted that it is not strictly speaking required that a rabbi be present for Kaddish to be said at a burial.
34 cf. Jonathan Rosenbaum, "Lost in Auschwitz: *Son of Saul*" posted February 7, 2016 From the *Chicago Reader* (January 28, 2016).
35 Georges Didi-Huberman, *Sortir du noir* (Éditions de Minuit, 2015); my translation from the original French: [Quelle épreuve que cette foule d'images et que cet enfer de sons rythmant inlassablement votre récit! Mais quelle épreuve nécessaire et féconde! [...] Votre histoire (votre fiction) sort du noir: elle-même « porte » ce secret [celui des Sonderkommandos], mais pour le porter à la lumière]. See Jacques Mandelbaum, *Le Monde*, November 4, 2015. www.leseditionsdeminuit.com/f/index.php?sp=liv&livre_id=3184.

36 László Nemes, *Son of Saul* (Saul Fia, 107 min, in Hungarian, English & Yiddish, 2015). 68th Cannes Film Festival, May 2015. Following a bidding war, the film was acquired on May 17, 2015 by Sony Pictures Classic for North American distribution. Nemes, the son of director András Jeles, served briefly as assistant to Béla Tarr whose insistence on an austere and rigorous film practice is legendary. Since its Cannes premiere in May 2015, *Son of Saul* has thus far won 36 international awards, 17 for best foreign film. It is worth noting, however, that the positive reception by most Hungarian critics and audiences has been tempered by dissenting voices, including those from the far-right Jobbik party who claim that Son of Saul is part of "a booming Holocaust industry," and that Hungarian filmmaking should focus on other parts of Hungary's history.

37 According to Nemes: "Of the twenty or so who are still alive many didn't reveal their work even to their families after the war because they were regarded so negatively. But in 2015, no one should call them part-killer." Some Sonderkommando committed suicide; most were murdered by the Nazis, and a small number survived. Lanzmann considered them to have been closest to the center of the Holocaust; their testimony is thus privileged in *Shoah* beyond that of other survivors. 430,000 Hungarian Jews were sent to Birkenau within eight weeks in 1944, among them more than 100,000 children (Shoard, 2015).

38 A 2001 film, *The Grey Zone*, based on a book by Dr. Miklós Nyiszli, takes its title from a chapter in *The Drowned and the Saved* by Holocaust survivor Primo Levi. The film tells the story of the Jewish Sonderkommando XII in the Auschwitz concentration camp in October 1944, the month and year during which *Son of Saul* takes place. These prisoners were made to assist the camp's guards in shepherding their victims to the gas chambers and disposing of their bodies in the ovens.

39 In the same interview Lanzmann compares the film *The Grey Zone* (1997) to *Son of Saul*: Il est vrai que les ressemblances sont troublantes. *The Grey Zone* raconte la révolte des Sonderkommandos d'Auschwitz du 7 octobre 1944 en empruntant un ressort fictionnel du même ordre: les détenus découvrent une jeune fille—vivante—sous un amas de corps dans la chambre à gaz. Ils décident de la sauver puis de la garder auprès d'eux, au secret, dans les baraquements, tout en préparant la mutinerie. Contrairement au héros de Nemes qui veut inhumer son fils à tout prix (il menace même les détenus qui se mettent sur son chemin), les personnages de *The Grey Zone* n'échappent pas aux questionnements sur l'obligation morale de sauver la jeune fille quand leur propre vie est en jeu. En ce sens, parce qu'il soulignait l'impossibilité d'être un homme parfait à l'intérieur d'un camp de concentration, *The Grey Zone*, qui a été très peu diffusé en France et en Europe, était peut-être plus troublant et moins acceptable que *Le Fils de Saul*, lauréat du Grand Prix du festival de Cannes 2015."

40 HBO Documentary Films has acquired the US Television rights. World premiere, April 25, 2015, Hot Docs Canadian International Documentary Festival, in Toronto. I attended a screening at NuArt Theater, Los Angeles, May 14, 2015, for Academy Award consideration. The film marks the directorial début of Adam Benzine who states:

> Claude Lanzmann is a filmmaking icon and a Jewish hero. His 12-year journey to make what is now considered to be the definitive Holocaust opus was really an against-all-odds story of defiant resilience in the face of tremendous adversity. I am deeply honored that he agreed to participate.
>
> (Rosser, 2015)

41 During the five-year editing process, Lanzmann was repeatedly confronted by hundreds of hours of footage of atrocities. The film features previously unseen material shot by the director and his team in the 1970s. The filmmakers are continuing to work with the US Holocaust Memorial Museum and Israel's Yad Vashem, who jointly own this material, to restore and digitize it. HBO will produce DVD and BluRay versions in 2016 including supplemental interviews. Sincere thanks to the director, Adam Benzine, for personal communications. Nominated for an Academy Award for best short documentary, the film is the only Holocaust-themed documentaries to have failed to win the award, and the first in that category to use the word "Shoah" in the title.

42 cf. Dominick LaCapra, 1998; Joshua Hirsch, 2004; Agnieszka Piotrowska, 2013.

43 "The Lord said, What have you done? Listen! Your brother's blood cries out to me from the ground" *Genesis 4:10, New International Version.* See also Geoffrey Hartmann, "What the Dead Have to Say to Us" (*Tablet Magazine*, 2013, February 4).

44 "Remain calm for the film … it was important that it not be easy…"

References

Adorno, T. (1955). Cultural criticism and society. In *Prisms* (pp. 17–34). Cambridge, MA: MIT Press.

Alexander, Z., & Kinder, M. (2002). The Danube exodus. *The Getty Musem Catalog Introduction.* Retrieved from www.forgacspeter.hu/prev_version/eng/main/installations/danube_exodus/articles/getty/getty.htm.

Altmann, M. (2010, January). [Personal interview]. Personal communication with Maria Altmann in her home in Cheviot Hills, Los Angeles.

Angelusz, I, Reich, A., Weisz G., Wittenberg, G. (Producers), & Gróo, D. (Producer & Director). (2013). *Regina* [Motion Picture]. Hungary: Katapult Film.

Barbalics, P., Hamori, A., Kemeny, I. Olsberg, J. (Producers), & Koltai, L. (Director). (2005). *Fateless*. Hungary: Hungarian Motion Picture Ltd.

Benzine, A. (Producer & Director). (2015). *Claude Lanzmann: Spectres of the Shoah* [Motion Picture]. USA: Home Box Office (HBO).

Blottière, M. (2015, May 24). Claude Lanzmann: " 'le fils de saul' est l'anti-'liste de schindler' ". *Télérama*. Retrieved from www.telerama.fr/festival-de-cannes/2015/claude-lanzmann-le-fils-de-saul-est-l-anti-liste-de-schindler,127045.php

Bouchara, O. (2015, May 24). Le fils de Saul: "Ce film ne pouvait que diviser." *Vanity Fair*. Retrieved from www.vanityfair.fr/culture/ecrans/articles/fils-de-saul-shoah-cinema-cannes/25988.

Chare, N., & Williams, D. (2016, February 4). *Searching for Feelings: The Scrolls of Auschwitz and Son of Saul*. Berghahn Books. Retrieved from http://berghahnbooks.com/blog/searching-for-feelings-the-scrolls-of-auschwitz-and-son-of-saul.

Dedio, F. (Writer & Director), Finger, B., and Karel, W. (Directors). (2014–2015). *Jusqu'au dernier: la destruction des juifs d'Europe*. France: TV5Monde.

Delbo, C. (1970). *Auschwitz et après: Aucun de nous ne reviendra*. Paris: Editions de Minuit.

Des Voix Sous La Cendre. *Mémoires des Déportations*. Retrieved from http://memoiresdesdeportations.org/fr/texte/des-voix-sous-la-cendre-extraits.

Didi-Huberman, G. (2015). *Sortir du noir*. Paris: Editions de Minuit.

Donadio, R. (2015, December 14). In "Son of Saul," Laszlo Nemes expands the language of holocaust films. *New York Times*. Retrieved from www.nytimes.com/2015/12/15/movies/in-son-of-saul-laszlo-nemes-expands-the-language-of-holocaust-films.html?_r=0.

Elek, J. (Producer & Director), Marmiesse, P., Ozorai, A., & Simó, S. (Producers). (1997). *Elie Wiesel Goes Home* [Motion Picture]. France: Les Films du Paradoxe.

Felman, S. (1987). *Jacques Lacan and the Adventure of Insight: Psychoanalysis in Contemporary Culture*. Cambridge: Harvard UP.

Felman, S., & Laub, D. (Eds.). (1992). *Testimony: Crises of Witnessing in Literature, Psychoanalysis and History*. New York: Routledge.

Forgács, P. (Producer & Director). (1996). *Free Fall* [Motion Picture]. Hungary: For-Creation Bt.

Forgács, P. (Producer & Director). (1997). *Class Lot* [Motion Picture]. Hungary: The Hungarian Motion Picture Foundation.

Forgács, P. (Producer & Director). (2001). *A Bibó Reader: Private Hungary 13, the Bishop and the Philosopher* [Motion Picture]. Hungary: Nextreme Film Ltd.

Forgács, P. (2002). *The Danube Exodus: The Rippling Currents of the River* [Multimedia Exhibition]. The J. Paul Getty Museum, Los Angeles CA.

Forgács, P. (2013). *Letters to Afar* [Video Art Installation]. POLIN Museum of the History of Polish Jews. Warsaw, Poland.

Forgács, P. (2014, November 2). Post-screening discussion, "The Alchemist: A Péter Forgács Film Retrospective." YIVO Institute for Jewish Research, New York.

Forgács P. (2016). *Attribution of Meaning* [Video]. Robert Capa Contemporary Photography Center, Budapest.

Frenkel, D., Krausz, D., Labadie, J., Stocker, K (Producers), & Lanzmann, C. (Director). (2013). *The Last of the Unjust* [Motion Picture]. France: Le Pacte.

Friedman, D. (2009, May 26). Peter Forgacs: Pariah to the people. Retrieved January 6, 2018, from http://forward.com/articles/106627/peter-forgacs-pariah-to-the-people/#ixzz3X6taWI1Z.

Freud, Sigmund. (1899). Screen memories. In *Standard Edition, 3* (pp. 301–322). London: Hogarth Press.

Gazdag, G. (Director) (1985). *Társasutazás* [Motion Picture]. Hungary: Objektív Film.

Gersht, O. (2012–2013). "History Repeating," August 25, 2012–January 6, 2013. Museum of Fine Arts, Boston.

Green, G. (Writer), & Chomsky, M. (Director). (1978). H. Brodkin's *Holocaust* [Television Miniseries]. New York: NBC.

Hamori, A., Lantos, R. (Producers), & Szabó, I. (Director). (1999). *Sunshine* [Motion Picture]. Germany: Kinowelt Filmverleih.

Himka, J., & Michlic, J. B. (2013). *Bringing the Dark Past to Light: The Reception of the Holocaust in Postcommunist Europe*. Lincoln, NE: University of Nebraska Press.

Hoberman, J. (2014, November 20). Péter Forgács' memory art brings phantoms of Eastern Europe to light. Retrieved from www.tabletmag.com/jewish-arts-and-culture/187009/forgacs-memory.

Hoberman, J. (2015, February 22). "Ida" wins: The count is now 20 out of 23. Retrieved from www.tabletmag.com/scroll/189157/ida-wins-the-count-is-now-20-out-of-23.

Hoberman, J. (2016, February 29). "Son of Saul" wins Oscar, cementing strength of Holocaust-themed films at Academy Awards. Retrieved from www.tabletmag.com/scroll/198028/son-of-saul-wins-oscar-cementing-strength-of-holocaust-themed-films-at-academy-awards.

Holocaust. (1978). (Television mini-series, 4 episodes). Release Date: April 16, 1978 (USA).

Imre, A. (Ed.). (2012). *Jewish Identities and Generational Perspectives in Hungarian Cinema: A Companion to Eastern European Cinemas*. London: Wiley-Blackwell. 101–124.

Jeffries, S. (2011, June). Claude Lanzmann on why Holocaust documentary Shoah still matters. *Guardian*. Retrieved from www.theguardian.com.

Kertész, I. (2002). Heureka! [Text]. Retrieved from www.nobelprize.org/nobel_prizes/literature/laureates/2002/kertesz-lecture-e.html

Lacan, J. (2001). La méprise du sujet supposé savoir. In *Autres Écrits*. Paris: Seuil.

Lanzmann, C. (1994, March 3). Holocauste, la representation impossible. *Le Monde*. Retrieved from www.lemonde.fr

Lanzmann, C. (2013 September). Q&A at the conclusion of the U.S. premiere of *The Last of the Unjust*, Alice Tully Hall, New York City.

Levi, P. (1988). The memory of the offence. In *The Drowned and the Saved* (p. 12). London: Simon & Schuster.

Liebman, S. (2014, March 4). Lanzmann's memory theatre. *The Criterion Collection*. Retrieved from www.criterion.com/current/posts/3084-lanzmann-s-memory-theater.

Messemaker, C. (Producer), & Forgács, P. (Director). (1997). *The Maelstrom: A Family Chronicle* [Motion Picture]. Hungary: For-Creation Bt.

Murphy, M. (2016, January 21). Laszlo Nemes narrates a scene from "Son of Saul." *The New York Times*. Retrieved January 6, 2018, from www.nytimes.com/2016/01/22/movies/laszlo-nemes-narrates-a-scene-from-son-of-saul.html.

Murphy, P. (2016, February 29). "Son of Saul": film on holocaust hell earns Oscar. *Yahoo*. Retrieved from www.yahoo.com/news/son-saul-film-holocaust-hell-earns-oscar-050113737.html.

Piotrowska, A. (2013). *Psychoanalysis and Ethics in Documentary Film*. New York: Routledge.

Portuges, C. (1993). *The Hungarian Cinema of Márta Mészáros*. Bloomington, IN: Indiana University Press.

Portuges, C. (1998). István Szabó's sunshine. *Cinéaste*, *xxvi*(1), 56–57.

Portuges, C. (2009). Intergenerational transmission: The Holocaust in Central European Cinema. In A. Sabbadini (Ed.), *Projected Shadows: Psychoanalytic Reflections on the Representation of Loss in European Cinema* (pp. 73–91). London: Routledge.

Portuges, C. (2011). Found images as witness to Central European history: Péter Forgács' a Bibó Reader and Miss Universe 1929. In B. Nichols & M. Renov (Eds.), *Cinema's Alchemist: The Films of Péter Forgács* (pp. 159–176). Minneapolis, MN: University of Minnesota Press.

Portuges, C., & Hames, P. (Eds.). (2013). *Cinemas in Transition in Central and Eastern Europe after 1989*. Philadelphia, PA: Temple University Press.

Reichbart, R (2008). Screen memory: Its relation to object relations and transference. Journal of the *American Psychoanalytic Association*, 56: 455–481.

Renov, M. (2013). *Psychoanalysis and Ethics in Documentary Film*. London: Routledge.

Rosser, M. (2015, April 30). HBO to debut "spectres of the shoah" doc. *Screen Daily*. Retrieved from www.screendaily.com/news/hbo-to-debut-spectres-of-the-shoah-doc/5087182.article.

Shatz, A. (2012). Nothing he hasn't done, nowhere he hasn't been. *London Review of Books*, *34*(7), 11–12.

Shoard, C. (2015, May 15). "Son of Saul"s astonishing recreation of Auschwitz renews holocaust debate. *Guardian*. Retrieved from www.theguardian.com.

Sigmund Freud: The Last Decade. (2017). Sigmund Freud Museum. London, UK. Screened 2017, November 2.

Varga, Z. (2005, May 23). Once they were neighbours [Interview by E. Szlanárs]. Retrieved from www.zsurlofilm.com/OnceTheyWereNeighbours/zsu_szom_a_ford5.htm.

Wiesel, E. (1960). *Night*. New York: Avon.

Wieworka, A. (2000). *La Shoah: témoignages, savoirs, oeuvres*. Paris: Presses Universitaires de Vincennes.

Wizner, B. (Producer), & Geller-Varga, Z. (Director). (2005). *Szomszédok voltak* [Motion Picture]. Hungary: Zsurló Film.

Chapter 7

Son of Saul

The remains of civilization

Clara Mucci[1]

Overture

The movie *Son of Saul* (Rajna, Sipos, & Nemes), by Hungarian director Lazlo Nemes, confronts the audience with a major riddle about what it means to be human when dishumanity and annihilation have prevailed in the world. For a day and a half of his life as Sonderkommando in Auschwitz's extermination camp, in October 1944, Saul devotes all his energy, and risks his own life (while at the same time his comrades are organizing a rising in the camp), in the effort to accomplish one deed, the burial of a boy, almost an adolescent, who might be (or might not be) his son: the movie leaves this point open, as a way of suggesting that this deed is not undertaken within the personal order or is at the level of attachment and individual involvement/affect that this deed is cast but at the universal order raised to protect the remains of a humane world. The act of burying the dead in the background of Auschwitz becomes both a duty and a spiritual connection with a "beyondness" that restores some kind of survival of meaning and memory beyond death and annihilation. The ritual of the burial in this brutal "waste land" becomes (in the intentions of the protagonist) a real act of witnessing to the divine order of humankind in the place where it has been most violated. It symbolically represents the persistence of the sacredness of human life when values and meanings have been deleted and erased, and results in an extreme celebration of the divinity of life against atrocity. Against the destruction of humanity and the total folly into which humanity has sunk, the movie affirms the value of a ritual that sustains the persistence of culture and civilization, a novel version of Antigone's ethical gesture cast against an order not only of conflict between laws (as was the case in Sophocles' play), but of total devastation and annihilation, a world where the existence of God has been seriously threatened.

While for Antigone the struggle was between the unwritten law of piety toward a brother, and the city law that condemned her brother as traitor of the State, Saul's struggle defines the limit to which individual moral responsibility has been taken in the *univers concentrationnaire*; for this reason he becomes a sort of hero in a landscape of totally erased human values. The value of a single body to be preserved from the erasure of the ovens becomes the obsession of the protagonist and highlights, for its very contrast with the landscape of destruction, the total madness and extreme barbarity into which humanity has descended in the extermination camps.

Porter to the gate of Hell: Saul as the hero of liminality

From the first open-air scene with some unclear details in the shallow focus of the background but with the singing of birds at a distance, a means to represent nature as unaware or innocent with regard to the unnatural acts that human beings are carrying out, the movie depicts a descent into Hell, as the protagonist approaches the interiors of the camp and enters the chambers of death: voices become cries, the light is reddish and dark, always murky and livid, similar to the "black milk of dawn" in the representation of the sun at Auschwitz, in the famous poem, "Death Fugue," by Paul Celan (Celan, 1948). The audience becomes the witness to the horror and insane destruction taking place there, perceived as going on at a hurried pace, in the hasty and business-like devastation and horror of the industry of extermination enacted by the Nazi Germans, fuelling the factory of annihilation.[2] As spectators, all around us we hear cries, made more real and concrete by the sound effects that take us realistically into a babel of a dozen languages (added to the movie afterwards: no soundtrack is in the movie, but the cries and multiple languages of this *Inferno* are the only "soundtrack"). The camera portrays the face of the protagonist in a narrow field of vision as if the horror were to pass through his own personal view and bodily perceptions. We "become" Saul the member of the Sonderkommando.

Entering this deadly space, we learn that the extermination machine is based first of all on a fraud: before the doors where they will be gassed, people are told to hurry up because they are going to take a shower, and will then receive a warm soup afterwards, before being assigned a job, to start some kind of necessary activity for the camps like carpentry, nursing, masonry, in an horrific mimicry of a frenetic busy "human" life. "Hurry up or the soup becomes cold," "Please remember where you have left your clothes, remember where your hook is so you can retrieve your clothes more quickly": the sentences resonate in their monstrous betrayal, as if there were a "beyond" after that door, a going back; this is what the Sonderkommando repeat endlessly, with a sense of an almost vital hustle and bustle, which reminds us of the hurly-burly of the murdering world of *Macbeth*. But the killing in this theater of death is not limited to one single king; it extends to a multitude of betrayed humans, like victims going to the slaughter. Beyond the doors, after they have entered with these promises, we hear banging, shouting, and cries of children and humans terrified, as they realize that they are going to be destroyed pitilessly: once again, before the reality of the extermination camps, only the imagination of an artist had represented so realistically the banging at the doors of a sort of Hell, as this representation appears in Shakespeare's *Macbeth*. The Sonderkommando men are the new porters to this gate of Hell, an inverted realm of liminality: they are the *Geheimnistrager*, "the bearers of secrets" in the German Nazi language, they are the keepers of the secrets of death and destruction, the "chosen" to become the destroyers, in this upside-down world into which humanity has sunk.

In the inverted order of the camps, where no one was supposed to survive to bring the news to the outside world, the ones who were in touch with the real bodies and would actually see the murder of millions carried out to these extremes were Jews themselves, in a careful, "shrewd," bureaucratically efficient and criminal organization.

In fact, these atrocities were perpetrated while at the same time the mechanism of moral responsibility on the part of the Nazis had been weakened through a bureaucratic machine that made it more difficult for the single individual to understand the total plan. As Zigmund Bauman (1989) argues cogently, writing about the "social production of the moral invisibility" of the extermination camps, the machine of bureaucracy annulled or weakened individual moral responsibilities: like automatons, in a way similar to what the Milgram experiment afterward proved, they carried out each command and each step to the extreme without realizing in full the moral and human consequences of the entire project. The moral inhibitions that would make the perpetration of atrocities impossible, as Herbert C. Kelman writes, tend to be erased in three cases: when violence is authorized; when violence becomes routine; and when victims are dehumanized. All three of these conditions were present in the *univers concentrationnaire* (Kelman, 1973).

The sudden cries inside the gas chambers last for the minutes of the actual gassing; soon afterward they will be echoed by other human beings in regular repetition of the same scene over and over again; only the people are different, and one group is moved on after the other, with the same illusion and betrayed hopes, in a sort of inverted, demonic deadly ritual. The Nazis repeatedly refer to the dead people coming out of the gas chamber as *Stucken*, German for "pieces," as if they did not count as humans, and had become totally dehumanized. We actually watch the Sonderkommandos as they very quickly and emotionlessly remove the gassed bodies and take them to the ovens—something never shown in a movie before, to my knowledge—without thinking or taking the time to feel. The gas chambers had to be cleaned and the whole operation begun again in haste.

Among the last group of gassed bodies Saul sees an adolescent, a boy, who is still alive: because he is still breathing, he has to be taken to the infirmary to be analyzed and to receive an autopsy. The Nazi doctor remarks in fact that all the "abnormalities" to the deadly routine had to be "documented." In a reversal of what would happen in any other order of life, the doctor killing the remnants of life in the young body is once again a horrific image of the upside-down horizon we are cast into, the death camps. Saul is a witness to this scene. The murder of one resonates for the multiplication of the many murdered. This one young male body becomes the representative of a form of survival, a form of extreme resistance to utter evil, and furnishes evidence to a kind of resilience, a last embodiment of a source of witnessing to the horror itself: Saul needs to bury this one body, remnant of a "superfluous" life in this inverted order of things, but, precisely for this reason, so much more meaningful.

In fact, one could ask, in the midst of the dozens and hundreds and thousands gassed and destroyed each day, why would this one person make a difference? He personifies the persistent survivor: in a sense the boy has been the one who "has faced death, and has remained alive," in the definition of survivorship given by Robert Jay Lifton, (1988, p. 18). For Saul, he is a symbol of resistance, of a relentless defying of evil and of destruction against all odds (even though he will, like the others, finally be put to death). Is he the son of Saul? He is the son of Humanity, of a kind of humanity that in its essence is not going to be exterminated, and will indeed remain alive in the sense that it will render testimony to what life is and should always be, a sacred form of existence, beyond animality, leaving a meaningful trace behind, a trace of dignity and meaningfulness. As we have heard in testimonies of Holocaust survivors, "the murderers haven't succeeded in exterminating the human spirit; they, the devils, the animals, haven't made us animals," or, in other words, "they wanted to reduce us to beasts, but they did not succeed."[3] While the exterminators wanted to reduce everybody to inanimate objects, to meaningless "pieces" devoid of sense and dignity, this one body, a symbolic "son of Saul," in an interlinear chain, shows that a vital force still lingers in the midst of the dead.

I would like to remind the reader that the name Saul, the first king of Israel, bears witness to a divine heritage, meaning "the long desired son"; while the surname of the protagonist, Auslander,[4] means the "foreigner," or, more appropriately, the "outcast," the one who comes from an outside place, therefore I would say the inhabitant of a liminal space, cast in-between human and divine, alive and dead, the inhabitant of a threshold, a symbolic *lieu*, powerful and ambivalent, as anthropologist Victor Turner has explained:

> The attributes of liminality or of liminal personae ("threshold people") are necessarily ambiguous, since this condition and these persons elude or slip through the network of classifications that normally locate states and positions in cultural space. Liminal entities are neither here nor there; they are betwixt and between the positions assigned and arrayed by law, custom, convention, and ceremonial. As such, their ambiguous and indeterminate attributes are expressed by a variety of symbols in the many societies that ritualize social and cultural transitions. Thus, liminality is frequently linked to being in the womb, to invisibility, to darkness, to bisexuality, to the wilderness, and to an eclipse of the sun or moon.
>
> (1977, p. 95)

While all of the Sonderkommandos are "liminal people" in the sense that they are the invisible people inhabiting the limits between the dead and the living, Saul is even more "liminal" within this community of cast-outs insofar as he inhabits the typical transgressiveness of liminal people, as I will clarify.

As a peculiarly aware and ethically driven inhabitant of the threshold, Saul the Auslander, the Sonderkommando, the Porter at the door of Death, decides to act, against the profanation of the dead and the dehumanization that the Nazis are programmatically accomplishing, the extreme act of transgression in this inverted world, in order to reassert civilization through an exercise of pity in at least honoring the dead: he will pay the proper respect to the corpse. If the Nazis have redesigned a universe in which they are the masters of death, taking possession of that extreme human limit always in the hands of the unknown that is death, in a delirium of criminal omnipotence or malignant narcissism (see Kernberg 1975, 2003a, 2003b for a discussion of malignant narcissism in totalitarian systems and leaders), Saul will use the most exquisite instruments a human being has toward a symbolic restoration of humanity and continuation of meaning to accompany the dead through the simple recital of the Kaddish, the prayers for the dead, and the performance of the sacred funeral rites. Performing the burial is a cultural act that resets an order of symbols and of civilization, which is what distinguishes the human: even if burial with the Kaddish is inscribed within the Jewish divine order, in these massively traumatic circumstances the burial itself is beyond mere religious tradition: it is intended to celebrate the divinity and sacredness of human life. It constitutes a basic cultural divide between humans and animals or the monsters, a cultural rite of celebration of the divine in Humankind, of a certain humankind, against the other so called "humans" who have become murders and animals.

It is also a means of restoring the humanity of the victims, against the dehumanization they have suffered even before the entering the camps. How the process of dehumanization had been carefully prepared and enforced by the Nazi regime has been described by several authors (Arendt, 1951; Bauman, 1989; Mucci, 2013). If the "beyond" of trauma consists, among other things, in the reconnection with and a reconstitution of a meaningful symbolic order, where all possible meaning had been shattered, the value of Saul's act embodies this intent of reissuing the value of a set of meanings enforced through rituals that reconnect and give sense to a social community. It celebrates the persistence of a bond between beings, even in the face of utter annihilation, it is a form of reconnection of a "we" that the Nazis were attempting to exterminate. Without symbolic and cultural meaning the community does not exist, and rituals are the last stronghold for saving meaning and civilization through a cultural act.

Burying the dead: "connectedness" and cultural community as the remains of civilization in the place of annihilation

Rituals as a symbolic human artifact at the foundation of culture define and mark the difference between culture and nature and are a means to sanction the divide between the two (Paul, 2015). Several authors have written on how community cannot exist without meaning, and how trauma cannnot be truly elaborated and overcome if some kind of meaning hasn't been restored within it, since trauma is precisely the shattering of meaning in representable terms. As Kai Erikson argues, "when the community is devastated ... one can speak of a damaged social organism in almost the same way that one would speak of a damaged body" (1991, p. 460).

The burial in the movie becomes a survivor mission within the community. The body of this child, the symbolic child of the Jewish lineage, needs to be celebrated by a Father figure. Against devastation, the rituals of death to honor this one body acquire a symbolic redemption and render some kind of solace, blunting the utter devastation and pain. After massive trauma and genocide, this ritual is symbolic of a form of reinstatement of a larger "communal body" (Erikson, 1976, p. 154). "Connectedness" (Mucci, 2013) in the camp was vital toward survival, as Primo Levi and his friend Alberto, Elie Wiesel, and his father and several others testify. Staying together, remaining with family or friends in the camp added a strong vital capacity to resist and remain alive, to survive atrocity and illness. Bonding and closeness among the prisoners afforded some stability, safety, and a sense of belonging, contributing to emotional, psychological, and physical survival. As Wiesel explains very clearly: "Those who retreated to a universe limited to their own bodies had less chance of getting out alive, while to live for a brother, a friend, an ideal helped you hold out together" (Wiesel 1995, pp. 80–81).

Maintaining a connection to other beings or a cultural connection through rituals reinforced relationships and was a stronghold against internal fragmentation. Loss, Judith Butler has argued, reveals our constitutional connectedness as human beings and shows us what it means to be human: "The question that preoccupies me in the light of recent global violence is, Who counts as human? ... And, finally, What *makes for a grievable life*?" (2004, p. 22, original emphasis). And also, I would ask, as does the director of the movie, what allows for the reconstitution of community? I would argue the answer is in a survived, ultimate form of connectedness, as bonding together and mourning even for a single life in the face of extermination, even if that life is not necessarily the life of a son. Connectedness is the persistence of the "human" even against atrocities, as I have written in *Beyond Individual and Collective Trauma* (Mucci, 2013). It is a way of reinscribing an empathic order when the "empathic dyad" (Laub, 2005a, p. 315) has been destroyed, both inside and outside. It is the way a semblance of community is resuscitated and reinscribed in the social order, as Kai Erikson argues, a source of reparation and healing:

> By collective trauma ... I mean a blow to the basic tissue of social life that damages the bonds attaching people together and impairs the prevailing sense of communality. The collective trauma works its way slowly and even insidiously into the awareness of those who suffer from it, so it does not have the quality of suddenness normally associated with "trauma." But it is a form of shock all the same, a gradual realization that the community no longer exists in an effective source of support and that an important part of the self has disappeared ... "I" continue to exist, though damaged and may be even permanently changed. "You" continue to exist, though distant and hard to relate to. But "we" no longer exist as a connected pair or as linked cells in a larger communal body.
>
> (1976, p. 154)

Rituals in these circumstances can help restore a sense of humane community and a sense of "we." Like any ritual reinforcing structure against anti-structure and disorderliness and chaos, this ritual becomes almost obsessively the mission of the subject *in lieu* of dehumanization, or, as André Green said, against deobjectification, a way of making culture resist un-civilization. As Clifford Geertz reminds us:

> Believing, with Max Weber, that man is an animal suspended in webs of significance he himself has spun, I take culture to be these webs, and the analysis of it to be therefore not an experimented science in search of law but an interpretive one in search of meaning.
>
> (1973, p. 5)

Rituals are the way these webs of meaning are created and reinforced, enacting culture and connecting humans into collectivity through patterns of shared meaning and value.

A horrific breach in culture and civilization, the Holocaust enacted instead a radical rupture of symbolic thread and a destruction of values and community, rendering shared meanings unrepresentable and rupturing the thread of connection between humans. As Jean Amery has written, echoed by other survivors, in Auschwitz and after the experience of the extermination:

> I was no longer an I and did not live within a We … I was a person who could not say 'we' and who therefore said "I," merely out of habit, but not with the feeling and the full possession of my self.
>
> (1980, p. 44)

Locating in "meaning" the main psychological feature of humanity, Robert J. Lifton argues:

> Anything that is psychological experience has to do with meaning. In that sense, meaning is the broadest kind of psychological entity. When one considers a life-death model or paradigm, it has to exist in relation to meaning, or in relation to how we symbolize our life process and our vitality, on the one hand, and our prospective end or individual death, on the other.
>
> (In Caruth, 2014, p. 7)

And he goes on: "What is causative from early on is the struggle for vitality and, ultimately, for symbolic immortality" (p. 8). It is toward this symbolic immortality that the gesture burial for the son of Saul's burial is cast/positioned.

Beyond Auschwitz, or what is left of Oedipus (and Antigone) at the end of civilization

I would say that Saul accomplishes in the movie what Jean Amery would define a celebration of "death" against mere "dying."

In distinguishing between the two, Amery uncannily writes:

> It was characteristic for the situation of the prisoner in regard to death that only a few decided to "run the wire," as one said, that is, to commit suicide through contact with the highly electrified barbed wire. The wire was after all a good and rather certain thing, but it was possible that in the attempt to approach it one would be caught first and thrown into the bunker, and then led to a more difficult and more painful dying. *Dying was omnipresent, but death vanished from sight.*
>
> (1980, p. 17, emphasis mine)

I think this distinction within a symbolic order (or dis-order) of brutal killing is very significant: Saul wants to pay a tribute to death in the camp, not to dying, which was an ubiquitous presence around him, and thereby wants to reinscribe for himself some kind of subjectivity in place of deletion. He regains some levels of moral freedom simply from his purpose and his desire to honor death; as Amery says: "the free person assume a certain posture towards death, because for him death is not totally absorbed into the torment of dying" (ibid.). Saul can see the difference, therefore his spirit even in the prison-hell can testify to some freedom, a form of moral liberation and redemption against being totally subjected. As Amery states: "The reality of the camp triumphed effortlessly over death and over the entire complex of the so-called ultimate questions. Here too, the mind came up to its limits" (1980, p. 18). Saul stretches these limits to embody moral resistance and spiritual liberation from the camps, defying the erasure of subjectivity as such.

In Western culture and philosophy, the burial of a loved one at any cost is powerfully reminiscent of Antigone's transgression of Creon's dictate not to bury Polyneices, Antigone's brother, who had been guilty of treason against the state, as narrated in the classical Greek theatre trilogy of the fifth century BC in Greece, which was the work of Sophocles.

An act of transgression and at the same time a characteristic way of inhabiting a liminal space of ambiguous and yet powerful threshold was at the origin of each of the plays centered on Oedipus, this exquisite psychoanalytic hero, dear to Freud and to Lacan among others, and used by them to exemplify the vicissitudes of human destiny and its development. Oedipus' transgressions are too notorious to need to be repeated here, and the consequences of his acts are the major theme of *Oedipus at Colonus*, in which Oedipus, after having blinded himself, is forced to leave Thebes and is exiled to Colonus, accompanied by his daughter Antigone. In a striking and extreme recognition of the desolation of human destiny, Oedipus once at Colonus utters the famous revelatory lines: "It is now that I have become nothing that I am made a man?" (Sophocles, 1991, *Oedipus at Colonus*, line 393).

Lacan has referred to this sentence to describe the peculiar destiny of the human subject as being marked by a radical split ("there is an-Other who speaks within myself," inhabited by an Unconscious unknown to oneself, as in the peculiar destiny of Oedipus (Lacan, 1966). For Lacan, and I follow here Shoshana Felman's seminal article "Beyond Oedipus: The Specimen Story of Psychoanalysis" (1983), Oedipus' destiny is emblematic of the human destiny in so far as any subject is forced to repeat a story, through repetition compulsion and death drive, precisely because he/she does not know his/her own origin (in Lacanian theory, this is because he has an Other within himself, the Unconscious split, *Spaltung* in the Freudian terms reappropriated by Lacan). As happened for all the other definitions and manifestations of humanity, Auschwitz expropriated and emptied out the human subject of any definition and meaning, even this extreme sentence, which seemed at the limits of possibilities: once humankind has been made null and has been lost, there is no other meaning left, the Holocaust victims are not made "human" ("man," in Oedipus' terms) by destruction, needless to say by the oven's ashes. Cast against this scenery, Auschwitz has operated in reality a radical shift not only in representation but in the definition of what Humankind is: a place of total devastation that has hollowed out even the definition of humanity—or of the subject—to nothing. The brutal reality of the place has erased the possibility of a symbolic representation—even the representation of the subject as inhabited by the Other, i.e. by a radical split within the Self—and it has left the breach of the Real open, has crushed any symbolic veil, leaving a void, a black hole underneath (as several survivors have defined the impossibility of making sense of the utter experience, a position of *Hilflösichkeit* to use the Freudian term for the helplessness of the traumatic experience). The Real as the extreme breach in the symbolic order as described by Lacan has revealed itself in the death camps. It is not incidental that in Lacan's view the Real is also connected to the traumatic per se, what cannot be symbolized. As Charlotte Delbo writes about her experience in the camps: "The reality was there, fatal. Impossible to withdraw from" (1985, p. 12).

In clinical terms, Auerhan and Laub have described this process in massive traumatization cogently:

> Since structure is built up by libidinal investments and identifications, we see that at its worst, trauma involves the annihilation, by aggression, of psychic structure and the total desolation that is tantamount to what we would experience in psychotic decompensation.
> (1984, p. 336)

The death instinct unleashed at Auschwitz has revealed its extreme reality, enacting the total loss or extermination of the good object (Kirshner, 1994; Green, 1996; Laub, 2005a, 2005b).

The third play rooted in the oedipal trilogy, *Antigone*, actually written before the second one, *Oedipus at Colonus*, but appearing as the last one in the traditional sequence, is based on the heroine who decides to bury her brother in defiance of the law of Thebes enforced by her uncle Creon, Oedipus' brother; ultimately Antigone takes her own life by hanging herself in the tomb into which she has been cast. Rivers of ink have been used from Hegel to Lacan to more recently Judith Butler to comment on Antigone's gesture of transgression as a basic divide between a law that is made by human beings and might be tainted and a law that goes beyond human intention and is divine and is cast against a wider and more comprehensive ethical order.

Jacques Lacan chose the powerful Greek heroine in his *Séminaire VII*, to discuss ethics as the relationship of human actions to a moral order, depicting her as a "turning point in the field that interests us, namely, ethics" (1997, p. 177), and eventually as the subject who casts her desire outside the symbolic order, which is in the end a desire of death, so that she is made to personify the death wish and the working of the death drive. In his desire to bury the child, Saul seems to rehearse Lacan's fundamental (ethical and human) question, defining precisely what it means to be human in conflict with an animal-like, non-symbolic world: "Given our condition as men, what must we do in order to act in the right way?" (p. 19). And furthermore:

> When we seek to explore the frontier between the animal and the human world, it is apparent to what extent the symbolic process as

> such doesn't function in the animal world … That man is caught up in symbolic processes of a kind to which no animal has access cannot be resolved in psychological terms.
>
> (p. 45)

But human beings are social and symbolic animals, among other things, and the constitution of society is based precisely on language, Law, and symbolic rituals and acts, even though these things are being denied around Saul, and the most unhuman and beast-like environment has been produced.

It could be said that Saul too, in a way similar to Antigone, is a subject who prefers death and performing the necessary rituals for the dead instead of embodying life or following some kind of life-drive actively fighting for his own escape or taking part in the uprising in the camps; but his exemplary and symbolic task gives resonance to another kind of (moral) survival as he gives voice to a deeper ethical quest that becomes also imbued with religious meanings. His search for a rabbi—in the midst of scenes in which people are shoveling ashes into the water of a nearby river, or are being taken to the gas chambers—his search for somebody who could properly recite the Kaddish according to the rituals, resonates as an utterly out-of-place quest for God in the place where God is most found dead, in the camps.

Once again, we find in Lacan's *Séminaire VII*, apart from several differences, a curious analogy with the absence of divinity in the camps. Here is what Lacan writes on *Antigone*:

> But if for us God is dead, it is because he always has been dead, and that's what Freud says. He has never been the father except in the mythology of the son, or, in other words, in that of the commandment which commands that he, the father, be loved, and in the drama of the passion which reveals that there is resurrection after death.
>
> (p. 177)

That God has never been the Father except in the mythology of the son seems a perfect image for the lack of God in the camps. Where was God in the camps?

In the movie, the search for a rabbi, a real rabbi, not an impostor, proves difficult; at one point when Saul flies out of the chambers to repair a door of the baracks, he finds someone who claims to be a rabbi, but as this presumed rabbi starts reciting the Kaddish his words fade and he can't go on: either he is a fake rabbi and does not know the words, or the very words that should sanctify the name of the Lord at Auschwitz are impossible to pronounce, and the (supposed/alleged) rabbi leaves Saul and tries to drown himself in the river (the Vistula river), but Saul saves him. When the man is later put to death by the SS guards, Saul asks him for his forgiveness.

The movie reminds us of the fundamental questions that have often been raised: "Why did God allow this to happen if he is in control of people's lives and destinies?" and "What were those creatures being created for, if they were to be exterminated?"

To the most atrocious questions, about the persistence of God in this realm and his agency, Wiesel (2006) notoriously responded in *Night* with the image of the hanged child; at Auschwitz God himself was made impotent, and abides, for Wiesel, in that very child: God himself is the victim of the dis-humanity of which certain beings were capable. As Hans Jonas has stated, for the Jew who sees earth as the place of the creation, of justice and of divine salvation, God is the Lord of History, therefore Auschwitz questions the very foundation of the divine presence in this world (Jonas, 1987).

A world beyond God at Auschwitz, or the legacy of Antigone for us

Obsessed with this extreme survival mission and with restoring the outside world, i.e. the burial (of the significant body) instead of the erasure of it, Saul commits only to this action, to the deed, in this one trait similar to Antigone's determination to bury her brother in defiance of the city laws. Against Lacan's view of Antigone as the one in love with death and the dead ones, other authoritative voices, as has already been mentioned, have been raised, the most recent of which is Judith Butler. In her essay *Antigone's Claim* Butler has written against Lacan's interpretation to maintain instead that Antigone's wish is not about death (as it is cast against the symbolic order) but reveals most urgently a sort of fallacy or lays bare a crisis within that symbolic order (Butler, 2000).

I would agree with Butler and I would go even further, saying that, within the extreme limits of the lack of signification of the symbolic disorder or psychotic criminal order enacted at Auschwitz, Saul's deed reveals and fights against a fallacy of the order, and performs the only highly symbolic cultural act and a simple act of pity that in the reign of death and murder can reinstate some humanity and some signs of culture and civilization.

It would seem that the director of *Son of Saul* (Rajna, Sipos, & Nemes) has stretched this view to an extreme as he makes of the transgressive act of burial the epitome of some kind of extreme homage to the survival of human dignity and its value in the face of extermination and total cancellation of humanity. It is an heroic act in so far as, through performing this ritual, he might be putting his life in danger (but all the men of the Sonderkommando will be put to death in a matter of days anyhow). In the moment in which Culture and Humanity are at risk of disappearing, his extreme gesture of pity and respect against the act not only of profanation of the corpse (as in Antigone, where the body of Polyneices is said to be the prey of dogs and scavengers), but of real extermination and reduction into ashes, thereby deleting the evidence of the crime and of evidence of the body itself, is seen as a redemptive act against the brutality and cancellation of the extermination in which bodies are "pieces," *Stucken*, and human beings are given numbers in place of their names, as is clear from numerous scenes in the movie where the appalling and numerous roll calls take place. In fact, do we know the name of this boy? It does not seem necessary to name him, as he is the body of the sacrifice of millions reduced to numbers and ashes. Giving burial is par excellence to restate the personal name and the family lineage through the origin to the end, even the nation of origin, in a Babel of tongues and confused nations, in the space between birth and death; significantly when the protagonist finds the "still-alive" body of the boy he asks if that very day new prisoners have arrived from Hungary, his nation of origin and that of the child possibly. The "son" is also the son of a nation, the future of a culture with precise and unique symbolic constructions, starting from the institution of language.

No name left: the erasure of language and burial as testimony

The exposure of the victims to numerous, repeated roll calls is particularly disturbing: no name, no identity, no family lineage, no national identity, everything destroyed in one act of reversal, of cultural inscription, the tattooing of a number instead of a family and personal name, another extreme act of the reduction of these people to pieces, *Stucken* or *Figuren*, with nothing human about them.

Primo Levi renders with his unique style and utter precision what it meant to have no name and no language left to describe the experience of the Lager:

> Then for the first time we became aware that our language lacks words to express this offence, the demolition of a man. In a moment, with almost prophetic intuition, the reality was revealed to us: we had reached the bottom. It is not possible to sink lower than this; no human condition is more miserable than this, nor could it conceivably be so. Nothing belongs to us anymore: they have taken away our clothes, our shoes, even our hair; if we speak, they will not listen to us, and if they listen, they will not understand. *They will even take away our name: and if we want to keep it, we will have to find ourselves the strength to do so, to manage somehow so that behind the names something of us, of us as we were, still remains.*
>
> (1996, pp. 26–27, emphasis mine)

Against the utter erasure of language and name for the subject, as described by Levi, in the ceremony of the burial, a name is being reinstated, a trace of belonging to a lineage and a human order.

Giving a name back, even if through burial, is a symbolic step toward a form of humane if not religious restoration and a rebirth, or an atonement and redemption after the ferocious encounter with evil. Every being receives a name in order to exist as a distinct being in the community of others and to keep the intergenerational transmission of his family's names. Renaming and burying is a collective act of restoration and truth, of testimony through a regaining of a collective meaning and place; as in any ritual, the purpose of rituals is precisely reinstating truth and value to the community, reinforcing community. When the community of real human beings is just the community of the dead, the most sacred act to celebrate community, and renewal of life, is the burial, against precisely the massive sacrifice, the Holocaust of thousands and millions. Stressing the fact that "it is man who invented the sepulchre" (Lacan, 1997, p. 276), Lacan writes: "One cannot be finished with his remains simply by forgetting that the register of someone who was identified by a name has to be preserved by funeral rites" (p. 279).

While Antigone's gesture was cast against a still human order of right and wrong, of life and death, of enforced laws and order, even though the human laws are viewed as unjust, *Son of Saul* (Rajna, Sipos, & Nemes) depicts a world beyond common moral divide and humane quest. The movie in fact is not properly or simply "violent" in a common way, it is in fact uniquely atrocious; it is not about aggressiveness but about erasure and annihilation; it portrays a world that has gone beyond the questions of the symbolic order in which even Oedipus casts his struggle and names his desire (to echo Lacanian language).

Although the common prisoners in this movie are shown to retain their usual appetites, like desire and possession of women, the movie depicts a world in which the normal human drives are out of place or misplaced. The protagonist acknowledges that he views desire of women in this place as appalling ("I wish I had not heard them; I don't remember women"). It is, as Bruno Bettelheim and other survivors of the camps have claimed, a world where the death drive has prevailed, a realm in which a psychotic and deeply perverse symbolic order has been realized and has replaced eros and the pleasure principle. As Robert J. Lifton says, describing the perversion at the roots of similar atrocities, "what is perverse is that one must impose death on others in order to reassert one's life as an individual and a group" (2014, p. 14: see also Kernberg 2003a, 2003b).

But not only would a burial reinstate in this upside-down world a sort of "local habitation and a name" against a brutally concrete "airy nothing" (if to quote *A Midsummer Night's Dream* (V.i) in this horrific context is not too irrespectful), but it would render to the extreme sacrifices endured some kind of redemption and make it a symbol of martyrdom (it is important to remember that the original meaning of Holocaust is sacrifice) and a permanent monumental testimony to human dehumanization. Against the ruins of civilization, it makes sense that several survivors testify that they had to hold on, together with family members or friends, to poetry or prayers, real monuments to civilization and humanity (see Levi and his friend Alberto's use of Dante, see Wiesel father and son who every morning recite the Jewish prayers: Levi 1996; Wiesel, 2006). Here the concept of "therapôn," in the sense of second in combat and at the same time ritual minister and double, as implied by

Homer in *The Iliad*, seems to me relevant and evocative. "Therapôn," a word with the same root as "therapy," would suggest the healing and reparative nature of the companion in the trip beyond death, the witness, the creator of a "testimonial community" (Laub, 2005b), in the tradition of the Jewish Tikkun Olam, "mending the world."[5]

While at the same time the reality of the camps have made a "nothing" of the most extreme violent imaginings of classic tragedies and cultural creations (as I have tried to show with the brief references to Sophocles' tragedies and mostly Shakespeare's plays), I would not say that no poetry is possible after Auschwitz, but that Auschwitz has incarnated and made real the most extreme nightmares the human imagination had been capable of until then (mostly in tragedy). The extreme nightmares made real became a daily reality impossible to withdraw from. The camps made it impossible for the survivors to have a universe of metaphorical language once back from the camps; they were left with what Ilse Grubrich-Simitis called "concretisation" (Grubrich-Simitis, 1984).

Coda: rebirth by water, memory and/or redemption for the subject through femininity?

In the movie, several attempts at testimonial forms, even within the Auschwitz camp, are depicted: some prisoners take notes about what is going on there, a form of diary and documentation (the famous "Auschwitz scroll," found not too long ago, which the director seems to have used); another inmate together with the protagonist tries to take pictures and Saul succeeds in hiding the camera before they can be caught. Pictures were indeed taken, as we know from the work of George Didi-Huberman, *Images malgré tout*, even if several authors believe that the *univers concentrationnaire* cannot describe and render what has happened (Didi-Hubermann, 2003). As Didi-Hubermann writes, the only ethical position in this terrible trap of history consisted in resisting in spite of everything and in attempting to do the impossible: to create *malgré tout* the possibility of a testimony, in defiance of the assumptions of the SS that even if there might be suspicions, discussions, or research by historians, all the evidence would have been destroyed and even if some traces were left they would seem too atrocious to be believable (as Wiesenthal reports, 1967). Shored up against the "unimaginable," the intended burial is raised, as a testimony and a form of memory to what has been destroyed, but will be sanctified and remembered for ever. Against the social production of moral invisibility created by the Nazis at Auschwitz, and against the triumph of the secret the Germans wanted to enforce, the sepulchre becomes a speaking testimony and a permanent visible trace of the horror perpetrated there.

In the ceremony of the burial, a name is being reinstated. Giving a name back, even if through burial, is a restoration and a rebirth. Renaming and burying is a collective act of restoration and truth, of testimony through a regaining of a collective meaning; as in any ritual, the purpose of rituals is precisely reinstating truth and value to the community, reinforcing community (even if in this case the community is that of the dead).

The movie is not about a fight between death and life, it is not about struggling to remain alive even though, on a minor level, this theme is also present in the narration. In the background of the burial, the major symbolic story and narrative pilaster of the movie, the insurrection of Auschwitz, is depicted. But the truly heroic gesture, however, the gesture that makes one say to Saul: "You have betrayed the alive for the world of the dead," is his ritual burial of the dead, the honoring of the living vestigia against animality and brutality. Animals do not bury their loved ones; only humans do, and in this simple link the mystery and the meaning of human civilization is all there: animals might have feelings but haven't created culture, they haven't enforced civilization. *Homo homini lupus* depicts on the contrary the unnaturalness of a world without civilization, without rules, where sheer aggressiveness has prevailed and destructiveness against each other has triumphed. And yet, animals do not kill each other for power and domination only, neither for a sadistic or paranoid impetus; and yet they do not endow their gestures and habits with symbolic meaning, nor do they inhabit a world of symbolic order and sacred rituals. Divinity is a precise construction of the human order; and this is why Saul wants the body of the child (of a human life against evil and brutality) to receive benedictions and prayers and to be buried.

The movie ends with Saul liberating himself with a few comrades from Hell and going back to life (and to a Partisan fight with the Polish nation, possibly); he hasn't succeeded in his own attempt and only wish, to give the dead boy definitive rest in the land. Crossing the Vistula (the river in fact where mountains of ashes had been shovelled by inmates), the wrapped body of the child he had been carrying on his shoulder (again, the Western thought of civilization goes to Enea's moving to Italy with his old father Anchise on his shoulders; and it is Enea again, the "pious man" who had given burial to Polydorus in *Aeneid* III, lines 13–68) falls into the waters and drifts among the ashes. Yet the water element is reminiscent or symbolic of a female creative rebirth, not so much death by water (in the waste-land form) but a kind of rebirth, rejuvenition, and restoration through the liquid element, feminine and restorative. It is significant to note the total lack of female characters in the entire movie, except for Ella, the woman who gives the "hero" Saul the powder for the uprising (which he loses, he is not the hero and the minister for the living but only for the dead). That contact with the female world of Ella and her barracks (is Ella a previous lover, even a wife for him? The movie does not say) suggests a moment of intense, dramatic connectedness with the feminine world).

The last image of the water involving and almost embracing the boy at last is not totally sad, is not a total failure for the anti-hero Saul, it is still, to my mind, a sign of rebirth and restoration, through the feminine and natural element of water. It is, if we may say so, a sort of *tomb-womb*,[6] a liquid shelter and a vessel for his sacred body, possibly the reverse of Eliot's (1992) "Death by water." Another sign of a not totally negative ending is that even though Saul seems shattered by the loss of the body and his failure to reach his objective and he is stumbling along in his escape sustained by one of the supposed rabbis he has encountered, the appearance of a young, blond boy of supposedly the same age as the "son," peeping through the hut where the refugees have sheltered themselves, seems to cheer Saul. The last scene leaves us with the protagonist smiling at the boy, as this young man (of civilization) escaped through the woods, high trees inundated by the sun; again, if culture (traditionally considered the creation of men—for the counterposition see the classic article by Sherry Ortner, 1972) has led humanity to the dead end of Auschwitz, nature (water, trees) is the open recipient of a renovated and hopeful humanity, witness to a different landscape of vitality and rejuvenation or at least possibility. At least, this is how I would like to see the end of this movie.

I would say that against the lack of moral responsibility toward the living demonstrated by the Nazis and in part by the other countries and regimes that remained silent while the horrors of the camps were perpetrated, Saul, the liminal minister in the realm of death, testifies to this exquisite human responsibility and form of piety, the act of burial, from

Antigone onward and revitalizes the sacredness of human life. Mourning the dead reinstates a form of hope between the alive and the dead, affirming, through a sacred form of connectedness, the value of ("even" a single) life.

Notes

1 I would like to express my gratitude to Diana Diamond for her precious comments on this paper.
2 The extent to which the modern state with its bureaucracy and distorted rationality have contributed to create this monstrous regime under the guidance of the Germans has been analyzed accurately by Zygmunt Bauman in *Modernity and the Holocaust*, 1989.
3 Taken from the Fortunoff Video Archives for Holocaust Testimonies, Yale University, founded by Dori Laub.
4 "The foreigner" is the attribute that Sophocles gives to Oedipus; I don't know if it is a coincidence with the surname of the protagonist, Auslander, the outcast or foreigner, or if the screen players had a connection with the tragic hero in mind.
5 I owe the suggestive reference to the "therapôn" in Homer to Dr. Diana Diamond, to whom I wish to give thanks here.
6 Again I find here an echo from Shakespeare, this time the powerful tomb-womb image is in *Titus Andronicus*, as well as in *Romeo and Juliet* and in *The Sonnets*.

References

Amery, J. (1980). *At the Mind's Limits: Contemplations by a Survivor of Auschwitz and its Realities.* Bloomington and Indianapolis, IN: Indiana University Press.

Arendt, H. (1951). *The Origins of Totalitariasm*. New York and London: Harcourt, Inc., 1973.

Bauman, Z. (1989). *Modernity and the Holocaust*. Oxford: Basil Blackwell.

Bettelheim, B. (1979). *Surviving and Other Essays*. New York: Knopf.

Butler, J. (2000). *Antigone's Claim: Kingship between Life and Death.* New York: Columbia University Press.

Butler, J. (2004). *Precarious Life: The Powers of Mourning and Violence.* London: Verso.

Caruth, C. (Ed.). (2014). *Listening to Trauma: Conversations with Leaders in the Theory and Treatment of Catastrophic Experience*. Baltimore, MD: Johns Hopkins University Press.

Celan, P. (1948). Death Fugue. In *Selected Poems and Prose of Paul Celan* (Trans. by J. Felstiner). Norton: W.W. Norton (2001).

Delbo, C. (1985). *Le Mémoire et les jours*. Paris: Berg International.

Didi-Huberman, G. (2003). *Images malgré tout*. Paris: Editions du Minuit.

Eliot, T. S. (1922). *The Waste Land.* London: Faber and Faber (1971).

Erikson, K. T. (1976). *Everything in its Path: Destruction of Community in the Buffalo Creek Flood.* New York: Simon & Schuster.

Erikson, K. (1991). Notes on trauma and community. *American Imago, 48*(4), 455–472.

Felman, S. (1987). Beyond Oedipus: The specimen story of psychoanalysis. In R. Con Davis (Ed.), *Lacan and Narration* (pp. 1021–1063). Baltimore, MD: Johns Hopkins University Press.

Geertz, C. (1973). *The Interpretation of Culture: Selected Essays*. New York: Basic Books.

Green, A. (1996). *On Private Madness*. London: Rebut Press.

Grubrich-Simitis, I. (1984). From concretism to metaphor: Thoughts on some theoretical or technical aspects of the psychoanalytic work with children of the Holocaust. *The Psychoanalytic Study of the Child, 36*, 415–450.

Jonas, H. (1987). The concept of God after Auschwitz: A Jewish voice. *The Journal of Religion, 67*(1), 1–13.

Kelman, H. C. (1973). Violence without moral restraint. *Journal of Social Issues, 29*, 29–61.

Kernberg, O. (1975). *Borderline Conditions and Pathological Narcissism*. New York: Jason Aronson.

Kernberg, O. (2003a). Sanctioned social violence: A psychoanalytic view. Part I. *The International Journal of Psychoanalysis, 84*, 683–698.

Kernberg, O. (2003b). Santioned social violence: A psychoanalytic view. Part II. *The International Journal of Psychoanalysis, 84*, 953–968.

Kirshner, L. (1994). Trauma, the good object, and the symbolic: A theoretical integration. *International Journal of Psychoanalysis, 75*, 235–242.

Lacan, J. (1966). *Ecrits*. Paris: Editions du Deuil.

Lacan, J. (1997). *The Seminar of Jacques Lacan Book VII. The Ethics of Psychoanalysis 1959–1960*. New York and London: Norton.

Laub, D. (2005a). Traumatic shutdown of narrative and symbolization: A death instinct derivative? *Contemporary Psychoanalysis, 41*, 2, 307–326.

Laub, D. (2005b). From speechlessness to narrative: The cases of holocaust historians and of psychiatrically hospitalized survivors. *Literature and Medicine, 24*(2), 253–265.

Levi, P. (1996). *Survival in Auschwitz*. New York: Touchstone.

Lifton, J. R. (1988). Understanding the traumatized self: Imagery, symbolization and transformation. In: J. P. Wilson, Z. Harel, & B. Kahana (Eds.), *Human*

Adaptation to Extreme Stress: From the Holocaust to Vietnam (pp. 7–31). New York and London: Plenum Press.

Lifton, J. R. (2014). Giving death its due: An interview with Robert Jay Lifton (June 8, 1990, New York. In C. Caruth (Ed.), *Listening to Trauma: Conversations with Leaders in the Theory and Treatment of Catastrophic Experience* (pp. 3–23). Baltimore, MD: Johns Hopkins University Press.

Mucci, C. (2013). *Beyond Individual and Collective Trauma: Intergenerational Transmission, Psychoanalytic Treatment, and the Dynamics of Forgiveness.* London: Karnac Books.

Ortner, S. (1972). Is female to male as nature is to culture? *Feminist Studies, 1*(2), 5–31.

Paul, R. A. (2015). *Mixed Messages: Cultural and Genetic Inheritance in the Constitution of Human Society*. Chicago, IL: Chicago University Press.

Rajna, G., & Sipos, G. (Producers), & Nemes, L. (Director). (2015). *Son of Saul* [Motion Picture]. Hungary: Sony Classics.

Shakespeare, W. (1997) *The Norton Shakespeare* (Eds. S. Greenblatt, W. Cohen, J. E. Howard & K. Eisaman Maus). New York and London: W. W. Norton & Company.

Sophocles. (1991). *Oedipus the King, Oedipus at Colonus, Antigone*. Chicago, IL: University of Chicago.

Turner, V. W. (1977). *The Ritual Process: Structure and Anti-Structure*. Ithaca, NY: Cornell University Press.

Virgil, P. M. (2008). *Aeneid* (Trans. F. Ahl). Oxford: Oxford University Press.

Wiesel, E. (1995). *All Rivers Run to the Sea. Memoirs*. New York: Alfred Knopf.

Wiesel, E. (2006). *Night*. New York: Hill and Wang.

Wiesenthal, S. (1967). *The Murderers among Us*. New York: McGraw-Hill.

Chapter 8

Sadomasochistic regression in *The Night Porter*

Bruce Sklarew

In Liliani Cavani's provocative *The Night Porter* (Edwards, De Simone, & Cavani, 1974), set in Vienna in 1957, Max (Dirk Bogarde), an ex-Nazi SS officer photographer reunites via a chance meeting in the elegant Hotel zur Oper with Lucia (Charlotte Rampling), gentile daughter of a socialist, his 15-year old "possession" in a concentration camp. Cavani describes the film as "the overture to the underground of the city—Vienna—where there was the highest percent of Nazi criminals" (Marrone, 2000, p. 221). Max and Lucia are a couple who have a taste for the underground. Marrone (2000, p. 89) speaks of the "supremacy of desire expressed though hallucinatory visualizations of expressionism as in the work of Munch, Klimt, and Schiele. Vienna is a city illuminated by a cold, gray light, a tonality that signals psychic disintegration." The establishment shot consists of Max walking under an umbrella to work in the hotel and the film ends on a bridge in Vienna.

Now the wife of an American orchestra conductor, Lucia eventually masochistically surrenders to Max's interest in his former "little girl" (Edwards, De Simone, & Cavani, 1974) The much older Max serves as a malignant oedipal father who in the guise of a protector sadomasochistically teases, tortures, and rapes her. His previous "protective role" in selecting her out from the death chamber line-up contributes to binding her to him as though Max would protect her as a witness from the surviving Nazis in Vienna. Max is a reluctant member of a supposed therapy group of former Nazi officers whose overt purpose of cleansing themselves of their guilt covers their goal of ferreting out and killing all witnesses to their concentration camp crimes. Max continues in the group while he is being investigated for his loyalty because he fears that the Nazis could "file him away." He drowns a witness from the camp who could identify Lucia. He wants to be left alone, just to live, he says, as a church mouse. Max claims that he prefers the role of "the keeper of the night because during the day he is ashamed, and night living is also a way of being in touch with the darkness within him" (Edwards, De Simone, & Cavani, 1974). It is as though the night porter character literally carries forth the baggage like the work of the pressing instinctual forces in the polymorphous perversities in the hotel. The sadomasochistic Sonderkommandos herd the arriving victims into the gas chambers, drag them to the incinerators like porters carrying luggage, and shovel their ashes into the river. The film, *Son of Saul* (Rajna, Sipos, & Nemes, 2015), poignantly displays sadism in identification with the Nazi aggressors and their limited existence before they are selected to be killed. Primo Levi said it was the worst job in the world.

In the hotel, Max and Lucia reengage in an embattled and sadomasochistic encounter. Then they retreat to his small apartment that recreates the Lager with its exhausted food supply and guarded isolation, and regress to sadomasochistic games and rituals. Max chains Lucia, and in a reversal of Max wounding her in the camp, she, in identification with the aggressor, breaks a glass that he walks on barefoot and bleeds. She attempts mastery rather than victimization in a reversal of roles. Max cuts Lucia's arm and sucks her blood like a vampire and repeatedly places his fingers in her mouth. The ex-Nazis follow them in a car as they walk to their assassination on a bridge. They are portrayed by Cavani as though they would be protected from the ex-Nazis as they were protected in the arrangement with the Nazis in the camp. Lucia may have also thought that Max protected her and perhaps "arranged" for her not to be shot on a merry-go-round and now wearing the same short white skirt. Max might have imagined that in uniform he had the power and seeming invulnerability he had had in the camp rather than his present life of being hunted by the ex-Nazis. In a haunting image, Max and Lucia recede as they walk away from the camera framed by large steel pillars on a Viennese bridge. The only sound is the echo of their footsteps, then gunshots, silence, and the distant toll of a bell. This black and deadly image suggests a metaphor for the smallness of Max and Lucia immersed and trapped in the immensity and continuation of the death camp's grim mechanisms and who now are entrapped internally in their deadly re-enactment—no escape from death.

The magnificence of this image attests to how much the viewer can be attracted by the aestheticization of the shocking. In Bertolucci's *The*

Conformist (1970) Dominique Sanda is also murdered as a witness to her husband's assassination by Mussolini's men. Dressed in white, surrounded by snow and birches, and with blood on her face, her murder is another highly aesthetic death scene. Both films were edited by the masterful Franco (Kim) Arcalli who, also in *The Conformist* (Bertolucci & Bertolucci, 1970), used complicated flashbacks and non-chronological flashbacks within flashbacks to reconstruct memories and rethink the film for the audience, leading to a rare example of a film surpassing a novel—Moravia's *The Conformist.*

Historically, flashbacks have been used to visualize the past, to explain motivation and character as in a psychoanalytic verbal reconstruction. They have also been used to explicate internal conflicts derived from recovered and repressed memories through free association, dreams, and the transference. Flashbacks are prominent in many complex films such as *Un Chien Andalou* (1928), *Citizen Kane* (1941), *Spellbound* (1945), *Wild Strawberries* (1957), *Hiroshima Mon Amour* (1959), *Belle du Jour* (1967), and the Holocaust films *The Pawnbroker* (1965), and *Sophie's Choice* (1982).

In its classic form, the flashback is introduced into the present through dialogue, voice-overs, or intertitles or dissolves through an image in the past understood either as narrative or a subjective memory.

Maureen Turim (1989, p. 2) wrote:

> The flashback is a privileged moment in unfolding that juxtaposes difficult moments of temporal reference. A juncture is wrought between present and past and two concepts are implied in this juncture: memory and history. It functions as a story-being-told or a subjective memory. Memory surges forth. It strengthens or protects or it repeats and haunts.

Arcalli builds tension by progressively lengthening the duration of the *Night Porter*'s (Edwards, De Simone, & Cavani, 1974) flashbacks, mimicking Max's growing obsession with Lucia, first identified when Max photographed her upon her arrival at the concentration camp. In contrast to most of the other victims, she does not wear a Jewish star. In a close-up we see her terrified stare as she turns away from the bright light aimed at her. The viewer of the film identifies with Max looking at her through his Leica lens, as though no longer watching the film, but witnessing an unfolding horrific event. "The complicity of cinema with transgression and voyeuristic compulsion becomes the subject of the film itself," according to Marrone (2000, pp. 8–9), the most prominent film scholar on Cavani's oeuvre. While filming Lucia, Cavani establishes an ambiguous form of communication between the prisoner and her torturer through the camera lens. The spectacle emphasizes the barbarity of the Third Reich. These sequences are enacted against an extreme close-up background in a shallow depth of field conveying a sense of hallucinatory memory repetitively trying to bring the past into focus. The flashbacks represent the visual memories of her trauma in the camp. They begin with the saving of her life and later approach her death. Lucia's flashbacks reflect her emotional state (dizziness, nausea, instability, nakedness) conveyed by the use of a bare light aimed at her face. The sequence of the intruding flashbacks into the present action develops a rhythmic montage for the film viewer's experience. This contrast in poignant flashbacks compounds a mechanistic rhythm reflected by the floating amusement park merry-go-round and multiple dance and sexual scenes. The circular ride is a central image of the film, condensing the eroticism of suspension with a blend of children's normal excitement, pleasure, and extreme frightfulness. We see the same short skirts and socks worn by the suspended little girls in the camp who were used as targets on a floating amusement park ride. [Cavani seems to be referring to the merry-go-round just outside the Warsaw Ghetto during the evacuation.] This scene is a sexualized sadistic shooting gallery captured by Max's camera. The flashback also displays sado-masochism (Freud, 1920). "Every pain contains in itself the possibility of a feeling of pleasure." The flashback suggests the rhythm and circularity of Max and Lucia's re-enactment and the horrific machinery of the Nazi's amusements. In another scene, Max sadistically teases the naked Lucia by shooting at her as she runs back and forth in an elongated room. Thus Lucia is shot at three times, including her final shooting on the bridge. Max is also shot at by the ex-Nazis when he walks on his balcony. They suffer near constant jeopardy of being murdered by the Nazis.

To divert from the description and interpretation of *The Night Porter* (Edwards, De Simone, & Cavani, 1974), Freud and others spawned various theories about the complexity of sadomasochistic behavior. Freud (1905) discussed the development of sadomasochism as a personality trait on a continuum to a perversion as a fixation and a hypertrophy from a partial component drive, here a combination of sadism and masochism. Freud (1915) saw masochism as aggression turned against itself in response to guilt from oedipal and anal-sadistic strivings and from castration fears. Sadomasochism and other perversions can serve as defenses from preoedipal fears of merger, diffusion, and annihilation. Freud paired the instincts of sadism and masochism as two intrinsic sides of a coin. Masochism is defined as sexual behavior that includes conscious sexual arousal and pleasure during the experience of pain or humiliation—sexual masochism. When either pain or humiliation is a requirement for maximum sexual arousal, the behavior becomes a sadomasochistic perversion. In contrast, in a masochistic personality disorder one's whole character is organized around the hidden search for suffering or disappointment without the action of an overt sadomasochistic relationship. Both forms include prominent self-defeating behavior, often including hidden gratifications. In his 1920 paper, *Beyond the Pleasure Principle*, Freud described the intimate linking of masochism with aggression from the superego.

Chasseguet-Smirgel (1985a, 1985b, 1986) describes the employment of a regressive "anal universe" that includes perversion with the malignant narcissism of the organized perversion. Kernberg (1991) said that his view of sexual excitement as a basic affect is akin to Erikson's (1963, p. 334), describing "infantile sexuality in terms of modes and modalities of object relations implied in the activation of zonal excitation. It serves as a defense against further development of genital sexuality to avoid oedipal threats including incest and castration."

In recent years sadomasochism is described as an internalization of both roles in their object relations. The reversal of roles as master–servant also contributes to the bisexual theme as Lucia dances topless in a Nazi uniform stimulating the Nazi officers, heterosexually and homosexually. The connection between cruelty and sexual instinct is derived from the need to subjugate the object because of the innate aspects of libido for every pain contained in pleasure. The pain and suffering of masochism may be the condition or price paid for any kind of pleasure or success. Kernberg (1991, p. 342) states that severe pain may intensify the attachment to the inflictor of pain and that the element of aggression is combined with the eroticization of the painful experience.

> It is as if one of its functions is the neutralization of aggression by incorporating it into the very fabric of sexual excitement. The

> unconscious identification with the aggressor linked with the erotization of pain facilitates sexualization of primitive omnipotence, a primitive condensation of love and hatred.

Eidelberg (1959) wrote of the factor of the magical control of the object and Lowenstein (1957) spoke of it being an attempt at "seduction of the aggressor" (p. 215). Others have connected masochism with an attempt to preserve a tie to an object with whom one has suffered in childhood. Kernberg (1991) describes sadomasochism as the potential for erotic masochism in both sexes linking an early capacity to combine aggression with the libidinal sexual excitement. Sexual excitement is a basic affect that overcomes primitive splitting of love and hatred. In this form of sexual excitement yearnings for symbiotic fusion and for aggressive penetration are combined. He also emphasizes bisexual identification and the desire to transgress oedipal prohibitions and the secretiveness of the primal scene and the violation of boundaries of a teasing and withholding object.

The film's intimate sadomasochism with Lucia's complicity, her willingness to reengage with an SS officer in the Holocaust rather than display revulsion to him, appalled many critics who could not recognize its underlying messages and artistry. Perhaps these critics had to deny any acknowledgment of sadomasochistic interest in themselves and project their self-condemnation onto the film. To them, this film implies a seeming complicity with and condoning of the atrocity of the Holocaust. The revulsion in some viewers is fed by unwillingness to recognize the universal potential for a sadomasochistic gratification, especially for someone like Lucia who is both internally and situationally so corrupted and debased yet gratified and saved by Max. Identification with Lucia is blocked. Although the film was praised by film critics, filmmakers, and intellectuals in Europe, it was savaged in the U.S. Critics bypassed its complex psychological, historical, and artistic fabric. It was described as a sadomasochistic thriller, romantic pornography, and hypnotically repellant. Critics begrudgingly acknowledged its technical mastery but placed Cavani in a snug fit between Visconti and Bertolucci, implying that it was nothing but a competent imitation of her (male) masters. It was termed "Next Tango in Vienna in Nazi uniforms" (Morandini, 1974, p. 71). Visconti ironically called it "an atrocious, cruel and terrible film that leaves you breathless!" (Marrone, 2000, p. 107).

Cavani's first major film endeavor was a four-part documentary series on the Third Reich shot in the early 60s. When she was commissioned to do a special on women in the Resistance, she interviewed many survivors. One non-Jewish partisan who had been confined for three years in Dachau spent her summer vacations near the camp, returning to the sadomasochistic experience. Another partisan woman who survived Auschwitz, chose to live nearby in very low-rent housing. She could not go back to her husband and children because she was treated like a wretch and made to feel she was an embarrassment, a reminder of something too disturbing. After the war this woman was shocked to see that others functioned as though nothing had happened, trying to forget anything unpleasant or sad, instead of radically changing their views and behavior. She became ashamed of having survived and thus serving as a stinging memory of what others wanted to forget. She was deeply disturbed by this forgetting by others because in the camp she had discovered the depth of her own nature, what good and, more importantly, what evil [stealing] she was capable of, emphasizing the word evil. She could not forgive the Nazis for making her aware of this capacity, saying to Cavani that she should not expect to be always innocent, because a victim is also a person. The director thus filmed a story that took human nature to the limits of credibility through sadomasochism made possible by the extreme situation in which the principles find themselves along with sadomasochistic proclivities. While filming a documentary in a camp:

> Bad weather had forced to a halt. Sitting under an umbrella in the mud she saw a smartly dressed woman walking through the drenching rain carrying a sheaf of red roses, and she watched as the woman searched among the sights of the long-demolished huts where the prisoners had been held. In time she found the place for which she had been looking, the brick angle, flushed to the ground, of the huts foundations, and knelt there placing the roses on the spot, and remained, head bowed, in the rain for a few moments, then rose and walked away. With Cavani in pursuit, she caught up with the woman "who had obviously come to mourn her family" but soon … found a more intriguing story than she had anticipated. There had been no family. She was not Jewish. She came back, she said, every year on the anniversary of her lover's death. He was a member of the SS, she was a girl who had been imprisoned for holding Socialist beliefs, and having a well known Socialist father.

> The hut foundation, where she placed her roses, were the site of the one in which she had been imprisoned; the day was the anniversary of the day on which her lover had been executed by the liberating Americans. She lived now in America and came back here every year on that day. It was simply told and unemotional. She left in the rain, leaving Cavani with a story which haunted her for months. What, she though, would have happened if the SS man had *not* been killed? Had escaped and gone to ground like so many others, and years later, in some unexpected place, at some unexpected time, the two had met again? What then? She wrote *The Night Porter.*
>
> (Bogarde, 2013, p. 185)

Primo Levi in *Survival in Auschwitz* (1969) described the "Gray Zone" in which depravity, cruelty, and inhumanity were taught and learned as a form of adaptive behavior necessary for survival. Victims felt extreme guilt about their aggressivity and competitiveness and stealing from other inmates and suffering with survival guilt. This guilt can lead to a masochistic character structure organized around a hidden search or a disappointment, suffering, or self-defeating behavior described by Freud as "moral masochism." Reik's (1939) idea of a fantasy of "victory through defeat" extends to the extremity of the Holocaust situation with sadomasochistic reengagement and death.

Seven months before his suicide, Levi, in an interview with Philip Roth, spoke of the "beautiful distillation, the reduction to the essential" and his own exceptional spiritedness while in Auschwitz.

> I had an intense wish to understand, I was constantly pervaded by a curiosity that somebody afterwards did, in fact, deem nothing less than cynical. Like a naturalist who finds himself transplanted into an environment that is monstrous, but new, monstrously new.
>
> (Roth, 1986)

Levi spoke of a friend who said that "your remembrances of before and after are in black and white; those of Auschwitz are in Technicolor." Levi agreed, saying that

> family, home, factory are good things in themselves but they deprive me of something that I still miss: the fascination for adventure.

> Destiny decided that I should find adventure in the awfulness of a Europe swept by war.... I found myself as uprooted as a man could be. Certainly, I suffered but this was far more compensated afterwards by the fascination of adventure, by human encounters, by the sweetness of convalescence from the plague of Auschwitz.
>
> (Roth, 1986)

His experience includes some aspects of dissociation. Other survivors, like Lucia and Max, never again feel at home in the world.

In her essay, "Fascinating Fascism" (1975), Susan Sontag says that:

> Fantasies about uniforms suggest community, order, identity (through ranks, badges, and medals ...). But SS uniforms convey a particularly powerful and widespread sadomasochistic fantasy because the SS was the ideal incarnation of fascism's overt assertion of the righteousness of violence, the right to have total power including sexual power over others. It is enhanced by serving and identifying with the hierarchy cumulating in the master, Hitler, and sadistically treating victims as absolutely inferior and disposable. They acted out in a singularly brutal and efficient manner, and dramatized it by aligning themselves to certain aesthetic standards.

The stiff uniforms were stylish and well-tailored, and promoted rigid posture. "The SS was designed as an elite military community that would be not only supremely violent but also supremely 'beautiful,'" suggesting a splitting (Sontag, 1975).

> Never before in history was the relation of masters and slaves realized with so consciously artistic a design. Sade had to make up his theater of punishment and delight from scratch, improvising the décor and costumes and blasphemous rites. Now there is a master scenario available to everyone.

In opposition to the aestheticization of the Holocaust, Theodore Adorno declared that "to write poetry after Auschwitz is barbaric" (Adorno, 1949, p. 34).

In *The Night Porter* (Edwards, De Simone, & Cavani, 1974), after her liberation, Lucia experiences a loss of intimacy with the idealized Max and with sadomasochistic gratification. Lucia would have wondered if Max had survived, and, in the surprise of finding him, would have accentuated the longing to reestablish a sadomasochistic relationship. Previously she wards off death by Max's selection and protection of her as long as she pleases him. She would feel sexual excitement and mastery while dressed in Nazi regalia in her earlier exhibitionistic topless dancing and singing like Marlene Dietrich for the mesmerized officers. She then reverses the victim role by controlling the officers whom she arouses but frustrates both heterosexually and homosexually. In other dancing scenes the ex-Nazi Bert is paid by Max to dance for him in a partially sublimated homosexual enactment, indicating a homosexual current; Bert also dances for the Nazi officers. In the barracks Lucia watches two male inmates in a sexual encounter. Max injects drugs into Bert's buttock.

As in the story of Salome, Lucia's dance culminates in the shocking presentation to her of a head of an inmate. She had complained about him to Max and only asked to have him transferred. He, as pseudo-protector and without empathy, sadistically and assaultively shocked her by his "gift." But it also served as a warning to her if she did not completely abide by Max's wishes. According to the Jewish historian Josephus, in the first century, Salome was the daughter of Herodias and stepdaughter and niece of Herod Antipas, ruler of Galilee. In the Gospel of Mark (6:14–29) and in Matthew (14:1–12), Herod imprisoned John the Baptist for condemning his marriage to Herodias, the divorced wife of his half-brother because it violated Mosaic Law. Herod was afraid to have the popular prophet killed. By promising to give her whatever she asked, Herod convinced Salome to dance before him and his guests at a festival. Because Herodias was enraged by John the Baptist's condemnation of her marriage she pressured Salome to demand the head of John the Baptist on a platter. Salome presented the head on a platter to her mother. The story was popular in Renaissance art and in a Strauss one-act opera, originally scripted as a play by Oscar Wilde. Herod thus lusts after Salome while Salome desires John the Baptist. She kisses the lips of the severed head of John, who has spurned her. An erotic symbol in art, she dances the provocative "dance of the seven veils," which ultimately ends in her nudity.

Lucia's immense survivor guilt is another motive for leaving her husband and for recreating the dangerous Lager with Max. Not only does she survive, but in contrast to the other inmates who were being deprived, humiliated, tortured, and exterminated, she exercised power and was gratified, excited, and narcissistically indulged. Intertwining herself again with Max partly expiates this guilt as she chooses to "arrange" her own death by the ex-Nazis. Her body thus becomes the scorecard of her trauma (van der Kolk, 1987).

Furthermore, her subjugation to extreme trauma in the Lager contributed to her vulnerability to repeat the fatal sadomasochistic disaster. She feared being beheaded and other forms of annihilation and was victimized by Max's extreme sadism in shooting at her and forcing her to dance topless in a Nazi uniform. Her sense of self, the quality of her object relations, her affect tolerance, her reality testing, and her secondary process thinking were impaired. Freud (1920) wrote that trauma leads to a breech in the stimulus barrier or protective shield of the ego, which is overwhelmed and loses it mediating capacity. He also described the vulnerability to potential traumatic dangers from the feeling of helplessness, including the fear of the loss of the object upon whom the infant has become dependent and the fear of the loss of the love of the object whose approval has become central to the child's sense of well-being. Lucia suffered a loss of trust in the value and safety of civilization. Shengold (1989) wrote of "soul murder," resulting in the child's loss of separate identity, an incapacity to love maturely and find joy in life, caused by seduction, overstimulation, cruelty, indifference, and/or neglect.

The Night Porter (Edwards, De Simone, & Cavani, 1974) illustrates Freud's repetition compulsion, or "fate neurosis," the compulsion to repeat distressing, painful situations often without recognizing one's participation. This compulsion is sometimes motivated by the wish to master the experience of loss as it manifests in the repetition of children's play. It is a means of transforming traumatic events from passive threats to active mastery. Freud saw the repetition compulsion as a derivative of the ultimate aim of a progressive "Death instinct" the return to an inorganic state, as this film's mutual deaths exemplify. In *Beyond the Pleasure Principle* (1920) Freud contrasted the life drive (*Eros*) aiming to preserve life, build organic complexity, and synthesize in opposition to the death drive (*Thantos*) which aimed to "undo connections and so to destroy things." Freud initially believed that the death drive operated with the Nirvana (or inertia) principle, the tendency to disburden the mind of energy. In 1930, linking it to aggression, he described it both working silently toward the self and directed outward in the destructiveness of hatred and sadism. The Kleinians used the death drive to explain both the seductive pull toward mindlessness and feelings of triumph and excitement in destruction of self and object, not only on an interpersonal level but in the outside broader level, exemplified in the Holocaust, other genocides, and war.

In conclusion, Max feels trapped by the other Nazis and enthralled by Lucia. By returning to the exhilarating Technicolor of her unique status and sexual power in the midst of the horrific, Lucia relives the intoxicating intensity of her sadomasochistic gratification. But at the same time they arrange to fatally punish themselves in this repetition compulsion.

Susan Sontag's last sentence in "Fascinating Fascism" (1975) is: "the color is black, the material is leather, the seduction is beauty, the aim is ecstasy, the fantasy is death."

References

Adorno, T. (1949). Cultural criticism and society. In *Prisms* (pp. 17–34). Cambridge, MA: MIT Press, p. 34.

Bertolucci, G. (Producer), & Bertolucci, B. (Director). (1970). *The Conformist* [Motion Picture]. Italy: Mars Film, Marianne Productions, Maran Film.

Bogarde, D. (2013). *An Orderly Man*. London: Bloomsbury.

Cavani, L. (Director), & Edwards, R. G., & De Simone, E. (Producers). (1974). *The Night Porter* [Motion picture]. United States: Embassy Pictures.

Chasseguet-Smirgel, J. (1985a). *The Ego Ideal: A Psychoanalytic Essay on the Malady of the Ideal*. New York: Norton.

Chasseguet-Smirgel, J. (1985b). *Creativity and Perversion*. New York: Norton.

Chasseguet-Smirgel, J. (1986). *Sexuality and Mind: The Role of the Father and Mother in the Psyche*. New York: New York University Press.

Eididelbert, L. (1959) Humiliation in masochism. *The International Journal of Psychoanalysis*, *71*, 279–289.

Erikson, E. H. (1963), *Childhood and Society* (2nd ed.). New York: Norton.

Freud, S. (1905). *Three Essays on the Theory of Sexuality. Standard Edition, 9* (pp. 123–243). London: Hogarth Press.

Freud, S. (1915). Instincts and their vicissitudes. *Standard Edition, 14* (pp. 109–140). London: Hogarth Press.

Freud, S. (1920). *Beyond the Pleasure Principle. Standard Edition, 18* (pp. 1–64). London: Hogarth Press.

Kernberg (1991). Sadomasochism, sexual excitement and perversion. *Journal of American Psychoanalytic Association*, *39*(2), 333–362.

Levi, P. (1969). *Survival in Auschwitz* (Trans. Stuart Woolf). New York: Collier.

Lowenstein (1957). A contribution to the psychoanalytic theory of masochism. *Journal of American Psychoanalytic Association*, *5*, 197–234.

Marrone, G. (2000). *The Gaze and the Labyrinth: The Cinema of Liliana Cavani*. Princeton, NJ: Princeton University Press.

Morandini, M. (1974). In portiere troppo chiacchierato. *Tempo*, August 2, 1974; reprinted in *Il portiere di note*. Rome: Itanlnoleggio Cinematografico, 1974.

Reik, T. (1939). The characteristics of masochism. *American Imago*, *1*, 26–59.

Roth, P. (1986). Philip Roth talks to the Italian writer Primo Levi about his life and times. *London Review of Books*, *8*(18), 17–19. Retrieved from www.lrb.co.uk/v08/n18/philip-roth/philip-roth-talks-to-the-italian-writer-primo-levi-about-his-life-and-times.

Shengold, L. (1989). *Soul Murder: The Effects of Childhood Abuse and Deprevation.* New Haven, CT: Yale University Press.

Sontag, S. (1975). Fascinating fascism. *The New York Review of Books*, February 6, 1975, *22*(1). Retrieved from www.nybooks.com/articles/1975/02/06/fascinating-fascism/.

Turim, M. (1989). *Flashacks in Film*. New York and London: Routledge.

Van der Kolk, B (1987). *Psychological Trauma*. Washington, DC: American Psychological Publishing.

Chapter 9

To know or not to know?

Common themes in *Ida* and *The Flat*

Emanuel Berman

Introduction

In November 2015 I participated in panel discussions of two films at the Eighth European Psychoanalytic Film Festival in London: Arnon Goldfinger's *The Flat* (Goldfinger & Kufus, 2011) and Pawel Pawlikowski's *Ida* (Abraham, Dzieciol, & Pawlikowski, 2013).[1] I was deeply moved by these films when I first saw them, and greatly admired the creative power of both directors; but initially I saw them as utterly different—in genre, style, and content.

Gradually, however, through repeated viewings and discussions, I realized that they do have common themes: the multiple ways in which massive defensive processes—particularly dissociation, repression, and denial—color and distort the memory of traumatic experience, and more specifically the memory of the extermination of Jews during World War II;[2] and the emotional upheavals resulting from the return of the repressed or the reconnection with the dissociated, among victims, perpetrators, and their next generations alike.

Let me start with a brief discussion of each film separately, and subsequently elaborate the common themes.

The Jewish nun: Pawlikowski's film *Ida*

At the beginning of this Polish feature film we meet Anna (Agata Trzebuchowska), a young woman at a Polish convent, who appears utterly dedicated to Catholic religion, wishing wholeheartedly to become a nun. It seems she has no memory (of any family life), and no (carnal) desire, just a spiritual non-conflictual dyadic fantasy union with Jesus Christ. Against the background of her sheltered and limited life, becoming a nun may be a necessity, not a free choice. Possibly this is what motivates Mother Superior to insist that Anna must meet her only living relative—her unknown aunt—before taking her vows. Anna feels no such need, but goes along with the request.

The meeting dramatically changes Anna's emotional world. Very quickly she learns of her Jewish roots, of her family's fate during the Nazi occupation of Poland (not long before, the year is 1962)—a heavy load of personal prehistory, which introduces a new option for recovered memory. In addition to exposing her to her original identity as Ida Lebenstein, her aunt Wanda (Agata Kulesza) attempts to arouse in her femininity and desire ("I won't let you waste your life"), an attempt that meets Anna's deep ambivalence.

Aunt Wanda introduces a new potential role model. This new model is exciting, but also disturbing. At some moments Anna/Ida is lured by the new life-options this model offers, and could identify with it; but at other moments she is appalled and deterred. Wanda's femininity appears to be expressed in casual one-night stands. She drinks heavily, at times dangerously. We gradually figure out that both her affectless sexuality and her alcoholism are post-traumatic manifestations.

We also learn that Wanda is a communist, who in the postwar years played an important role in Poland's judicial system, persecuting the enemies of the new regime and sending some of them to their deaths. Her senior position during the Stalinist period now belongs to the past (she was demoted to a marginal role of a provincial judge), but may have left traces of guilt. However, as the plot thickens we realize that guilt may be even more central element in Wanda's emotional life, because her valiant role as a fearless partisan in the anti-Nazi underground during the war may have heavily damaged her own family. Her beloved sister (Ida's mother), her brother-in-law, and Wanda's own little boy were murdered by the Polish peasants who initially gave them shelter, but eventually became too threatened by the Nazi determination to execute any Poles who help the persecuted Jews. Little Ida, who was blonde (and as a girl could not be identified as Jewish—her cousin was circumcised and therefore doomed), was handed to the local priest and sent to the convent.

In attempting to uncover the details of their tragic family history, Anna/Ida and Wanda—momentarily united—encounter the anti-Semitic undercurrents of Polish society. Peasants ask for Anna's blessing, but they might have betrayed her had they known her true Jewish identity as

Ida. The Church turns out to be less pure and honest than it pretends to be; the local priest denies any knowledge of Anna/Ida's origins, covering up his own role in her life. After Anna/Ida and Wanda manage to uncover the circumstances of the murder of their loved ones, they bury their remains in a Jewish cemetery.

Anna/Ida searches for a better life, but the film offers no easy solutions. New memories and new desires arouse conflict, not tranquility. The protagonist rarely verbalizes her thoughts, but her expressions seem to indicate that she absorbs all her new experiences and struggles to integrate them into a fuller and more multi-dimensional identity.

Anna/Ida returns to the convent, but postpones taking her vows, probably needing to digest the discovery of her deeply repressed past. Meanwhile, Wanda cannot tolerate the harsh renewed awareness of her tragic history, and commits suicide.

Anna/Ida comes to her funeral and to her empty apartment. She momentarily steps (both literally and metaphorically) into Wanda's shoes, but seems to realize they do not fit her. She drinks, she smokes, she starts a love affair with the young musician Lis (Dawid Ogrodnik) whom she got to know when traveling with her aunt. They contemplate a life together, but she soon leaves when her lover is asleep. She may be on her way back to the convent, but the film ends before she reaches it, so the ending is deliberately open-ended.

The period covered by the plot may be seen as an intense period of initiation into adult life for Anna/Ida, who is forced to abandon her naive and idealized adolescent world view but clearly wishes to broaden her understanding of life and of history without sacrificing her humanity and honesty. The unique circumstances make this challenge more intense and immediate, a condensed version of coming of age.

The film is both very specific in its exploration of recent Polish history and of Polish–Jewish relations, and most universal in its portrayal of the development of the identity of a sensitive young woman in a conflict-ridden and stormy world.

Unheimat: Arnon Goldfinger's film *The Flat*

The Flat (Goldfinger & Kufus, 2011), an Israeli documentary film, opens with a universal situation: grandmother Gerda dies at age 98, and her children and grandchildren gather in her apartment, trying to empty it.

Naturally, opposite impulses appear: some wish to do it quickly and efficiently, keep just a few pretty and amusing items ("linking objects," as Volkan [1981] called them), get rid of all the old letters from people they never knew; others—like the director, one of the grandchildren—are more curious, see it as an opportunity to figure out parts of the family history that is barely known to them.

A unique cultural element is also crucial: Grandpa Kurt and Grandma Gerda Tuchler were immigrants. They left their native Berlin in 1936 and moved to Tel Aviv. It appears that they attempted to recreate Berlin in their new home. They kept furs, which surely were not needed in the Mid-Eastern climate. The books are mostly in German. Grandma never learned Hebrew, and her grandson communicated with her in English. They were part of a generation of German Jews who escaped their native country but remained deeply identified with it and with its culture. In a way, they no longer had a homeland—they came to have two non-homelands, "*Unheimats*,"[3] a situation that must be uncanny, "*unheimlich*" in Freud's (1919) vocabulary, a term that literally refers to the opposite of feeling at ease, "at home."

Whereas this may be the situation of many immigrants, an added factor colors this documentary film: not only were the grandparents forced to leave their original country, this country developed a murderous hatred toward them, and killed their family members who stayed behind. The contrast between the deep attachment and the painful wounds must have been unbearable. It appears to have mobilized rigid, powerful defenses.

Grandma's own mother, Susanna Lehmann—who insisted on staying in Berlin, and refused to join her daughter and son-in-law, even after she visited them in Tel Aviv in 1937—was murdered by the Nazis, but Grandma never told her own children about her horrible fate. And the children did not ask, they maintained the pact of silence. When a letter from that great-grandmother is found in the apartment, her granddaughter—the director's mother—appears embarrassed. The writer of the letter addresses her granddaughter Hannah (she was a little girl at that time), asking her to pray for her, but Hannah is unable to believe it, and keeps saying this letter must be from another person and cannot refer to her.

The wish not to know, we learn later on in the film, is shared by the children of the victims and by the children of the perpetrators. "Where illusion reigns supreme, curiosity is felt to spell disaster" (Britton, 1998,

Figure 9.1 Hannah reads her grandmother's letter in Arnon's presence (from *The Flat*).

Source: courtesy of Arnon Goldfinger.

p. 37). Only the next generation may be able to become curious and inquisitive, and start asking the tough questions.

The toughest question relates to the most dramatic discovery of the film: the warm relationship that could be maintained secretly between some Jews and some Nazis, even after the horrors of the extermination period became fully known. Goldfinger and his family find in the grandparents' apartment old Nazi newspapers documenting a visit of a high-ranking Nazi official, Von Mildenstein, in Palestine in 1933; and it turns out that Grandpa—on behalf of the Zionist Federation of Germany—and Grandma accompanied that Nazi and his wife on their trip. The trip was actually part of the Nazis' search for solutions for what they viewed as the "Jewish problem" in Europe, before the "Final Solution" of mass murder was chosen.

This is unsettling, but even more unsettling is the discovery that not so long after the end of World War II, the friendship between the Tuchlers and the Von Mildensteins blossomed again, culminating in many warm meetings in Germany, joint tourism, and exchanges of gifts. This renewed friendship was kept secret from family and Israeli friends alike.[4]

The director follows in their footsteps, and visits Edda—the daughter of Von Mildenstein—and her husband Harald, who host him cordially.

But the pleasure of this new surprising bond is marred by Edda's need to deny the Nazi identity of her beloved father and see him as an innocent journalist, even though Goldfinger's thorough research gradually documents that Von Mildenstein remained part of the Nazi apparatus throughout the war, as a department head in Goebbels's Ministry of Propaganda .

What forms of massive denial and splitting made all this possible? Was some kind of identification with the aggressor in operation among the victims? Or perhaps a grandiose wish to bypass historical reality, to maintain an alternative subjective reality based on blind idealizations? Or a desperate need to find confirmation of one's lasting German identity (on the Jewish side), and to overcome guilt and achieve some reparation and forgiveness (on the German side)? Does it imply striving for a fantasy world governed by illusion, in which evil is not acknowledged?

Goldfinger's powerful film makes no pretense to supply clear answers, but it raises these questions in an open and courageous way.

Trauma and its aftermath: victims and their offspring

In their divergent styles, these two films—one a subtle work of fiction, the other a strictly factual documentary—explore the fate of two European Jewish families in the shadow of the Nazi era. In one family, the Lebenstein family, Polish Jews, a young couple and their little nephew are butchered by Polish peasants fearful of Nazi retribution after they helped these Jewish neighbors to hide; the survivors are the woman's sister and her orphaned niece. In the other family, the Tuchler-Lehmann family, German Jews, the mother is murdered in a Nazi concentration camp, while her daughter and son-in-law settle in Palestine before World War II breaks out, and are survived by numerous children and grandchildren in Israel and in the U.S. At the core of both films we find the dilemmas and turnabouts of memory and its avoidance. Let me start with the victims and their descendants.

At the beginning of *Ida* (Abraham, Dzieciol, & Pawlikowski, 2013), young Anna seems to have no interest in her family background. "Do I have to, mother?" she asks the Mother Superior when the latter tells her to meet her unknown aunt before taking her vows. It seems that her early childhood experiences are utterly repressed; though it can be argued that the disjointed fragmentary visual images and sounds with which the film opens point to her traumatic background, expressing disturbing residues of lost memory, unconsciously present but represented vaguely (Dudai, 2015).

When Aunt Wanda tells her of her Jewish identity and shows her old family pictures, she appears to be mostly perplexed. Similarly, Wanda herself appears restless and impatient in their first meeting, and ends it abruptly, in line with her refusal in past years to accept the invitations from the convent to come for her niece. She rationalizes this avoidance as resulting from her duties as a senior prosecutor and her lifestyle, but we can understand that she is attempting to disconnect herself from the traumatic past, especially from the murder of her family members, while her life as a partisan was saved.

Wanda's survivor guilt focuses on the death of her little boy, when she was not there to protect him; practically abandoning her niece is a continuation of that earlier abandonment. When showing her niece old family photos (such photos play a role in both films) she avoids identifying the boy. Only later in the day she apparently regrets sending Anna/Ida back to the convent so speedily, and she fetches her from the bus station.

This act makes a more intimate conversation between them possible, and it results in their joint project of trying to decipher the exact circumstances of the death of their close family members, and to discover their grave. It is evident that Wanda had made no such attempt before, even though her powerful position in the Stalinist years would have made it quite feasible. Her brutality as a prosecutor (she was nicknamed "Bloody Wanda"; the English subtitles change this title erroneously to "Red Wanda") can be understood as a displaced vengeful rage, and her alcoholism and promiscuity as post-traumatic reactions functioning to avoid painful memories and guilt.

The joint mission is accomplished successfully, but Wanda's subsequent suicide suggests that this fuller contact with the trauma was more than she could bear. In the figure of Anna/Ida we can sense more hope for a future integration, making her more able to contain the wounds of the past.

Turning now to the protagonists of *The Flat* (Goldfinger & Kufus, 2011), Gerda Tuchler was evidently unable to deal with the murder of her mother Susanna, and she hid this tragic story from her children and grandchildren. When the director's cousin interviewed her about her life, she pretended not to know the fate of her mother, and the cousin felt asking more about it would be too intrusive. Survivor guilt may have played a role too, even though Susanna would have saved her own life had she accepted the desperate appeals of her daughter and son-in-law to stay with them in Palestine and not to return to Germany after visiting them as a tourist in 1937. There is no indication of Gerda and Kurt attempting to find out more about Susanna's fate during their numerous visits to Germany after the war. Their need to reestablish their German identity and German ties apparently took precedence.

Defensive denial (probably conscious) is evident in an interview Gerda Tuchler gave to an Israeli magazine in the 1980s. When asked about their tour of Palestine in 1933 in the company of the Nazi leader Von Mildenstein and his wife (also named Gerda), she added proudly that right after the war her late husband Kurt refused to resume contact with Von Mildenstein, who wanted him to help in clearing his name. What she did not disclose was the fact that a few years later this friendship was indeed reestablished and it flourished for many years.

Turning now to the next generation, Gerda's daughter Hannah (who was born in Germany and came with her parents to Palestine as a little girl) collaborated for many years with the repression and denial in her family. When Hannah's son Arnon (the director) asks her about it, she says: "I never asked … I wasn't interested," and then adds: "I don't really care about what happened many years ago." Her impulse is to throw away the old letters stacked in her grandparents' apartment. Goldfinger—who insists on keeping and reading those letters—comments that his was a "family with present only."

Parenthetically, political currents contributed to the disengagement with the painful past both in Poland and in Israel. Many Polish communists, like Wanda, were deeply dedicated to the creation of "a new Poland"—hopefully free of the shadows of nationalism and anti-Semitism—after the war. Many Israelis like Hannah were deeply dedicated to the establishment of "a new Jewish nation"—hopefully free of the tragic fate of persecuted diaspora Jews—in Israel. The utopian aspects of both communism and Zionism, both of them cultivating the illusory "New Person Fantasy," may have eventually backfired (Berman, 1988, 2000, 2010); but this is another topic.

Returning to *The Flat*, one of the most powerful scenes in the film is the one in which Arnon reads to his mother Hannah the letter of her grandmother Susanna, written not long before Susanna was exiled from Berlin to Riga and then murdered by the Nazis. "I hope sweet little Hannah remembers Grandmother," she writes, and then asks Hannah "to keep praying for Grandma—so God will help." Hannah appears to desperately ward off what she hears: "It's not from her…" she claims; and then in another attempt, "There was another Hannah in the family." When Arnon insists that it is her Grandma's letter, addressing her, she only says: "Interesting." This scene gains added weight when we see a photo taken in 1937 in Tel Aviv, portraying Susanna, Gerda, and the little girl Hannah together.

As discussed in the film, only the third generation—indeed represented by the director Arnon Goldfinger himself—can break the pact of silence. But as the film progresses, Hannah changes, joining her son's search for the truth about his grandparents and their friends, the Von Mildensteins. In the last part of the film the two of them travel together to Germany and become a fearless investigative team, resembling in some ways Anna/Ida and Wanda at the peak of their collaboration.

Perpetrators and their descendants

In *The Flat* (Goldfinger & Kufus, 2011) the German side is consistently characterized by denial: conscious forging of historical truth by the father, a more complex and probably unconscious pattern concerning his daughter.

Leopold Von Mildenstein (1902–1968) was a Nazi activist since 1929. In the 1930s he headed the Department for Jewish Affairs of the SS, and hired Eichmann to join it. Later on his pro-Zionist views (support of Jewish immigration to Palestine) were rejected by the Nazis and he left that position, but—as Goldfinger documents—he joined instead the Propaganda Ministry headed by Goebbels. After the war he became the press officer of Coca-Cola in Germany. In 1956 several British newspapers described him as a former Nazi; he sued for libel and won the case. But this flat denial was no longer possible after the Eichmann trial in 1961, in which Eichmann himself discussed Von Mildtenstein's role in the SS.[5]

Edda, his daughter, who lived in Britain for 30 years, relies on the successful libel suit as proof of her father's innocence; she reads the verdict published by *The Times* triumphantly. She explains that her father spent the war years as a journalist traveling around the world. She condemns the Nazis, but is very proud of her heritage, of her family tree starting in 372. Arnon—with whom Edda and Harald form a warm relationship against the background of the past bond between their families—hesitates for a long time about confronting her with the bitter truth. Eventually he shows her the handwritten CV submitted by her father, located in the National Archive, which remained inaccessible for decades in the former East Germany. In this document Von Mildenstein states that in 1938 he became department head in the Nazi Ministry of Propaganda.

Edda is perplexed, and cannot give up her idealized image and her blindness. "I don't quite believe that," she first says. "This gives nothing," she subsequently states. Yes, she wants to know the truth, but "I wouldn't know where to start." And finally: "I'd like to see different sides of it … Anything else?"

In *Ida* (Abraham, Dzieciol, & Pawlikowski, 2013), it becomes clear quite early on that the Skiba family—Catholic Polish peasants who hid the Lebensteins in the nearby forest—must have eventually murdered them. Wanda mostly suspects the aging and ill Szymon Skiba, who was

Figure 9.2 Edda reads her father's incriminating CV, in Arnon's company (from *The Flat*).

Source: courtesy of Arnon Goldfinger.

the head of the family during the German occupation. She and Anna/Ida visit the former Lebenstein home, now occupied by the next generation of the Skiba family. The younger Skiba denies everything bluntly: "No Jews ever lived here." We know he is lying. But when they locate old Szymon in the hospital and put pressure on him, his son appears and offers Anna/Ida a deal: he will bring them to the grave, they will leave the father alone and make no attempt to retrieve the family property. She agrees and apparently convinces her aunt too.

The deal seems mostly motivated by the son's wish to let his father die in peace, and by his fear of losing their home. But at the secret grave in the forest, when digging out the remains of the victims, he unexpectedly confesses that he was the one who murdered them. He appears troubled; the feeling is that some guilt and remorse finally became possible, after being warded off for years.

The reception of the films and their significance

The Flat (Goldfinger & Kufus, 2011) was warmly accepted both in Israel and in Germany, among other countries. German analysts screened it on several occasions, inviting the director to participate. I assume that this interest is related to a coming of age of German culture and German psychoanalysis, which in earlier decades had great difficulty with handling openly the Nazi era (see Moses & Hrushovski-Moses, 1986).

Israeli culture also went through a radical change, which according to some scholars started around the Eichmann trial. In the 1940s and 1950s the wish to let go of the traumatic past was prevalent, along with the contemptuous attitude toward "passive diaspora Jews" who supposedly "went like sheep to the slaughter," and were seen as the very opposite of the active and courageous "New Israeli Jew." Psychiatrists often disregarded the traumatic burden of the survivors who came to Israel. The ambivalent attitude toward the survivors is powerfully portrayed by a story written in 1980, "The Witness," by Shulamith Hareven (1930–2003). In this story a boy who barely survived the war in Europe comes to a kibbutz and is condemned as a liar when he talks about the atrocities he witnessed. An ideologically committed teacher (the unreliable narrator of the story) makes all possible efforts to convince him that in order to become "one of us" he must stop dwelling on the past and should instead orient himself only to the future.

Ida (Abraham, Dzieciol, & Pawlikowski, 2013), which was admired around the world and awarded an Oscar, aroused mixed reactions in Poland. Many critics praised it. But there were also protests. A Jewish critic commented that according to this film Polish Jews have only two options: suicide or conversion to Christianity; paradoxically, this implied demand for "a positive example" in art brings to mind the cultural climate of the Stalinist period. Wanda's figure was seen by some as anti-Semitic. From an opposite angle, certain journalists protested that the film portrays the Poles as murderers, instead of identifying the Nazi occupants as the real villains (Mroz, 2015). This multiplicity of opposing viewpoints surely supports the view that subjective transferential responses play a major role in any interpretation of literature and film (Berman, 2003).

The view of *Ida* (Abraham, Dzieciol, & Pawlikowski, 2013) as anti-Polish is related to the storm aroused in Poland a dozen years earlier by Jan Tomasz Gross's (2001) book *Neighbors*. In that book the Polish-American historian explored the 1941 massacre of the Jewish population of a small Polish town, Jedwabne, by their Christian Polish neighbors. The book split Polish society into two camps: in liberal and left-wing circles the book was praised as stimulating truthful awareness of Poland's complex past, of Poles being both victims and perpetrators during World War II; in nationalistic right-wing circles the book was condemned as distorted and anti-Polish (Polonski & Michlic, 2004). Gross was awarded the Order of Merit of the Republic of Poland in 1996 by Polish president Kwaszniewski. Recently, after the nationalistic Law and Justice party won the 2015 elections, it has been proposed that the award should be revoked, and some demand Gross be prosecuted for libel.

Against this background, it is not surprising that when *Ida* was shown on Polish television early in 2016, a caption was added stating that numerous Poles rescued Jews during the Nazi occupation. This is indeed true; but the need to counterbalance the film this way proves that the issues of wanting and not wanting to know, so powerfully portrayed by this film—as well as by *The Flat* (Goldfinger & Kufus, 2011)—are far from resolved today.

Notes

1 I am grateful to my co-participants in these two panels, Gabi Bonwitt, Arnon Goldfinger, and Shimshon Wigoder (discussing *The Flat*), Ian Christie and

Matilda Mroz (discussing *Ida*), as well to the Festival's organizer, Andrea Sabbadini.

2 I deliberately avoid the word "holocaust." I view the popularity of this term, originating in theological discussions of ceremonial sacrifice (Patraka, 1997), as an unfortunate historical distortion. It gives the horrible reality of the systematic Nazi persecution and murder of European Jews a pseudo-spiritual significance utterly foreign to the experience of the victims, and it can be viewed as an expression of denial regarding the arbitrary brutality of that genocide. The Hebrew word "Shoah" (meaning a great disaster) is free of these forced theological connotations, but is less widespread in the English-speaking world.

3 This term, and additional points in this section, were suggested by Shimshon Wigoder.

4 Bonwitt (2015) sees this friendship as an expression of the German–Jewish negative symbiosis (Diner, 1990) created by World War II. He compares it to the Arendt–Heidegger friendship also resumed after the war.

5 A detail not mentioned in the film is Von Mildenstein's subsequent claim for immunity as a CIA agent, which was neither confirmed nor denied by the CIA.

References

Abraham, E., & Dzieciol, P. (Producers), & Pawlikowski, P. (Director). (2013). *Ida* [Motion Picture]. Poland: Solopan.

Berman, E. (1988). Communal upbringing in the Kibbutz: The allure and risks of psychoanalytic utopianism. *Psychoanalytic Study of the Child, 43*, 319–335.

Berman, E. (2000). The utopian fantasy of a New Person and the danger of a false analytic self. *Psychoanalytic Psychology, 17*, 38–60.

Berman, E. (2003). Reader and story, viewer and film: On transference and interpretation. *International Journal of Psychoanalysis, 84*, 119–129.

Berman, E. (2010). My way. *Psychoanalytic Inquiry, 30*, 116–132.

Bonwitt, G. (2015). Discussion of "The Flat." 8th European Psychoanalytic Film Festival, London.

Britton, R. (1998). *Belief and Imagination*. London: Routledge.

Diner, D. (1990). Negative symbiosis: Germans and Jews after Auschwitz. In P. Baldwin (Ed.), *Reworking the Past: Hitler, the Holocaust and the Historians' Debate*. Boston, MA: Beacon Press.

Dudai, R. (2015). The trauma speaking its own margins. Presented at the Tel Aviv Institute of Contemporary Psychoanalysis.

Freud, S. (1919). The "uncanny." *Standard Edition, 17*, 217–252. London: Hogarth Press.

Goldfiner, A. (Producer & Director), & Kufus, T. (Producer). (2011). *The Flat* [Motion Picture]. Israel: Ruth Diskin Films.

Gross, J. T. (2001). *Neighbors*. Princeton, NJ: Princeton University Press.

Moses, R., & Hrushovski-Moses, R. (1986). A form of group denial at the Hamburg Congress. *International Review of Psychoanalysis*, *131*, 175–180.

Mroz, M. (2015). Discussion of *Ida*. 8th European Psychoanalytic Film Festival, London.

Patraka, V. M. (1997). Situating history and difference: The performance of the term holocaust in public discourse. In J. Boyarin & D. Boyarin (Eds.), *Jews and Other Differences* (pp. 54–78). Minneapolis, MN: University of Minnesota Press.

Polonski, A., & Michlic, J. (Eds.). (2004). *The Neighbors Respond.* Princeton, NJ: Princeton University Press.

Volkan, V. (1981). *Linking Objects and Linking Phenomena.* New York: International Universities Press.

Chapter 10

Inheriting Nazism

Reflections on the film *Two or Three Things I Know About Him*

Régine Waintrater

Introduction

> The fathers eat the sour grapes, but the children's teeth are set on edge.
>
> —Ezechiel 18:2

After the war, a wall of silence fell upon Germany. For several lengthy years, a kind of iron curtain shut out speech and blocked off history: history in the big-H sense, but also familial history experienced day by day in the privacy of homes, where the fathers and mothers had been adolescents or adults under Nazism. For the wartime generation and the one born after, exploring the past remained impossible. It was too recent, unapproachable. Any questioning or confrontation was barred. Germany, vanquished and destitute, harnessed itself to the work at hand: rebuilding materially. We know how successfully and rapidly Germans accomplished that goal, which demanded repression bordering on foreclusion in the Lacanian sense. Denazification, imposed from the outside, did not open up any space for questioning. Rather, it held examination of the past at bay. For many, intergenerational dialogue never took place.

Two or Three Things I Know About Him

The film I shall discuss here, *Two or Three Things I Know About Him*, (Svarcová & Ludin, 2005) premiered in Berlin in 2005. It provoked much debate, proving, as though it were necessary, that Germany's recent past is far from having been digested. The film's director, Malte Ludin, was born in 1942 in Slovakia, where his father, Hanns Ludin, had served as ambassador and minister of the Third Reich. Arrested at the end of the war, Hanns Ludin was hanged in 1947, when Malte was a mere five years old. In this film, the director sets off in search of a father he hardly knew, sifting through official documents, archives, family papers, and conducting interviews with relatives and witnesses. Most of the latter were Jewish victims of his father.

Barbel, Ellen, and Andrea, who accompany us throughout the film, are Malte's three surviving sisters; an older sister, Eri, and a brother, Tilman, had already died. All were born under the Third Reich, some before the war, others during the conflict. Thus they belong to "the 1.5 generation," the term Susan Suleiman (2002) uses to designate those too young to have taken active part in events of the war, but old enough to have memories of them.

In one scene of the film, Ludin opens a family album. We are treated to a close-up of adorable blond children similar in age, all lined up. They smile at the camera with an innocence all the more startling since we know what will ensue. As the images and interviews unfold, we become acquainted with the three surviving sisters, nephews, and nieces, as well as some who have died: not only the elder brother and sister, Eri and Tilman, but also their mother, Erla, who departed this world in 1997 at the age of 92. The director confesses that he "would never have dared to make this film during her lifetime," and adds ironically, "She lived quite a long time."

A typical German story

This film presents the typical story of a German family, as the director himself puts it. We see how his search for truth runs up against his family's denial. Obstinately, sometimes brutally and inquisitorially—and despite the pain it causes him—he attempts to lift this denial. Ludin makes himself into the historian not only of a family but also of a period that continues to reverberate in the lives of his fellow citizens. A pact of denial was the rule, on the collective as well as the individual level.

The pact of denial, as defined by René Kaës, is an unconscious alliance that "condemns to repression, denial or disavowal ... and keeps unrepresented ... whatever could question the formation and maintenance of a relationship" (2003, p. 32). Essentially, it is the treatment accorded to negative elements and their transmission. Here, the negative element is the Nazi past, and the pact of denial is the means whereby two generations of an entire people managed to keep silent regarding the legacy they held. Silence, repression, and denial caused a break in filiation, keeping far from thought anything having to do with that period of history.

German psychoanalysts Alexander and Margarete Mitscherlich (1967) interpreted this denial by German society as a strategy to avoid sinking into melancholia. The unconscious process went thus: "if we in Germany were to deny the events of the Third Reich, their consequences need not be acknowledged." Not recognizing consequences allowed the generation of adults under Nazism to keep from examining the past and admitting guilt. Failure to accept consequences likewise served members of the generation after; thereby, they could elude the reality of having criminal parental figures and maintain a necessary idealization of their parents.

The pact of denial let both generations escape confronting an unpleasant reality and kept at bay pain caused by the loss of idealizations and the resultant ideations that can de-structure personality. By treating Nazism as a natural catastrophe that had stricken the German people, the collective attempted to surmount the collapse of the strong ego represented by Hitler. Deprived of a tradition, unable to hold onto tarnished and officially disavowed ideals, Germans after Nazism threw themselves into their day-to-day activities. One can say that the German economic miracle was built on avoidance of reality. The psyche of those involved did not remain unharmed.

The encounter between personal and collective history

Ludin's film confirms Freud's assertion that in psychic life nothing vanishes; everything is conserved one way or another and is destined to reappear (1912–1913). Though presented as a general documentary, the film traces most of all the strategy one particular family develops to deal with a legacy we would be tempted to call a curse. Most emphatically, this is not just a film about a family or a chronicle of private life. Whatever is private here has been marked by the collective, and the collective dimension is required in order to externalize what is private.

As in many German homes, the private life of this family was constructed around rejection of anything on the outside that could reveal the unbearable truth. Thus the filmmaker looks toward the outside to escape his family's isolation and find what he is seeking. By addressing his film to the public, he introduces a kind of third party into what until then had remained confined to the familial sphere.

Any psychic or social catastrophe affects the mental space not only of the individual but also of the groups to which he belongs, destroying the institutions that constitute the basis of those groups. The subject, deprived of the usual recourse to mediating agencies, requires a third to restore to him the nullified intermediate space. Here, the central third is the director's wife, whom he met after the fall of the Berlin Wall. Born in 1962, thus well after the war, in Bratislava where the director himself came into the world and which was also the scene of his father's crimes, filmmaker Eva Svarcova is unequivocally "on the victims' side." Close enough to his origins, but far enough from the past of the German people and his family, she underpins the entire making of the film. Simultaneously, she contains the rush of emotions but demands he go further, accompanying him in his labor of reappropriation, transformation, and creation, and never yielding to the siren call of denial. Throughout the film, the "he" who speaks becomes an "I" addressing an "us," through the mediation of the Other, personified by his wife.

The task of any familial group is to articulate and perpetuate itself, permitting the individuation of the subjects who compose it. Perpetuation requires transmitting, beyond the death of individuals, a familial ethos embodied by them, made up of values, myths, and history. Verbalization provides an interface between the external world and the familial core, in a permanent process of exchange and transformation of events experienced. These two functions contribute to the chain of signifiers without which the subject cannot construct his identity. When a break occurs in that linkage of meaning, an alteration is observed in the capacity of the group and its members to work through what has happened. The event that has caused that breach weighs heavily on the subject, rendering impossible the psychic and mental task of working-through.

In such cases, "rough objects of transmission"—psychic contents that remain omnipresent due to their never having been thought or represented—are transmitted in diffracted, partial form, subject to splitting and denial: "words, verbalizations, strange and oft-repeated expressions … Such transgenerational débris becomes toxic vestiges that occupy the familial and individual psyche" (Granjon, 1989). No space is left for sharing. Individuals are isolated, abandoned to solitude within a group, a loneliness that can be lifted only at the cost of attempting to rip away from the group and thereby risk shattering it or oneself. In shooting his film, Malte Ludin knows he is taking a risk: that of being left out of the family or wrecking it. He confronts the risk with the willfulness of a man who knows he has no other choice.

Film credits as genesis

The opening credits plunge us directly into the dilemma of self-individuation versus family loyalty. The film opens in the middle of a conversation in which the eldest sister, Barbel, a classically elegant figure, expresses her disapproval of her brother's endeavor and proclaims her right to "see my father as I wish to see him." Her off-screen interviewer, who we presume to be Malte Ludin, tries to argue that this question goes beyond her feelings toward their father. Barbel reasserts her position, obstinately and angrily; throughout the film, she will not waiver. The responsibility she feels is to defend her father's memory, in a loyalty that nothing—official documents or photos—can assail.

On the screen, archival images and well-known Nazi emblems skillfully scroll before us, as we hear a man's voice uttering these chilling words: "This is the story of my father, a war criminal. It is the story of my mother, my sisters, my nephews and my nieces." A uniformed Nazi dignitary, baby-faced, stares at us while the voice continues: "It is a typical German story." The irony of the last sentence is underscored by dissonant, farcical trombone notes that will sound every time the Nazi past and its symbols are shown.

The tone of the film is thus set at once. This sequence *in medias res* is followed by an unusual formal opening. We are immediately transported into the aisles of what appears to be a storage area brimming with voluminous files. On its floor appear the title of the film and the credits. As Mihal Friedman convincingly notes (2009), this presentation immediately underscores the link here between the private and public spheres, a link that will continue to be suggested, enhanced, or even brought into being by the expert montage. Far from merely illustrating what is said, the cinematographic articulation here functions as a language in its own right. By fostering associations, it inspires a multiplicity of reactions on our part that we imagine to be shared by the filmmaker. Voiceovers, documents read before the camera, conversations, and interviews are the means whereby Ludin invites us to join him on his voyage to his father. The pace of the film may be compared to that of a psychoanalytic cure.

After the abrupt opening sequence and the credits, the conversation with Barbel shifts without transition to the subject of how she learned of her father's death from her brother Tilman. What remains most vivid is her mother's bursting into tears, an obviously traumatic scene for the little girl she was at the time. In turn, Ellen tells us of how she became aware of her father's shameful death: from schoolyard playmates who mocked her. Andrea, the youngest, was simply told that her father fell on the battlefield.

Family loyalties and defense strategies

The diverse protagonists' portrayals, elaborated through details recorded during exchanges with their brother, illustrate perfectly the multiplicity of psychic reactions in the face of a common legacy. Each contributes a particular element to the defenses that shield them from the history of which they are the product. Their differing attitudes, ranging from defenses of the most rigid kind (denial and foreclusion) to more flexible ones (such as rationalization), can be charted on a gradient, so clearly does each embody the aspect of the familial strategy that he or she was assigned—without their necessarily being conscious of it.

The notions of delegation and loyalty, as defined in the field of family therapy, are particularly enlightening in the case playing out before us. It is worth noting that these concepts were developed in large part by a German psychiatrist, Helm Stierlin, whose theories were the direct result of clinical work undertaken with German families after the war. The notion of delegation uncovered by Stierlin stands at the heart of the intergenerational relationship (1977). Delegation is necessary to the construction of identity, for it inscribes the subject in a relational process at once horizontal and vertical. However, it can become pathogenic, especially when a conscious or unconscious conflict obtains between the mission entrusted to the subject and his individual development. Loyalty, as described by Ivan Böszörményi-Nagy, may be viewed as an extension of delegation, wherein emphasis lies on the process that links the subject to his familial or some other group (1973). While delegation gives meaning to the subject's life, loyalty represents the relational ethics linking generations together. In this sense, we can say that transgenerational transmission is entirely governed by the phenomena of delegation and loyalty; they are the very conditions of its existence.

Delegation and loyalty often act unconsciously in the case of heirs to a group trauma. They are forced into an allegiance of which they can free themselves all the less, the more it operates unbeknownst to them. The way the Ludin family functions is paradigmatic of such an allegiance that extends undifferentiatedly to all generations, in a morbid repetition that hinders the labor of thought and individuation each family member must accomplish.

Mother Erla is the archetype of the Nazi female, a beautiful, athletic, healthy Aryan who remains unshaken in her convictions. The two segments where she speaks allow us to understand the major role she played in her husband's life. She provided him unflagging support, even encouraging him to go on at moments of doubt such as occurred with the elimination of the SA, which he escaped only thanks to his close relationship with Hitler. Deeply disturbed by the murder of his comrades, Hanns Ludin considered abandoning his career. Evoking that moment, Erla accompanies a frightful phrase she utters with a little smile to the camera: "I just about said to him: 'Hanns, you can't make an omelet without breaking eggs.'" She viewed her husband as an honorable man to the very end, and portrayed herself as the widow not of a criminal, but of a hero.

In another segment of the same interview done by a TV director, she recounts how at Bratislava, where her husband was stationed during the war, the Swiss ambassador's wife confided to her that she was sheltering a Jewish child she had saved from Auschwitz. When Erla asked what Auschwitz was, her interlocutor replied with astonishment: "Don't tell me you don't know. It's where they gas the Jews." Returning home she queried her husband, who responded: "Auschwitz is a weapons factory." Not batting an eyelash, Erla adds: "All of us knew nothing, my husband included."

Even though Ludin did not conduct this interview, his use of it supplies nonverbal cues that further his point. The smiles and gestures accompanying Erla's account show the pleasure she takes in evoking a past that she never reconsiders in the light of historical information garnered later. The discomfort the viewer feels in the presence of this nostalgic old woman, indifferent to what occurred around her, no doubt reflects the unease her own son experiences. More than explicit words could do, the close-ups he offers of her, which capture all her facial expressions, force us to pose the questions he cannot ask. What Erla fails to admit comes out through her silence, which endows her words with the force of testimony.

In the interview he conducted a year before her death, his mother appears weakened by her advanced age, but as firm as ever in her convictions. In that respect, she is no different from other Nazis, who rarely expressed any regret other than for having been defeated. It is striking that in the presence of his haughty, distant mother, Ludin—capable of such incisiveness with his sisters—stays in the grip of an icy respect. After all, has he not admitted he could not have made this film during his mother's lifetime? Erla is the perfect embodiment of the certainties and lies of the generation complicit in Nazism. To the very end, she seems to have remained a mystery to her son. Without going so far as to assert, as Mihal Friedman does, that the film could have been called *Two or Three Things I Know About Her*, I find that his mother's unshakeable faithfulness to Nazi ideals remains an unresolved question for Ludin.

The three sisters appear as a subgroup charged with defending the family memory, in the face of a brother who looms before them, and sometimes before us, as a prosecutor drawing up a list of charges. From the beginning, Barbel implicitly appoints herself spokeswoman for the family's honor. Refusing to acknowledge the reality of documents and arguments her brother presents, she remains attached to the figure of a father noble and loyal to a cause that cost him his life. She sees her father as a victim. The only wrong he committed was to allow himself to be tricked by an omnipotent father figure who turned out to be weak and unreliable: the Führer, who dragged down with himself honorable men who stayed faithful to him. She echoes the words of her father, which we hear quoted at the film's start, in a voice-over: "I cannot consider myself guilty." He thus identifies himself as a miserable, vanquished man, radically reversing the figures of victim and executioner, as did many Germans who lived under the Nazi régime.

Throughout the film, Barbel opposes her brother. When the latter, in a scene difficult to watch, dissects all the euphemisms she employs to designate extermination, we see how denial operates to allow her to reject evidence. When her brother brandishes the document, signed by their father, that ordered the deportation of Jews from Slovakia, Barbel shifts her glance and continues her monologue exculpating their father; she claims he could not have known the fate to which he consigned those people. Not for a second does she fail in the mission she has assigned herself, forcefully rejecting her brother's arguments. He sometimes loses his calm in the face of her denial.

In comparison to Bardel armed with certainty, Ellen, a younger sister, appears less radical and open to doubt. The close-ups of her repeatedly wringing her hands or smoothing the fringes of her shawl, her choked voice, and her moist eyes make her inner conflict clear. She is torn between family loyalty and an awareness from which denial can no longer protect her. The interviews show her as a powerless victim of fate, resigned to never knowing a truth she refuses to seek. The youngest sister, Andrea, who might seem to be freer and more "modern," refuses no less than the others to see her father as a criminal, and becomes truly angry when her brother dares to doubt the authenticity of a document asserting that her father saved some individuals. Of the three sisters, she is the hardest to grasp, the most ambiguous.

Eri and Tilman, now deceased, are made present in their absence through their evocation by those near to them. Eri, the eldest sister, so close to her father, seemed never to have gotten over the shock of his death. From the description her daughter Alexandra offers of her, we discover that she sank into alcoholism and that her self-destructive conduct led to her divorce and death. Regarding the latter, nothing is explicitly stated, but in researching the family I learned that she had committed suicide in a way particularly horrible and traumatizing for those nearest to her. We may wonder why Ludin does not reveal her end. Was it because of feelings of shame or pressure from the others to remain silent?

From the scrutiny she applies in the book she published on her family, we see just how much Eri's daughter has meditated on her mother's fate and the problematic familial relations. To her mind, her mother could never deal with seeing her beloved father as a criminal. His shameful death represented a double abandonment for her. She was abandoned by the father she knew as a child, and she had to renounce her idealization of him as a hero. This is a hallmark of the conflict experienced by many children of Nazis.

For his part, Tilman found a way out of this dilemma by leaving the family home at 16 and going off to live in South Africa. As before, a daughter's voice—that of his daughter Astrid—tells us that Tilman never breathed a word about his father's story, even though he kept on his desk a photo of himself as a child in the arms of a uniformed man, whom he identified as his uncle. Astrid asserts having respected her father's silence, all the while knowing that the picture actually showed her grandfather. We discover as well that Tilman was a voracious reader of books on the Nazi period, which indicates a solitary obsessive search for the truth. Had he learned of his brother's film project, she maintains his reaction would have been: "Better that he, and not a stranger, make the film." And he would have expressly requested that his children "be kept out of it."

Do the questions themselves bear guilt?

On the whole, as lively as the interaction becomes, the film never falls into caricature. The director's sometimes indignant or accusatory tone does not preclude his expressing empathy and affection for his sisters. He shows them in all their complexity and contradictions, thereby making us actually feel attached to them.

Ludin puts himself in the position not of observer but of full family member. Even as he takes on the mission of breaking silence and ending denial, he does not place himself on a pedestal, but instead makes us privy to his hesitations and evasions. Thus, in his voice-over, he comments on his own successive stances regarding his father, which in earlier years went from veneration to hatred. "At the outset, as was the case for many Germans, my father was a war hero … In the sixties, he became a criminal, a Nazi pig."

Then came the fall of the Berlin Wall in 1989, followed by his meeting the woman whom he would marry. Understanding the importance of the role he was to play, Ludin admits that his cut-and-dry positions had often become an embarrassment or an irritation to himself. Like his sisters, he attempted to sneak around an all too brutal reality. An example of this attitude on his part occurs in the scene where he meets a Jewish poet from Slovakia, whose parents and young sister were murdered by the Nazis. Ludin's revelation to him of his father's identity constitute a greatly effective moment in cinematographic terms; Ludin hems and haws in the survivor's presence. When the latter says, "So, your father sent my family to their death," Ludin, despite himself, offers rationalizations, arguing that his father was simply carrying out orders from above. Thus he takes the tired line of defense Nazi functionaries used. Later on in the film, he discusses the scene and the shame he feels at his own evasiveness.

In a process analogous to psychoanalytic treatment, Ludin searches for himself even as he sometime resists his own discoveries and insights. We see this at the beginning of the film, as he reads a letter addressed to the prosecutor by his father, beseeching the judges' indulgence "for the sake of his honor and the honor of his children." The purposefully neutral tone he assumes melts away when he reaches the sentence, "I cannot plead guilty," which he repeats four times, first ironically, then scornfully, and finally choked with rage. This son cannot resign himself to read that phrase, the sole testament from a father about whom he adds: "Throughout all my research, I kept hoping I'd find something that would get him off the hook." The wish to absolve his father, a wish he shares with his sisters, remains present, even though he chooses to confront a truth from which the others flee.

In another sequence, we see him taking on the responsibility of dealing with the explicit denial of their father's guilt. In deliberately dramatic fashion, the scene contrasts two simultaneous and totally opposite experiences. On the one hand, there is the elder sister Barbel, who evokes her childhood in their beautiful home in Bratislava, "an aryanized house," in which the Ludin family happily spent their days. On the other hand, Professor Stern, who teaches at a Czech university, recounts how his family had to leave the neighborhood and hide among peasants. Starting at age three, he spent several years ensconced in a stable, condemned to complete silence. The joyous atmosphere of the Ludins' childhood, recalled innocently by Barbel, juxtaposed with the terror experienced during the same years by Professor Stern, shows us the courage the director needed to work through the guilt and shame that his family refused to feel.

The contribution of cinema to history and to psychoanalysis

Far from simply presenting information on what had happened, the cinematographic narrative here performs a collective construction of an aesthetic and psychic experience that helps us better understand the multiple links between an individual psyche and the world around it. The visual dimension offered by cinema, a dimension that written media cannot provide, allows for a multiplicity of narrative structures, which

Ludin employs to transmit to the viewer the complexity of the questions he approaches.

Thus his use of archives, documents, and letters shows us how he had to proceed to reveal the family's story. Over and again, he is filmed reading and sifting through documents, in an exemplification of his quest. One section of the film is entitled "The Crate of Sorrows" (*die Kummerkiste*); this is the name the director gives to the box in which the family kept all the items relating to their father: letters, weapons, military decorations, photos. As we see the filmmaker searching through the contents, forcing the trunk to cough up its secrets, we realize to what extent his film is an unveiling, an opening-up of the closed suffocating space of the familial past.

For historian Arlette Farge, "the cinematic experience enables the historian to widen her narrative field, the better to approach a past reality, one that is crisscrossed with gaps and strange discontinuities" (1998, p. 125). Cinema allows tension to be maintained among different loci and temporalities, thus opening new spaces for interpretation. This dimension cannot fail to evoke Freud's notion of the "return of visual residue" (1923) as a privileged manner of entry into thought processes.

However, I find Wilfred Bion's theory of the work of thought to be more useful in proposing an analogy between working with visual images and the work of the cure (1967). It is worth noting that Bion's theories of thought and group processes built upon the basis of his experience as a military officer and army psychiatrist during the two world wars (1961). Bion saw early functioning of thought as relying first of all on visual formations, before hearing and words come into play. The emergence of cognitive activity originates through the senses, and visual images are at the very onset. Bion thus hypothesizes that conscious thought is linked to sensory perception and sees the cure as the place where associations between knowledge and emotional experience are woven and restored. For him, knowing is simultaneously affect and perception (1977).

The future of a generation

The dialogues here with the husbands and wives of sisters, nieces, and nephews can teach us much about the processes whereby transmission of a legacy takes place. The husband from whom the deceased Eri has divorced, and Barbel's and Ellen's spouses, assume positions analogous to those of their wives. Barbel's husband shares his wife's denial, whereas Ellen's spouse tries to apply shades of meaning and cannot make up his mind. It is the divorced husband of the deceased Eri who confronts the past most radically; while not condemning anyone directly, he minimizes no responsibilities. It is worth noting that he had studied abroad and thus escaped the climate of collective denial in postwar Germany.

The relationship that their children's generation maintains with the family's history is not characterized by denial; it is freer but also more distant. Familial narratives and legends are met with far less massive strategies of delegation and loyalty. Once again, this freedom owes much to the collective climate in Germany, which by their time had partially lifted the denial on history. Unlike their mothers and fathers, who had to struggle to regain trust in their own parents, the youth of the new generation did not experience such conflict. Those implicated were "only" their grandparents, and all too common oedipal guilt did not come into play, even if the latest book of Harald Welzer on the subject shows it is not so easy even for the grandchildren (Welzer, 2002). Ludin shows us how various individuals face the challenges posed by that legacy, as each elaborates his or her own personal version of their family's history and deals with what is left unsaid. To conclude, let us recall the irony of fate that has given Barbel a Jewish son-in-law.

Conclusion

After years of research on extreme trauma, it appears to me that for the generations after, creativity can be a means of mastering and transforming the traumatic history they bear. To my mind, creativity embraces any kind of work, art, or thought that attempts restoration after transforming the family's and group's indelible history. Novelists, essayists, filmmakers, painters, but also witnesses try each in his or her own way to transform a legacy that has kept them from separating reality from fantasy, a hindrance that otherwise might have definitively crushed their ability to let their thoughts follow their own path.

By exploiting the very gaps in transmission, creativity is a process of working-through and anaclitic propping-up that can operate in the psyches of heirs to an individual and collective catastrophe. But for the unthinkable to be thought, there must be an Other to whom may be addressed what is being created. The Other opens the spaces of thought closed off by trauma, thereby sustaining the subject as he crosses over from fright and shock into artistic creation. Thus, heirs to silence may find the space that was lacking to them, occupied as it was by psychic contents that previous generations had not worked through. Creativity allows such contents to be transformed into symbolic objects that may be transmitted to and shared by others.

Nobody can be "insured against history." However, Ludin's well-wrought film shows us that one can, through treatment, testimony, or creativity, break the vicious cycle of passive transmission by working out one's history as a particular subject in order to occupy one's own place in the succession of generations. Such is the way, the only way, that the crate of sorrows can mutate into a treasure chest and not remain a coffin in which to bury lost illusions.

References

Bion, W. R. (1961). *Experiences in Groups*. London: Tavistock.

Bion, W. R. (1967). *Second Thoughts: Selected Papers on Psycho-Analysis*. London: William Heinemann.

Bion, W. R., (1977). *Seven Servants*. New York: Jason Aronson.

Böszörményi-Nagi, I., & Spark, G. M. (1973). *Invisible Loyalites: Reciprocity in Intergenerational Family Therapy*. New York: Harper & Row.

Farge, A. (1998). Écriture historique, écriture cinématographique. In A. de Baecque & C. Delage (Eds.), *De l'histoire au cinéma* (p. 125). Bruxelles: Complexe.

Freud, S. (1912–1913). *Totem and Taboo. Standard Edition, 13*. London: Hogarth Press (1955).

Freud, S. (1923). *The Id and the Ego. Standard Edition, 19*. London: Hogarth Press (1953–1966).

Friedman, R. M. (2009). The "Second Generation," a view from Germany: On Malte Ludin's *Two or Three things I Know About Him. History and Theory*, Bezalel, 14.

Granjon, E. (1989). Transmission psychique et transferts en thérapie familiale psychanalytique. *Gruppo, 5*, 47–48.

Kaës, R. (2003). Réalité psychique et souffrance dans les institutions. In R. Kaës (Ed.), *L'institution et les institutions*. Paris: Dunod.

Mitscherlich, A., & Mitscherlich, M. (1967). *The Inability to Mourn: Principles of Collective Behavior* ... http://germanhistorydocs.ghi-dc.org/sub_document.cfm?document_id=1049.

Stierlin, H. (1977). *Psychoanalysis and Family Therapy*. New York: Jason Aronson.

Suleiman, S. Rubin (2002). The 1.5 generation: Thinking about child survivors of the Holocaust. *American Imago*, *59*, 277–296.

Svarcová, I. (Producer), & Ludin, M. (Director). (2005). *Two or Three Things I Know About Him* [Motion Picture]. Germany: National Center for Jewish Film.

Welzer, H. (with Moller, S., & Tschuggnall, K.) (2002). *Opa war kein Nazi. Nationalsozialismus und Holocaust im Familiengedächtnis*. Frankfurt: Fischer-Taschenbuch-Verlag.

Chapter 11

Discussion

Nanette Auerhahn and Dori Laub

The language of film

In certain ways, of all the modes of representation, the visual, and cinematic in particular, comes closest to immediate experience and closest to the psychoanalytic attempt to achieve verisimilitude with the primary process, which primarily transpires visually, as we see in dreams. Waintrater notes that Bion saw early functioning of thought as reliant first of all on visual information, before hearing words comes into play. The formal qualities of films and the palette of techniques available to a filmmaker—such as flash cuts (as short as a sixth of a second), long tracking shots by a handheld camera, shifting angles of filming, movement to different times and places, interweaving of different periods that bleed into each other, color palettes that interpenetrate (Weinstein, Chapter 3), flashbacks that portray memories that provide motivation and explicate internal conflict (Sklarew, Chapter 1)—i.e. the language of film, all approximate the language of a psychoanalysis with its unencumbered flow of free associations from the unconscious, which is structured like a language (Lacan, 1953). Cinematic techniques like voice-over, documents read before the camera, and interviews, to name a few, are different modalities or dialects, if you will, of cinematic speech, which reveal character as surely as does free association allow entrée into the internal world of an analysand. Waintrater (Chapter 10) notes:

> Far from simply presenting information on what had happened, the cinematographic narrative … performs a collective construction of an aesthetic and psychic experience that helps us better understand the multiple links between an individual psyche and the world around it. The visual dimension offered by cinema, a dimension that written

> media cannot provide, allows for a multiplicity of narrative structures … to transmit to the viewer the complexity of … questions.
>
> (pp. 221–222)

Diamond and Jurist (Chapter 5) track the close relationship between cinematic technique and depiction of character in their analysis of the film *Hannah Arendt* (Brokemper, Rexin, & von Trotta):

> In the film, the multiple selves of Hannah Arendt are depicted through a complex interplay of image and dialogue, black-and-white archival footage interspersed with fictional scenes in color, present-time narrative intercut with past flashbacks, with each register amplifying, commenting on, and even contradicting the others. Each cinematic dimension provides another layer of meaning to Arendt's reactions to, and account of, the trial. It is this multiplicity of perspectives conveyed through a variety of techniques that makes the film a work of the creative imagination—one that inexorably draws us into the workings of the passionate thinking, creative intellect, and even unconscious of its intrepid and multifaceted heroine as she covers the Eichmann trial.
>
> (p. 98)

The questions that we address are: What is the specific relationship between cinematic language and trauma? What are the advantages of this primarily visual medium and what are its limitations? What does it reveal and what does it conceal? We suggest that films have much in common with dreams. A dream reveals conflict, instinct, and desire, but just as effectively obscures, hides, and erases, revealing defenses against knowing. Traumatic dreams are never exact replicas of trauma; each reveals attempts to cope, process, and move away from trauma. Every dream has a navel—a point that reaches into the unknown, beyond the reach of the attribution of meaning (Freud, 1900). So, too, with movies, with each failing to fully encompass and master the Real of the Holocaust.

Cinematographic techniques used to convey traumatic experience

Both trauma and film are encoded in imagistic rather than lexical modes of thought (Diamond & Jurist, Chapter 5). Images allow for representation of the vertical splits in trauma victims that indicate concomitant dissociative states and the existence of multiple selves, which have the purpose of holding the traumatic experience in a separate register, so that it does not destroy the mental apparatus and can be thought about and integrated at a later point. Film can convey trauma's affective experience without attempting to put it into words; indeed, it can convey what cannot be captured in words. Horror cannot be presented openly; sudden, absolute horror cannot be transmitted. Once shown, it disappears. Oblique presentation that arouses a sense of horror is achieved in films such as *Night and Fog* (Dauman, Halfon, Lifchitz, & Resnais, 1955) and *Son of Saul* (Rajna, Sipos, & Nemes, 2015) by desynchronization and disjunction between visual material, spoken words, and soundtrack, a suddenness of shifts, shocking quick transitions, switches back and forth from color to black and white to indicate different time frames, and abruptness and shortness of flashbacks (as short as four frames). All these replicate our experience of the traumatic and of shattered selves and shattered time. The viewer imbibes the trauma, feels overwhelmed, and instantly flees.

The only ethical response to trauma is bearing witness and transmitting information. The attempt to do so drives survival even while it is also a precondition (not a guarantee) of survival. Paradoxically, fully bearing witness is made impossible by the shutdown of symbolization in the trauma-impacted mind. There can be no single trauma narrative but, at best, successive expansions of a network of images that are continually symbolized and increasingly integrated into novel narrative contexts. The repetitive nature of an analysis, as well as the multiplicity of the language of films, allows for an unfolding of this process. Creation of a narrative is but one step in an ongoing, never completed effort at symbolizing trauma (Weinstein, Chapter 3). Creative works such as novels, essays, paintings, and films can be means of mastering and transforming traumatic history, but there must be an other to whom the work that is being created can be addressed. The other opens spaces closed off by trauma (Waintrater, Chapter 10). The trauma that bypasses the eyes and ears and goes straight to the brain can be conjured by the multimodal sensory elements of film, but can only be processed in the presence of an other, utilizing a symbolic system that can always only approximate representation. Something is always left unarticulated.

Psychodynamic interpretations

We cannot assume the truth of what we see and are shown precisely in part because what is shown is constructed for us and what we see is constructed by us—the former, as in Nazis' stagings (e.g. of Theresienstadt as a supposedly model camp, of the entrance to the gas chambers as a shower), is intended to create a certain effect while the latter is limited and circumscribed both by our defenses and by our inability to know. The inability to know is intimately connected to limitations to symbolization. With our psychoanalytic third ear, we hear via symptoms what is not only repressed but also what is not yet formulated, the latter in part due to deficit—the mind's limits regarding formulation of trauma, but also the psyche's limits, i.e. the unbearableness of knowing trauma. The survivor of trauma often refuses to know. This lacuna is equivalent to the navel of a dream, which defeats representation.

Hiroshima Mon Amour (Dauman, Halfon, & Resnais, 1959) explores questions such as one's capacity to truly see, metaphorically to know the experience of another's trauma, the veracity of memory, the questionable truth of the visual record, and concern with the distinction between living and dead, body and object. *Hiroshima* (Dauman, Halfon, & Renais, 1959) also represents a reworking of the filmmaker Resnais' traumatic memories of the Holocaust, induced during the filming and editing of *Night and Fog* (Dauman, Halfon, Lifchitz, & Resnais, 1955) (Weinstein, Chapter 3).

The Arendt film creates a space for the viewer to witness witnessing (Diamond & Jurist, Chapter 5), while *Six Million and One* (Fisher, 2011) explores variation among children of survivors in experiencing their parents' Holocaust history, which subverts generalizations. The totalistic trauma of being in the Holocaust has many individual meanings (Winer, Chapter 4). One reaction illustrated in the movie is the slow replacement of defensive anger by compassion and the experience of genuine feelings. *Two or Three Things I Know About Him* (Svarcová & Ludin) also illustrates the multiplicity of psychic reactions among different family members inheriting a common (Nazi) legacy. With perpetrators, even more than with survivors, only the third generation, the grandchildren, is capable of breaking the bond of silence and initiating a dialogue that faces the truth (Waintrater, Chapter 10).

But truths are screened out as well. Hannah Arendt, eager to cover the Eichmann trial in order to understand Eichmann himself, is unaware of the driving force underlying her passion—her need to make sense of her own experiences with Heidegger. Diamond and Jurist suggest that Arendt projects her sense of betrayal by Heidegger and her German colleagues onto the Jewish councils (Judenräte) who unwittingly assisted in the destruction of their Jewish communities. In *Ida* (Abraham, Dzieciol, & Pawlikowski), the promiscuity, alcoholism, and vengeful rage of the survivor Wanda serve to avoid painful guilt feelings and the experience of posttraumatic stress disorder (Berman, Chapter 9). Wanda cannot let herself mother her niece Ida or know how much she loves Ida and loved her son, because she is unable to know and work through her guilt at the boy's death, her rage at her sister, Ida's mother, for failing to protect the boy, and her unbearable sense of loss over her son's death. Instead, she punishes herself by living out a meaningless objectless sexuality deprived of the role of nurturer. She cannot let herself bring up a child, having failed to secure the life of her son, because she holds herself responsible for his death. She is not dissimilar to the pawnbroker in the movie by that name who remains deadened rather than experience inexcusable guilt and crippling shame regarding his failure to save his family. He resolves never to be vulnerable again by being engaged with other human beings. He cannot let himself know that he loves the boy who works for him, for fear that it would revive his love for his murdered children and, along with such love, the agony of loss and the gaping void of their absence.

The different essays in this book bring readers closer to the protagonists in the films under discussion by offering psychodynamic interpretations of their character traits and of their repetitious actions as seen in the films. Frequently, information that is not in the film is added in support of these interpretations. A good example is Diamond and Jurist's essay on Hannah Arendt. Diamond and Jurist draw on Arendt's other writings and biography to demonstrate convincingly and in fine detail how the film tells the story of Arendt's desire. The film

> provides us with a portrait of Arendt's psychic reality – that mélange of historical (both individual and collective) experience and fantasy, memory, wish and desire, past and present, that lies at the heart of both cinematic and psychoanalytic narrative.
>
> (Chapter 5, p. 87)

Diamond and Jurist put particular emphasis on the notion of passionate thinking—thinking without banisters, thinking about one's own thinking and that of the other—that must be pursued as an end in itself, transcending knowledge. This concept resonates with the present-day psychoanalytic concept of mentalization. Thinking entails being alive; thinking together is a form of survival.

Defense and the repetition compulsion

Trauma, as noted, initiates vertical splits into multiple, dissociated self-states. Additionally, defensive responses to trauma occur through horizontal splits—through trauma's repression, denial, disavowal, and reaction formation. In the Israeli movie *The Flat* (Goldfinger & Kufus, 2011), the producer's grandparents, the only survivors in the family, renew their close, prewar secret friendship with an ex-Nazi and his wife. This official had been involved in the persecution of Jews. The couples exchange gifts, visit together in Germany, and travel together without disclosing this to anyone. The grandmother pretends not to know about the fate of her mother, living out a fantasy of being a new person in Israel. The survivors act as if nothing has happened, perhaps gratifying a grandiose wish to bypass reality and live in an illusion. Or are they identifying with the aggressor?

The repetition compulsion is ubiquitous and leads to a fate neurosis originating in the death instinct. In most of the films under discussion, involuntary repetition and re-enactment of trauma along with defensive strategies employed to ameliorate its impact are the central driving forces of the plots. In *Ida* (Abraham, Dzieciol & Pawlikowski, 2013), Wanda's abandonment of her niece in the convent is on one level a repetition of her earlier abandonment of her little boy—of leaving him with her sister—but psychologically is a repetition of her experience of abandoning him to his death—of not being present to protect him. The murder of a child always represents a failure of the maternal figure to preserve life. Given this experience, Wanda could not believe in her capacity to sustain the life of her niece and therefore gave her up to a convent, thereby precipitating the loss of a Jewish child to Judaism, and hence initiating a figurative death of a Jewish soul—constituting for Wanda a repetition of her murderousness for which she punishes herself by living a soulless life alone and then suiciding when affect is reawakened. In *The Pawnbroker*

(Langer, Lewis, & Lumet, 1965). Sol repeats his failure to save the life of his son through the death of the Puerto Rican boy who befriends him. In *The Night Porter* (Edwards, De Simone, & Cavani, 1974), Luca and Max recreate the Lager and their intoxicating, sexualized, sadomasochistic master–slave relationship in it in the latter's beleaguered, impoverished apartment. Eventually, they both get themselves killed by ex-Nazis.

Intrusive memories that circle, bespeak, and cover over an absence

Winer, in his essay on *The Pawnbroker* (Langer, Lewis, & Lumet, 1965), emphasizes the intrusive nature of memories of trauma, which arise unbidden and are experienced as alien—not of one's own authorship. Many of these memories unconsciously sculpt the life of the dissociated self (Winer, Chapter 4), as seen in the brief, intrusive memories of the pawnbroker as well as the German lover in *Hiroshima Mon Amour* (Dauman, Halfon, & Resnais, 1959). In the latter film, scenes of Nevers and Hiroshima intercut. For Claude Lanzmann, the making of the film *Shoah* (Lanzmann, 1985) was a kind of hallucinatory voyage. Being

> a pioneer in the desolate ruins of the camps, 'spellbound, in thrall to the truth being revealed to me...I was the first person to return to the crime...
>
> (Portuges, Chapter 6, p. 126)

What is to be filmed is the very impossibility of filming itself. "What needs to be captured and bound is itself a gap in the experience of both time and identity" (Weinstein, Chapter 3, p. 59). "Hiroshima, much like the Holocaust, is an absence … unrepresentable in the usual forms: its memory exists only in the potential for action, or … written on the body as mutilation, as deformity" (Weinstein, Chapter 3, p. 62). The absolute horror can never be openly represented. It cannot be transmitted. Portuges (Chapter 6), in her discussion of *Son of Saul* (Rajna, Sipos, & Nemes, 2015), writes that one can sense this unrepresentability in the Sonderkommando's cinematic body, see it through the terrorized eyes of the main character Saul, see the crush of images, hear the hell of sound, feel the cadence of the narrative, but the narrative itself remains focused on an "absent subject".

Trauma as identity

Amidst destabilizing rage and powerlessness, one fears losing one's mind and identity. In an insane situation, wherein one cannot tell right from wrong or control one's actions, the experiencing "I" disappears and one becomes trauma. *Hiroshima Mon Amour* (Dauman, Halfon, & Resnais, 1959) explores the manner in which trauma becomes protagonists' identity. The lovers in the movie say to each other: "Hiroshima. Hiroshima, that is your name." "Your name is Nevers. Nevers in France."

Winer discusses how Sol Nazerman, in *The Pawnbroker* (Langer, Lewis, & Lumet, 1965), recreates the past because he can neither remember nor forget it, but holds on to it because it is experience that gives life meaning, bestowing the only truth that he accepts: never to be powerless again. The past confirms for Sol not only "This is who I am," but also, "This is why I am." To let go would mean feeling truly estranged. When life is no longer a possibility, death comes to be celebrated. Sol forges an unconscious Faustian bargain with his conscience—he is allowed to live as long as he agrees to remain dead. He is allowed sexual release, as long as he feels no passion (Winer, Chapter 4).

Levels of remembering and knowing

Most of the films discussed in this book do not deal with the Holocaust directly but rather with its aftermath. The exceptions are *Night and Fog* (Dauman, Halfon, Lifchitz, & Resnais, 1955) and *Son of Saul* (Rajna, Sipos, & Nemes, 2015). The others do not attempt to present what is not representable, but instead focus their lens on the manner in which survivors and their families deal with their horrendous, haunting, and fragmented memories. Thus, these movies are at least one step removed from the experience itself and focused on the ways the Holocaust is mirrored in the memory of those who survived or who were impacted by it. These movies reflect a stage or step in the never to be completed process of symbolization, a point on the continuum from the self becoming trauma to trauma being witnessed by a self.

What protagonists know can range from minimal conscious knowledge (cf. *The Pawnbroker* (Langer, Lewis, & Lumet, 1965) and *The Night Porter* (Edwards, De Simone, & Cavani, 1974) in which characters are targets of merciless, haunting flashbacks and move like automatons through unavoidable traumatic re-enactments) to re-enactments occurring as consciously willed but unconsciously determined life events (see *Ida* (Abraham, Dzieciol, & Pawlikowski, 2013) and *The Flat* (Goldfinger & Kufus, 2011) to the repetition and sublimation of unconscious conflicts (such as Hannah Arendt's wish to understand Eichmannn in an attempt to come to terms with her experience with Heidegger, or her possible projection of her own betrayal by Heidegger and her German colleagues onto the Jewish councils of Hungary). Protagonists may attempt to approach the traumatic and indeed to visit it, as in *Six Million and One* (Fisher, 2011), *Two or Three Things I Know About Him* (Svarcová & Ludin, 2005), and *Hiroshima Mon Amour* (Dauman, Halfon, & Resnais, 1959). In *Hiroshima Mon Amour*, trauma begins to be known by being relived in an immediate, intimate, sexual relationship.

Filmmakers create knowledge either implicitly via their structuring of the plot and building of the characters or explicitly through bringing individuals together, interviewing them, and having them interact and speak to each other (as in *Six Million and One* (Fisher, 2011) and *Two or Three Things I Know About Him* (Svarcová & Ludin, 2005). A next level of knowing resides in the authors of these essays who view the films multiple times, reflect on them, interview filmmakers, bring in additional sources of information, and draw on clinical expertise to psychodynamically interpret deficits, repetitions, and the multiplicity of defensive strategies.

But after all this, do we really know?

Screens and fetishes: the case of *Son of Saul*

Invariably, defenses and obstructions are major components of knowing trauma, extending as they do from total denial and dissociation to the creation of screen memories involving a conscious, fetishistic attachment to facts that is used primarily to defend against the Real (Weinstein, Chapter 3), to obscure the vision of the real past.

In all the films reviewed herein, there is an attempt to represent the Real through the Symbolic without descending into the barbaric, into Hell, which would inevitably cause us to look away. They follow the spirit of Claude Lanzmann who stated that had he found footage of actual gassing, he would have destroyed it. Even *Night and Fog* (Dauman, Halfon, Lifchitz, & Resnais, 1955) and *Son of Saul* (Rajna, Sipos, &

Nemes, 2015), the former a documentary and the latter a dramatization of the Holocaust itself, turn to the symbolic for denotation and connotation. *Night and Fog* engineers our imaginative reconstruction of the horrors of the Holocaust via metonymic signifiers: mountains of hair that are turned into cloth, human bones that are turned into fertilizers, a barbed wire fence, fingernail scratches on gas chamber ceilings made by people trying to escape, frenetically paced group scenes from the past and rapidly cut archival still footage in black and white, contrasting with the soothing, bucolic landscapes of the present sites where camps once stood, shot in Kodachrome color, an ironic description of the different architectural styles of watchtowers, the naming of people and cities from which deportations originated, and a voice-over that ceases when events become extreme. The atrocities themselves are not and cannot be represented. The accumulation of signifiers does not recreate the Holocaust but rather its signification. Against our will, our imaginations are commandeered to do the work of conjuring up the horror.

Son of Saul (Rajna, Sipos, & Nemes, 2015) is the only dramatization of the Holocaust in our series of films and the least removed from immediate experiencing. Its attempt to explore not displacements but the heart of the Holocaust represents a continuation of Lanzmann's *Shoah* which continually goes eastward until it reaches the central moment of the film—an interview with a Czech member of the Sonderkommando. *Son of Saul* (2015) picks up there. Mucci (Chapter 7, p. 162) writes:

> [T]he movie depicts a descent into Hell, as the protagonist approaches the interiors of the camp and enters the chambers of death: voices become cries, the light is reddish and dark, always murky and livid … [N]o sound track is in the movie, but the cries and multiple languages of this Inferno are the only "soundtrack" [added to the movie afterwards]. The camera portrays the face of the protagonist in a narrow field of vision as if the horror were to pass through his own personal view and bodily perceptions. We "become" Saul, the member of the Sonderkommando.

The Sonderkommando were the Jewish Geheimnisträger—the bearers of the secrets of death and destruction whom the Germans had chosen to lure victims into gas chambers with false entreaties to hurry lest their soup that was waiting get cold. These secret bearers heard (as we hear through them) victims' desperate banging on crematorium doors (along with shouts, screams, and agonized death cries), only to drag bodies to the crematoria to be burned. We see body parts, not recognizable faces, with people being referred to as pieces, in a narrowed field of vision amidst an auditory sensory bombardment by a confusing polyglot of languages, a multilingual word salad. We are in the dominion of death, which is always happening in the present and whose too-muchness engenders a fragmentation that is an attack on linking, parallel to this psychotic defense (see Bion, 1959) against the experience of whole ideas and whole affects that would otherwise be too huge to absorb. Trauma severs associations among memories, ideas, affects, and words, thereby sabotaging the ability to know.

The plot that moves the movie forward *appears* to be a redemptive one: Saul's unrelenting struggle to give a murdered adolescent a proper Jewish burial that includes recitation of the Kaddish, the Jewish prayer for the dead. Mucci posits that for Saul, performing the Kaddish and the sacred funeral rites acquires the meaning of symbolic immortality. "[R]ituals are the last stronghold for saving meaning and civilization through a cultural act" (Mucci, Chapter 7, p. 166). The ubiquitous presence of Saul's struggle *appears* to soften the impact of the Real as represented in the movie by an investment in prewar values that transcend the meaninglessness of the camp.

But all is not as it *appears*. Žižek (1992, p. x) posits the fetishist as a realist who clings to the fetish "to cancel the full impact of reality." He argues that the existence of the fetish allows the individual to pretend to accept reality, and that should the fetish be destroyed, reality emerges and the individual breaks down. Saul's obsession with (dare we say addiction to?) burying the boy can be understood as a kind of fetish or idol that stands for reality, directing our attention to facts and ideas, but also a barrier that stands in the place of reality, blocking our view and hiding what we dare not face directly. The interpretation of the reinstatement of values screens out what the victim and his witnesses are unable to cope with. A (movie) screen serves three different functions. It is projected onto; it filters, letting some materials through and others not; and it screens out.

Son of Saul (Rajna, Sipos, & Nemes, 2015) resembles an Escher painting whose perusal is unremarkable but whose close scrutiny reveals a disquieting failure of lines to meet at a common horizon and to exist on the same plane. Events in the movie are haphazard and due to chance: people move inexplicably from place to place; some are killed, and there appears to be no order or guiding principle for events. Saul moves from work detail to work detail; a boy may or may not be his son; a man tries to drown himself or instead is merely trying to retrieve his shovel; the man is killed, although he hides whether or not he is a rabbi, while a second man is killed after revealing he is a rabbi, perhaps thinking that will save him. Saul meets with a woman who may or may not be his wife, and so on. Events happen, rather than being organized by a purposeful plot. There is an illusion of purpose when in fact there is no purpose. The only plot propelling the movie in a particular direction (forward) is Saul's obsession with burying his son. On first glance, this quixotic quest appears to be a wresting of meaning from meaninglessness. It is a focus on ritual and civilized values that will survive the Nazi bestiality, and hence appears to be on a par with Saul's peers' plot to blow up the crematorium. On a first level, the viewer puzzles at Saul's investment in death, in contrast to his fellow inmates' attempt to live via a revolt. But, in fact, the members of the Sonderkommando knew that their revolt was doomed and that they would all be killed. Both Saul and his fellow workers then, in the face of death, were focused on dying, on their experience of death. More specifically, in the face of annihilation anxiety, one cannot face feelings of helplessness and hopelessness without either surrender to death (as was the case with the so-called Muselmen) or via the development of a fantasy of hope. In the face of total and certain annihilation, any fantasy that develops is psychotic, involving an inability to name feelings, an inability to distinguish reality from fantasy in the realm of the forbidden, the impossible, and the perverse, and a shift away from reality to soothing fantastic mechanisms. It is only when we relinquish the idea of a redemptive narrative and understand the death immersion of *l'univers concentrationnaire* that the discrepancies and lacunae of the movie make sense. For example, otherwise why would Saul forego participation in a rebellion that might lead to freedom only to bury a boy who is dead anyway?

Ostensibly *Son of Saul* (Rajna, Sipos, & Nemes, 2015) presents a valorization of the spiritual world via the rabbinic, when in fact a rabbi is not needed for a funeral and burial and the rabbis in the movie do not, will not, or cannot step up. It is questionable who is a rabbi and who is not. Water eventually takes the boy, but this is not a redemptive womb, for Saul almost drowns, as does an inmate earlier, because of Saul's actions. At the end, a second boy is seen, but this boy (whom Saul hallucinates?) is a harbinger of being found and killed. Is the son a delusion as well? The body in the water at the end—is this return to an oceanic feeling that is visually represented by Saul's smile at the local boy? Was the Kaddish for Saul, who knew he was about to die? The illusion of forward motion during the course of the movie, as well as the appearance of purposive action, gives way to psychosis by the end, to the illusion that the boy who was suffocated after surviving the gas chamber has returned to life, revealing that the more we have descended into the actual details of the killing machine, paradoxically, the more the mind has lost its bearings and anchoring in reality and the more defense, fantasy, and madness hold sway.

It only appears that Saul and his comrades are engaged on opposite tracks, that of death and burial (Saul), or of resistance and life (comrades), one communal, the other a private, individual quest. In fact, comrades' comments about Saul's quixotic quest—that to bury a boy is futile—apply to their own as well. Members of the Sonderkommando knew from the start that they would not succeed. Nanette Auerhahn's mother worked in the Canada Kommando with a woman from her town whose brother worked in the Sonderkommando. The night before the revolt depicted in the movie, this young man came to his sister and bid her goodbye. "Tomorrow I die," he informed her. The men rebelling knew they would die. They were retaining the option of saying "no," of choosing how they would die, within the constraints of the camp. Hence their quests were as hopeless, quirky, and individualistic as Saul's. One kept a diary with little hope that it would be found. Another took pictures, knowing full well that there would be no responsive action even should the photos be smuggled out. Each was reaching for another—for the Allies, for history, for future generations, for God, for ritual, for some other beyond and past themselves and out of reach of Nazi ideology.

Some of the contradictions and paradoxes disturb the viewer. For someone who is deadened, Saul generates a lot of loyalty and investment while living in a system in which people die anonymously, en masse, and the individual has lost significance (even hair and name). Yet people go out of their way to save and include Saul, as if he in particular does matter, even when he is lost to others as he focuses on his own individual goal. A comrade who appears to know Saul from before, saves him from drowning, as if for this man the connection to before, a time when people did matter, is the source of continued connection. For Saul, this at first appears to no longer be the case. Only when the Boy Who Lived defies the death machine by surviving the gas chamber, does Saul become enlivened and desperately search identity papers to see if the boy's transport was from Hungary, as Saul is. It is the boy's survival that makes Saul search for a connection in the past, rather than the past connection in and of itself being the driving force behind Saul's investment in the boy. We see this clearly by the contrast between Saul's obsession with the dead boy who may or may not be his son and his unresponsiveness to the woman Ella who knows him and reaches out to him. While following his obsession to bury the boy, Saul has no reaction to his loss of the gunpowder she risked her life to smuggle to the Sonderkommando and for which she likely will be hung. She is alive and will be killed—therefore she is decathected, as are the individuals he herds through the "showers" on their way to their deaths.

This narrative makes little rational sense, but deep metapsychological sense. It is the boy's survival in the gas chamber that enlivens Saul, creating the hope that if he can survive, so can Saul's loved ones—that the death machine is not invincible. It is this survival that makes Saul search for a connection to the boy, not the connection that leads to the investment. The Boy Who Lived cannot have an autopsy (which is against Jewish law) and must have a Jewish burial (cremation is also against Jewish law) to continue the fantasy that he has escaped the Nazi death machine. The boy represents not just a continuation of Jewish values (via the attempt at a Jewish burial) but a continuation of life itself, which in the camp resides only in the past. The fantasy that what was past can be revived enlivens and drives Saul. Symbolically, burial of an intact body will allow for resurrection in the future. On a psychotic level, preservation of the boy's body and its internment via a Jewish ritual represent the promise of resurrection of life and those values that give life meaning.

We are alerted to the otherness of genocidal reality starting with Saul's name: Auslander means outsider, alien, reminding us of one survivor's reaction to Auschwitz—that surely she was on another planet. The movie depicts the complexity and dark side of victimization on this alien planet. Saul, the main character, is responsible for the deaths of others, e.g. the rabbi who denies he is a rabbi, presumably to save himself, but who may not be, or who may be abandoning someone asking for his spiritual services, evincing a compromised morality. This man appears to try to drown himself (or perhaps just retrieve his shovel) and is shot due to having thereby called attention to himself, the final result of actions initiated by Saul. A second man admits to Saul's questioning that he is a rabbi, perhaps thinking this will save him, or perhaps because he is new to the camp and does not yet know that identifying himself as a rabbi is a death sentence. In any case, he too is shot as a result of Saul's actions. Has director Nemes, by implicating Saul in the deaths of others, drawn us into the Nazi universe in which inmates felt implicated in the murder of others, or has he himself succumbed to the Nazi and postwar perspective that saw Jews as deserving their victimization? Is the viewer compromised, feeling a distrust and disapproval of Saul, who no longer can be seen as a mere innocent non-actor? Along these lines, Saul's loss of the gunpowder is troubling given the historical reality that women smuggled gunpowder to the Sonderkommando at the risk of their lives. Several were hung for doing so after the revolt. Saul appeared cavalier about the loss of a package that might have cost the woman who gave it to him her life. Is the viewer meant to be ambivalently uncertain as to who is victim and who is perpetrator in this world where meaning has been turned upside down?

It is important that filmmaker, viewer, and critic all guard against ensnarement by the poisonous libel that Jews were responsible for their own deaths. We see this libel in society's condemnation of members of the Sonderkommando, as if they had chosen this descent into the nadir to prolong their lives, rather than been condemned to the work of Satan. This toxic critique reveals adherence to the false fantasy that members of the Sonderkommando retained agency as well as a vision and hope of survival, when in fact they, more than any other inmates of Auschwitz, knew that the death machine was inexorable and would swallow them all. A 13-year-old cousin of N.A., who worked in the Canada Kommando, watched daily as hordes of people entered the gas chambers never to leave, fantasizing that surely there was an exit on the other side of the building that she could not see. Other inmates could hope that if they worked hard, they would survive. The Sonderkommando had no illusions that their work would save them, as their first job was to dispose of the bodies of the prior members. They knew more about death than any other inmates, being immersed in it day and night, unable to push it aside.

But to understand the Sonderkommando's particular hell, think of Lanzmann's barber Bomba's description of a colleague cutting his wife's hair before she entered the gas chamber. Although speaking of another, Bomba gives the impression of narrating a story about himself that can only be told in the third person. We think, too, of N.A.'s uncle who, as a member of the Sonderkommando, came across the bodies of his wife and children and "lost his mind." (That is all N.A.'s mother could tell her. To say more would have risked losing *her* mind, as certain things cannot be talked about, because it is not possible to live with them.) We disagree with Sontag's statement (cited by Sklarew, Chapter 8) about the black SS uniforms that "convey a particularly powerful and widespread sadomasochistic fantasy … a military community … supremely violent but also supremely 'beautiful.'" In real life, those uniforms were terrifying, not beautiful. They looked obsessively well-tailored and inhabited by baby-faced, machinelike nonhuman robots. Sontag's other statement—"The color is black, the material is leather, the seduction is beauty, the aim is ecstasy, the fantasy is death"—betrays a fascination with and libidinization of Nazism that cannot withstand Arendt's conclusion that there was nothing extraordinary or demonic about Eichmannn, that what made it possible for him to become a mass murderer was precisely his failure to think, his inability to imagine the other person's experience. Above all, we disagree with a libidinization of the Sonderkommando that sees its members as part of a sadomasochistic cycle. This is a countertransference response applicable to some viewers, perpetrators, and perhaps even some survivors after the Holocaust, but has no application to the members of the Sonderkommando during the Holocaust, who looked death in the face without even the defense of perverse sexualization.

Whose fetish are we talking about now?

Annihilation anxiety and transitional objects: wherein lies hope?

Even traumatic dreams are not exact replicas of the trauma but often include some change, some defense. In *Son of Saul* (Rajna, Sipos, & Nemes, 2015), the director depicts ways several different characters defend against annihilation anxiety and reveals his own defense against traumatization. The director understood that the story of the Holocaust is a story of death, and that the focus on survivors in cinema and literature represents denial of the fact that most of the targets of the Nazi genocide were killed. He understood that to be accurate, a story of the Holocaust must have nothing redemptive about it. It is therefore that he has most of the protagonists in the movie killed at the end. Perhaps they are killed off-screen due to the director's need to protect himself (and viewers) from a death immersion that nevertheless sensitized him to the protagonists' defenses. With the breaking of dyadic bonds, each character is alone in his defensive pursuit whose utility is mocked, not shared, by others. There is the individual who hides his diary of events and who is threatened with exposure by Saul who believes that this activity is futile. Another individual takes pictures while a fellow inmate mocks the expectation that Allies, seeing the devastation, will send planes. Saul wrestles with the director's way out of the situation of total death via investment in a Christ figure (The Boy Who Lived) who enlivens Saul/Nemes by a fantasy of life after death. Saul comes alive when a boy survives the certain death of the gas chambers. From then on, he seeks to bury the boy in a pursuit that feels more Christian than Jewish. The boy is a Christ figure who captures Saul's imagination, whom Saul lives through vicariously (claiming "He is my son"), and who Saul believes is resurrected at the end of the movie after immersion in water, which represents return to the womb and/or baptism. Saul's beatific smile at the end is about the fantasy of life after death—again, a Christian, not Jewish, defense against death and a way for the director to protect himself from his immersion in *l'univers concentrationnaire*.

The last rites, which on first glance are imagined to be redeeming, are understood to be a fetish in a universe where there is no meaning. *Son of Saul* (Rajna, Sipos, & Nemes, 2015) is not about the survival of meaning but about what remains when meaning dies and relationships and God are unavailable. It is about disintegration and annihilation anxiety. As we note contradictions in the movie, funeral rites seem increasingly abstract and imaginary, as no longer representing themselves (comforting acts implying inscription in a meaningful spiritual community), but a hedge against hopelessness and a nod toward mythic (Christlike) immortality, as well as a retreat into madness as an escape from an unbearable reality. That the community no longer exists can be seen by others' reactions to Saul's quest and their pursuit of their own defenses against hopelessness, which in turn are mocked by the others. Each person's dream or goal is his alone. We are dealing with the Imaginary, not the Real, not return to a community but individuals' final, desperate gasps for air. There is no actual community any longer that would give death and burial meaning. It is therefore that Kaddish—which traditionally is recited not by a rabbi but by a mourner and only in the presence of a minyan (ten men) who responsively utter the prayer's central line affirming God's greatness and eternality—cannot be said and is not said in the end. We witness psychotic dissolution of a ritual that for centuries had served as a soothing social link. *Son of Saul* (Rajna, Sipos, & Nemes, 2015), like the story of the Holocaust itself, is not about redemptive survival but about horror and annihilation.

It is this that the fetish of the boy screens out. The "son" represents the fantasy and hope that something that is dead can be alive again. There is knowledge that what is alive can die, so that the living are decathected (as is Ella in *Son of Saul* (Rajna, Sipos, & Nemes, 2015), the Puerto Rican boy Jesus in *The Pawnbroker* (Langer, Lewis, & Lumet, 1965), and Ida in the movie by that name). The delusion is that death does not exist. Burying the boy becomes an obsession as a way to keep him alive by preventing his disappearance among the anonymous mounds of ashes and instead ensuring his survival as part of the earth and chain of Jewish souls.

When there is no hope, what is left? Nemes portrays inner survival as a madness, a revolt. When nothing is left, we can still say "no." The forms this "no" takes in *Son of Saul* (Rajna, Sipos, & Nemes, 2015) are of armed rebellion, a burial, a camera, and a diary. Each action presupposes an addressee. There is a reaching out to an implicit thou who, when not present, is imagined in a form of madness. The other is recreated in psychosis.

In *Son of Saul* (Rajna, Sipos, & Nemes, 2015), when Nemes tries to represent the death immersion by having the main character and his colleagues killed, events transpire off screen. All we hear is gun shots. Events are reduced to their most basic; hearing is the most passive sense and the last one to go when we die, as well as the first way by which we know our mother in the womb and recognize her at birth—by the sound of her voice, suggesting the Isakower (1938) phenomenon: the dream as breast. In their Introduction, Diamond and Sklarew discuss the regressive experience of movies that lulls viewers into imbibing the affects organized on screen, like an infant seduced at mother's breast. With Holocaust films, we are all as if drinkers of Paul Celan's (1955) "black milk" (p. 242) of mourning. We suck in characters' terror and melancholy as we imaginatively form relationships with them, feeling suffocated. Yitzchak Zuckerman, a survivor of the Warsaw Ghetto uprising, warned: "If you could lick my heart, it would poison you." The Holocaust represents actualization of the bad breast and persecutory object, which cannot be directly represented and instead are replaced by obsessional defenses (Auerhahn, in press).

In massive psychic trauma, annihilation anxiety is at its apex. One cannot face one's feelings because of utter helplessness, a shutdown of cognitive functions resulting in an inability to name experience as well as an inability to distinguish reality from fantasy. One finds oneself in the realm of the psychotic, where the only choice is either to succumb and die (the Musselman) or to shift to soothing mechanisms that exist in fantasy. That is what Saul does—he becomes addicted to hope. The boy represents a fantasy of hope that one can survive the death machine. It is not that Saul realizes that the boy is his son and hence rekindles an investment via recognition of a relationship. Rather, the boy represents a fantasy of survival, that the death machine is neither invincible nor inevitable, and, if he could survive, perhaps Saul's loved ones could as well. To this day, some survivors retain the fantasy that their loved ones are alive somewhere and just cannot find their way back home. The Boy Who Lived is a dike against powerlessness for Saul. He is a transitional object that restores a sense of omnipotence to salve the deep wound of injured narcissism due to helplessness. A rabbi is needed because Saul cannot remember the words of the Kaddish and so cannot mourn within an accepting community (read holding environment). Saul needs a rabbi to maintain memory, a connection to the past, to reality, and to an avenue for the expression of grief. In fantasy, Saul creates a son, a community, and a rabbi as a way to work through his bottomless grief with others.

Saul's obsession takes the form of an addiction or perverse defense in the sense that it involves a shifting from reality to fantasy, in that fantasy becomes more important to him than reality through the hope that powerlessness will be changed via a fantasy of omnipotence. It is therefore that to him his quest to bury the boy is more important than the rebellion that preoccupies his peers.

Grief from the Holocaust resembles waterboarding in that it is a suffocating death sentence and source of fantasies and losses, which, after the war and as we see in movies such as *The Pawnbroker* (Langer, Lewis & Lumet, 1965) and *Ida* (Abraham, Dzieciol & Pawlikowski, 2013), become a source of retraumatization. Grieving connected to an experience of annihilation persists after the Holocaust and is impossible to fully work through. Protagonists in most of the films discussed in this book look back at the Holocaust from the position of knowing that they survived. Thus their narratives have a beginning, a middle, and an end—a before and after. But survivors are exceptions. Most of the targets of the Nazi genocidal system did not survive. During the Holocaust, the past was obliterated, a future could not be imagined, and the present was overpoweringly fragmented. Only *Son of Saul* (Rajna, Sipos, & Nemes, 2015) attempts to represent the Holocaust not via survivors' repetitions and remembrances, but via recreation of the conditions that give rise to the impossibility of representing the Real. Only in *Son of Saul* do we meet those who did not survive and who constituted the majority of European Jewry.

Analysis of this extraordinary film makes clear that any story about the Holocaust is a delusion. Belief in the redemptive value of the Kaddish in Auschwitz, like the fantasy that photos will bring about bombing, like Wanda's guilt in *Ida* (Abraham, Dzieciol & Pawlikowski, 2013), like the pawnbroker's defenses against powerlessness, are all fragments of defenses enlarged into central phenomena, delusional beliefs and pieces of psychological functioning meant to obscure the terror and horror of being devoured in the dominion of death. Of all the movies, only Nemes' looks directly at the void. It is therefore in the last scene that we see Saul's odd, incongruous, and psychotic smile at a local boy; the viewer wishes for meaning, but views, instead, a main character who is out of his mind. A minute later, Saul and the men with him are murdered—this is reality. Even the men's talk of joining the partisans is illusory; there is no way of finding the partisans, and, of course, German troops can find them a few kilometers from Auschwitz. The men's comments about being free are wisps in the air. From these, humans spin films.

References

Abraham, E., & Dzieciol, P. (Producers), & Pawlikowski, P. (Director). (2013). *Ida* [Motion Picture]. Poland: Solopan.

Auerhahn, N. C. (in press). "I Could Eat You Up": Philomela, Trauma, and Enactment. In E. Schreiber (Ed.), *Healing Trauma: The Power of Listening*. New York: International Universities Press.

Bion, W. R. (1959). Attacks on linking. *International Journal of Psycho-Analysis*, *40*, 308–315.

Celan, P. (1955). Death fugue. *Commentary*, *20*, 242.

Dauman, A., Halfon, S., & Lifchitz, P. (Producers), & Resnais, A. (Director). (1955). *Night and Fog* [Motion Picture]. Paris: Cocinor Films.

Dauman, A., Halfon, S. (Producers), & Resnais, A. (Director). (1959). *Hiroshima Mon Amour* [Motion Picture]. France: Dajei Stdios, Argos Films, Como Films, Pathe Entertainment, Pathe Overseas.

Edwards, R. G., & De Simone, E. (Producers), & Cavani, L. (Director). (1974). *The Night Porter* [Motion Picture]. United States: Embassy Pictures.

Fisher, D. (Producer & Director). (2011). *Six Million and One* [Motion Picture]. Israel: Fisher Features Ltd.

Freud, S. (1900). *The Interpretation of Dreams. Standard Edition, 4* (pp. ix–627). London: Hogarth Press.

Goldfiner, A. (Producer & Director), & Kufus, T. (Producer). (2011). *The Flat* [Motion Picture]. Israel: Ruth Diskin Films.

Isakower, O. (1938). A contribution to the patho-psychology of phenomena associated with falling asleep. *International Journal of Psycho-Analysis*, *19*, 331–345.

Lacan, J. (1953). The function and field of speech and language in psychoanalysis. Discours de Rome. In *Ecrits* (Trans. B. Fink). New York: W.W. Norton and Co., 2006.

Langer, P., Lewis, R. (Producers), & Lumet, S. (Director). (1965). *The Pawnbroker* [Motion Picture]. United States: Allied Artists Pictures.

Lanzmann, C. (Producer & Director). (1985). *Shoah* [Motion Picture]. United States: New Yorker Films.

Rajna, G., & Sipos, G. (Producers), & Nemes, L. (Director). (2015). *Son of Saul* Motion Picture]. Hungary: Sony Classics.

Svarcová, I. (Producer), & Ludin, M. (Director). (2005). *Two or Three Things I Know About Him* [Motion Picture]. Germany: National Center for Jewish Film.

Žižek, S. (1992). *Enjoy Your Symptom! Jacques Lacan in Hollywood and Out*. New York and London: Routledge (2008).

Index

Page numbers in *italics* denote figures.

accountability, *Night and Fog* as statement of 72
Adorno, T. 143, 192
affective responses, to viewing Holocaust films 34–38
Allied forces, footage documenting the liberation of concentration camps 3
Altmann, Maria 137
American Gas Company 74
American Jewish History (Leff) 74
Amery, J. 169–170
Andersson, Bibi 35
Anderst, L. 66
Anne Frank Remembered (Blair) 123
Annenberg Centre for Communication 133
Antigone 22, 161–162, 169, 172–175; comparison of *Son of Saul* with 169–174
Antigone's Claim (Butler) 174
Arcalli, Franco 186
archaeological palimpsests, documentary projects as 131–136
archival footage 85, 90, 125, 137; as body of evidence 2–4; in *Hannah Arendt* 90–91, 98; Resnais's use of 52–56; use of in fictional films 5; use of in *Hannah Arendt* 85, 90
Arendt, Hannah 6, 21, 27, 109; *see also Hannah Arendt* (von Trotta)
Army Signal Corps Motion Pictures Unit 73
"Attribution of Meaning" (Forgács) 135
Auerhahn, N.C. 23, 58, 172
Auschwitz concentration camp: Arendt on the shock of learning about 101–102; István Kertész's autofictional account of his deportation to 127; portrayal in film 52; Scrolls of Auschwitz 6, 138–139, 178; Wittgenstein on 71
Auslander, Saul 21
Avisar, I. 36
awards: first Hungarian filmmaker to be awarded the Erasmus Prize 131; *Ida* 26, 208; Palme d'Or 26; *Regina* 131; *Son of Saul* 1, 138, 155; winner of the inaugural World Jewish Congress Recognition Award 137

banality of evil, Arendt's concept 27, 95, 107
Barthes, R. 37
Bauman, Z. 163
Belle du Jour (Buñuel) 186
Benzine, Adam 145
Bergen-Belsen concentration camp, portrayal in film 52
Berlin Holocaust Memorial 36
Berlin Jewish Museum 36
Berman, E. 15, 25–26
Bertolucci, Bernardo 185
Beyond Individual and Collective Trauma (Mucci) 168
"Beyond Oedipus: The Specimen Story of Psychoanalysis" (Felman) 171
Beyond the Pleasure Principle (Freud) 188, 194
Bibó, István 132
A Bibó Reader: Private Hungary 13; *the Bishop and the Philosopher* (Forgács) 132
Bion, W.R. 222, 226, 236
Bloch-Bauer, Adele 137
Blücher, Heinrich 92, 98, 104
Blumenfeld, Kurt 94

Bogarde, Dirk 38
Bomba, Abraham 21, 23–24, 143, 146, 241
Bromberg, P.M. 97–98, 105
burial, *Son of Saul* and the symbolism of the ritual 161–162, 166, 167–169, 175, 175–178
Butler, J. 167, 174

Cartier-Bresson, Henri 36
Caruth, C. 18, 28, 30
Cavani, Liliana 18, 38, 190
Cayrol, Jules 53
Chaplin, Charlie 73
Chasseguet-Smirgel, J. 188
Cinemas in Transition in Central and Eastern Europe after 1989 (Portuges) 122
cinematographic techniques, use of to convey traumatic experiences 227–228
Citizen Kane (Welles) 186
Clift, Montgomery 75
Comité d'historie de la Seconde Guerre Mondiale 53
communism, impact of the fall on representation of the Holocaust 136–137
comparison of *Ida* and *The Flat*: common themes 197; *The Flat* 199–202; *Ida* 197–199; perpetrators and their descendants 205–207; reception and significance of the films 207–208; victims and their offspring 202–205
concentration camps: depictions in film 3; documenting the liberation of 3
Conversation on Psychoanalysis (Forgács) 132
The Counterfeiters (Ruzowitzky) 123
Cowie, E. 5–6
Crowther, B. 83
Curtis, Simon 137

Danieli, Y. 14, 22, 24
The Danube Exodus: The Rippling Currents of the River (Forgács) 133
de Beauvoir, Simone 145, 147
"Death Fugue" (Celan) 162
Death Mills (Wilder) 5
Delage, Christian 137
Delbo, C. 171
denazification 211
denial: of the extent of barbarism and complicity in the Nazi era 16; German pact of 212–213
depicting the Shoah in film: cinematic traces and intergenerational dialogue 122–148; families' Holocaust experiences 6–7; identity recovery and integration 24–27; liberation of the camps 3–5; mourning process 21–24; psychoanalytic themes 12–13; repetition compulsion 17–21; role of film in fostering understanding and integration 27–30; survivor guilt 13–17; survivor testimony 5–6; types of representation 3–7
Diamond, D. 9, 25, 27–28
The Diary of Anne Frank (Stevens) 74, 123
Didi-Huberman, Georges 143, 178
dissociation/dissociative mechanisms 15, 25, 86, 104–105
documentary evidence 3; *see also* archival footage
documentary films: "Attribution of Meaning" 135; *A Bibó Reader: Private Hungary 13*; *the Bishop and the Philosopher* 132; *Conversation on Psychoanalysis* 132; *The Danube Exodus: The Rippling Currents of the River* 133; documentary projects as archaeological palimpsests 131–136; *The Dybbuk* 134; *Elie Wiesel Goes Home* 130; and the fall of communism 136–137; *Free Fall* 132–133; the genre 51–52; influence of *Shoah* 129–130, 131, 131–136; *Letters to Afar* 133, 135–136; Lumière brothers' influence 135; *The Maelstrom: A Family Chronicle* 132; *Once They Were Neighbors* 129; *Package Tour* 129; Péter Forgács 131–136; *Private Hungary* 132; *Regina* 131; *Synagogue for Sale* 130; *see also Shoah*; *The Flat*
The Drowned and the Saved (Levi) 139, 144
Duras, Marguerite 58
The Dybbuk (Der Dibuk) (Waszynski) 134

Eichmann, Adolf: anti-Semitism 106; appearance in *Hannah Arendt* 90; Arendt's interpretation 112; Arendt's view 9, 86; discusses Von Mildenstein's role in the SS 205; explains decision to go to Argentina 111; kidnapping 90; letter to the President of Israel 89; the trial of 74, 102–107

Eichmann, Edda 205–206
Eichmann in Jerusalem: A Report of the Banality of Evil (Arendt) 85, 95, 103, 105–106, 108
Eisenhower, Dwight 73
Elek, Judit 130
Elie Wiesel Goes Home (Mondani a mondhatlant: Elie Wiesel üzenete) (Elek) 130
Erasmus Prize 131, 151
Erikson, E.H. 188
experience of watching Holocaust films 34–38

Fairbairn, W.R.D. 105
fall of communism, impact on representation of the Holocaust 136–137
Farge, A. 222
"Fascinating Fascism" (Sontag) 192, 195
Fateless (Sorstalánság) (Koltai) 127–128, 143
Felman, Shoshana 146, 149, 171
fictional films: *Fateless* 127–128, 143; as first representations of the Holocaust 127; and presentation style 128–129; *Sunshine* 127; transgenerational 127–128; use of archival footage 5; *see also Son of Saul*
film, the language of 226–227
filmic depictions of the Shoah *see* depicting the Shoah in film
"Filming the Camps: From Hollywood to Nuremberg" (Delage) 3, 137
Fisher, David 13, 21, 25, 40
Fisher, Joseph 13, 22, 42–44, 47
flashbacks 18, 21, 34, 68, 77, 79, 98, 100, 186–187, 226, 228
The Flat (Goldfinger) 7, 29; Hannah reads her grandmother's letter *201*; outline of the film 199–202; reception and significance 207–208; *see also* comparison of *Ida* and *The Flat*
Fonagy, P. 110
Ford, John 137
Forgács, Péter 131–136
Free Fall (Forgács) 132–133
Freud, Anna 135
Freud, Sigmund 30, 116, 135, 187, 194, 213
Freudiger, Pinhas 88
Friedman, R.M. 215
Fuller, Samuel 137

The Garden of the Finzi-Continis (De Sica) 123
Gazdag, Gyula 129
Geertz, C. 168
Geller-Varga, Zsuzsanna 130
Genocide (Schwartzman) 123
genocide, Arendt's contribution to changing our way of thinking about 106–107
Getty Centre 133
Grand Prix Award 1
Grant, B. 53
Grapes of Wrath (Ford) 30
"The Gray Zone" (Levi) 16, 88, 91, 139, 191
gray zone, definition 16
The Great Dictator (Chaplin) 73
The Grey Zone (Nelson) 28, 155
Gróo, Diana 130
Gross, Jan Tomasz 208
Gusen camp *see* Mauthausen-Gusen concentration camp

Hamburger, A. 19, 24, 28
Hannah Arendt (von Trotta) 27, 85–116; aim of the film 85–89; Arendt celebrates her assignment to cover the Eichmann trial 99; as compelling portrait of a woman academic at work 107–110; as courtroom drama 112–116; depiction of Arendt's self-reflective inner dialogue 95; depiction of Arendt's thinking process 89–91; depiction of the relationship with Heidegger 92, 99–100; the Eichmann trial 102–107; examination of Arendt's multiple selves 91–97; Hannah Arendt thinking *108*; Hannah watches the Eichmann trial from the press room *96*; interspersing of fictional film footage with archival footage 90–91, 98; opening scenes 89–90; portrayal of multiplicity and disassociation 97–102; privileging of narrative truth over historical 95; thinking as action 110–112
Hannah Arendt: The Last Interview and Other Conversations (Arendt) 87, 93, 101, 105, 117
Hareven, Shulamith 207
The Heart is a Lonely Hunter 75
Hebard, S. 53
Heidegger, Martin 27, 89, 93; Arendt's relationship with 92, 100; endorsement of Nazi ideology 99

Hiller, Arthur 75
Hiroshima Mon Amour (Resnais) 5, 20, 51, 58–67; comparison with *Night and Fog* 51–53, 59, 61–62, 65; inserted film 60; opening scenes 61; outline of the film 60, 62–66; prologue 61; repetition in 66; and Resnais personal feelings around documenting of the Holocaust 58–60; use of flashbacks 186
history, cinema's contribution to psychoanalysis and 221–222
History beyond Trauma: Whereof One Cannot Speak, Thereof one Cannot Stay Silent (Davoine & Guadilliere) 103
Hitler, Adolf 73
Hollywood, Holocaust films and 122–124
"Holocaust" (miniseries) 72, 122–123
Holocaust fatigue 127
Hotel Terminus (Ophüls) 123
Howe, Irving 89
humour 48–50, 54, 102
Hungarian National Film Fund 138
Hungary 128

Ida (Pawlikowski) 21–22, 26, 36, 123; anti-Polish perceptions 208; caption added when shown on Polish television 208; outline of the film 197–199; reception and significance 208; *see also* comparison of *Ida* and *The Flat*
identity: destruction of 175; trauma as 233
Imaginary Witness: Hollywood and the Holocaust (Anker) 72
The Imperial War Museum (London) 136
Indelible Shadows: Film and the Holocaust (Insdorf) 38
Insdorf, A. 38
interpretations, psychodynamic 229, 231
Into the Arms of Strangers: Stories of the Kindertransport (Harris) 123
Invention of Hysteria: Charcot and the Photographic Iconography of the Salpêtrière (Didi-Huberman) 143
Israel 15

Jarvis, J. 72
Jaspers, Karl 93, 95
Jewish councils, Arendt's view 87–88
Jonas, Regina 131
Judenräte 87–88, 91, 101, 230
Judgment at Nuremberg (Kramer) 74, 114, 123
Jurist, E. 9, 25, 27–28

Kaës, R. 212
Kant, Immanuel 109
The Karski Report (Lanzmann) 125
Kearney, R. 66
Kelman, H.C. 163
Kernberg, O. 115, 188–189
Kerner, A. 3
Kertész, István 127
Klein, M. 115
Klimt, Gustav 137
knowing and not knowing, conflict between 15
Kohler, Lotte 115
Kracauer, S. 38
Kristallnacht 73

Labyrinth Project 133
Lacan, J. 124, 171–173
LaCapra, D. 6
Landau, Ely 75
Langer, E.J. 37
language of film 226–227
Lanzmann, Claude 5, 23, 142, 144
The Last Days (Moll) 123
The Last of the Unjust (Lanzmann) 125–126
Laub, D. 23, 58, 172
Laub, M.D. 19, 24, 28
Lauder, Ronald S. 137
Le Sang des Betes (Franju) 51
Leff, L.J. 74
Letters to Afar (Forgács) 133, 135–136
Levi, Primo 16–18, 36, 88, 144, 167; death 147
Lewin, B. 35
liberation of the camps: Allied forces footage 3; depicting in film 3–5; differences in American, British, and Soviet filming styles 4–5; inclusion of American liberators in *Six Million and One* 46; Mauthausen-Gusen 46–47; Paris exhibit of documentary footage 3; silence among the survivors 47
Liebman, S. 4
Life Is Beautiful (Benigni) 123
The Life of the Mind (Arendt) 110
Lifton, J.R. 164, 169
liminality, ambiguous nature of the attributes 165
Lithuania, killing fields 36
The Long Way Home (Harris) 123
Los Angeles, Forgács' multimedia installation 133

loss, Butler's argument 167
loss of humanity, Resnais' depiction 56–57
Love Inventory (Fisher) 40
Lowenstein, R.M. 189
Ludin, Hanns 17, 211–212
Ludin, Malte 211–212
Lumet, Sidney 75
Lumière, Louis and Auguste 135

The Maelstrom: A Family Chronicle (Forgács) 132
Marrone, G. 184, 187
matzeva 36
Mauthausen-Gusen concentration camp 13, 40–49; liberation 46–47; portrayal in film 52
McCarthy, Mary 92, 95
Medusa, Kracauer's recounting of the myth 38
memories of trauma, intrusive nature 232
"Memory of the Camps" (Bernstein) 136
Milgram experiment 163
Mirren, Helen 137
Mitscherlich, A. & M. 213
Mori, M. 56
Moses, J.W. 59
Moses, Siegfried 90
Mossad 90
Mostar Round Trip (Fisher) 40
mourning process, depicting in film 21–24
Mucci, C. 10
Murmelstein, Benjamin 125
Muselmen/Musselmen 56, 237, 244

National Socialism, Levi on 88
Nazism, treatment of in Hollywood films 73
Neighbors (Gross) 208
Nemes, László 1, 6, 22, 138
Nietzsche, Friedrich 109
Night (Wiesel) 71
Night and Fog (Resnais) 4–5, 20, 23, 34–35, 51, 53–58, 126; comparison with *Hiroshima Mon Amour* 51–53, 59, 61–62, 65; culminating scene 56; directional shift 54; genre 51; humour in 54; implication of the viewer 57–58; intercutting of archival footage with present-day view 56; moral imperative 57; opening scenes 54; source of the idea for the film 53; as statement of accountability 72; suggestion of time 52
The Night Porter (Cavani) 5, 18–19, 195; audience reactions 38; critical reception 189; inspiration for 190–191; storyline 184; use of flashbacks 186–187
Night Will Fall (Singer) 136
not knowing, conflict between knowing and 15
Nuremburg 3

objective representation, words *vs* photographs 36
objectivity, expectations of in the documentary genre 51
Once They Were Neighbors (Szomszédok Voltak) (Geller-Varga) 129
Ophüls, Marcel 126
organized forgetting 127
Ornstein, A. 25

Package Tour (Társasutazás) (Gazdag) 129
Palme d'Or 26
The Pawnbroker (Lumet) 5, 14, 35, 71–84; crucial nude scene 75; and Hollywood's relationship with the Holocaust 72–74, 75; loss 80–82; memory 76–78; opening scene 76; power and impotence 79–80; repetition 82–84; resistance to the film 74–75; synopsis 76–84; use of flashbacks 186
Perrott , K. 66
Persona (Bergman) 35
photographic image, as means of objective representation 36
photographs, shock value 37
The Pianist (Polanski) 123
Picker, Arnold 74
Podhoretz, N. 116
"Portrait of Adele Bloch-Bauer I" (Klimt) 137
Private Hungary (Privát Magyarország) (Forgács) 132
psychoanalysis, cinema's contribution to history and 221–222
psychoanalytic themes, in Holocaust films 12–13
psychodynamic interpretations 229, 231

Rajk, László 141, 154
Rampling, Charlotte 38
Regina (Gróo) 131
Reik, T. 191
remembering, levels of knowing and 233–234

repetition: banalizing effect 5; defence and the compulsion for 231–232; in depictions of the Holocaust in film 17–21; in *Hiroshima Mon Amour* 66; in *The Pawnbroker* 82–84
Resnais, Alain: cinematographic style 52; examination of two films by 51–68; personal feelings around documenting of the Holocaust) 58–60; reluctance to make *Night and Fog* 53; *see also Hiroshima Mon Amour*; *Night and Fog*
Rilke, R.M. 83
Riviere, J. 115
Röhrig, Géza 139
Rosenblum, R. 77

sadomasochism: Freud on 187; Kernberg's description 189
Sartre, Jean-Paul 145
Sassen, Willem 106
"Saying Goodbye to Hannah" (McCarthy) 95
Scarry, E. 71
Schindler's List (Spielberg) 74, 123, 142; comparison of *Son of Saul* with 142–143; Lanzmann's criticism 148
Scholem, Gershom 94
Schubert, Heinz 146
Screen Memories: The Hungarian Cinema of Márta Mészáros (Portuges) 122
Scrolls of Auschwitz 6, 138–139, 178
Shoah (Lanzmann) 21; the "barber of Treblinka" 143; commissioning of 123; influence on documentary filmmaking 129–130, 131–136; Lanzmann describes the making of 126; Lanzmann's vision 123–124; and the release of *Claude Lanzmann: Spectres of the Shoah* 145–148; subsequent documentaries made from unused material 125; and the third post-war generation 130–131
Shop on Main Street (Kadár & Klos) 123
Sigmund Freud: the Last Decade 135
silence, as response to the unspeakable 35
Singer, André 136
Six Million and One (Fisher) 7, 15, 21, 25, 36, 40–50; David's visits to the camp 44; depiction of the end of the war 50; as film about sibling intimacy 48–50; historical and geographical context 40–48; inclusion of American camp liberators 46–47; insight into the question of transmission of the Holocaust trauma 48; Joseph Fisher's diary 42, 44, 47; Mauthausen-Gusen concentration camp 40–42; meaning of the title 45; other films in the trilogy 40
Sklarew, B.H. 18, 184
Sloniowski, J. 53
Sobibór (Lanzmann) 125
Son of Saul (Nemes) 21–23, 34, 36–37, 138–144, 181; annihilation anxiety and transitional objects 241–245; awards 1, 138, 155; basis of the film 6; the boy survivor 164–165; claustrophobic style 140; comparison with Antigone 169–174; comparison with *Schindler's List* 142–143; depiction of descent into Hell 162–166; depiction of the Sonderkommando 138–144; emotional toll for filmgoers 37; ending 179–180; focus on the "gray zone" 88; legacy of Antigone for us 174–175; outline of the film 161; role of the audience 162; screens and fetishes 234–241; set design 141; style of filming 147; and the symbolism of the burial ritual 161–162, 166, 167–169, 175, 175–178; synopsis 138–142; testimonials 178–181
Sonderkommando: depiction in *Son of Saul* 138–144; depiction in *The Grey Zone* 28; liminality of 165; mutiny 144; Primo Levi's view 139; role and behaviour 162–164; summary execution 139
Sontag, Susan 192
Sophie's Choice (Pakula) 72, 123, 186
Sophocles 22, 161, 170, 178, 181
The Sorrow and the Pity: Chronicle of a French City Under Occupation (Ophüls) 126
Spellbound (Hitchcock) 186
Spielberg, Steven 74
Stangneth, B. 111
Steiger, Rod 35
Steiner, G. 35
Stevens, George 137
Sukowa, Barbara 103
Sunshine (Szabó) 127
Survival in Auschwitz (Levi) 191
survivor guilt 82; meaning and variants 13–17
survivor testimony, depicting in film 5–6
survivorship, definition 164
Svarcova, Eva 214

Synagogue for Sale (Zsinagógát Vegyenek) (Geller-Varga) 130
Szemző, Tibor 133

testimony of survivors, significance of film as a vehicle for 5
thinking: Arendt on 87; Arendt's theory of 107–110
trauma: as identity 233; intrusive nature of memories of 232
traumatic experience, cinematographic techniques used to convey 227–228
Triumph of the Will (Riefenshtal) 54
Turim, M. 186
Turner, V.W. 165
Two or Three Things I Know About Him (Ludin) 7, 15, 17, 21, 29, 211–224; and cinema's contribution to history and psychoanalysis 221–222; dilemma of self-individuation *vs* family loyalty 215; as the director's way of dealing with family guilt 220–221; encounter between personal and collective history 213–215; family loyalties and defence strategies 216–220; and the future of a generation 222–223; opening sequence and credits 215–216; tone and pace of the film 215–216; as typical German story 212–213

Ullman, Liv 35
Un Chien Andalou (Buñuel) 186
United States Holocaust Museum 36
University of Southern California 133

Varga, János 133
viewing Holocaust films, the experience of 34–38
Violence: Thinking without Banisters (Bernstein) 110
A Visitor from the Living (Lanzmann) 125
Von Mildenstein, Leopold 205
Vrba, Rudolf 148

Waintrater, R. 16, 25
Ward, J. 59
Weinstein, L. 20
Welzer, H. 223
Wetzler, Alfred 148
Wiesel, Elie 36, 71–72, 123, 130, 147, 174
Wild Strawberries (Bergman) 186
Winer, R. 14, 16
Winnicott, D.W. 28, 105
"The Witness" (Hareven) 207
Woman in Gold (Curtis) 137
words, *vs* photographs 37
World Jewish Congress Recognition Award 137
Wurmser, L. 113

Young-Bruehl, E. 88, 106, 115

Zimmerman, Bill 74